FREEDOM COLONIES

NUMBER FIFTEEN

Jack and Doris Smothers Series in Texas History, Life, and Culture

Freedom Colonies

INDEPENDENT BLACK TEXANS
IN THE TIME OF JIM CROW

BY THAD SITTON AND JAMES H. CONRAD

With research assistance and photographs by Richard Orton

UNIVERSITY OF TEXAS PRESS
Austin

Requests for permission to reproduce material from this work should be sent to
Permissions, University of Texas Press, P.O. Box 7819, Austin, TX 78713-7819.

The paper used in this book meets the minimum requirements of
ANSI/NISO Z39.48-1992 (R1997) (Permanence of Paper).

LIBRARY OF CONGRESS CATALOGING-IN-PUBLICATION DATA

Sitton, Thad, 1941–
Freedom colonies : independent Black Texans in the time of
Jim Crow / by Thad Sitton and James H. Conrad.
p.   cm. — (Jack and Doris Smothers series in
Texas history, life, and culture ; no. 15)
Includes bibliographical references and index.
ISBN 0-292-70618-9 (cl. : alk. paper) — ISBN 0-292-70642-1 (pbk. : alk. paper)
1. Freedmen—Texas—History.   2. African American farmers—Texas—History.
3. African Americans—Land tenure—Texas—History.   4. African Americans—
Texas—Economic conditions.   5. Agricultural colonies—Texas—History.   6. Land
settlement—Texas—History.   7. Texas—History—1846-1950.   8. Texas—Race
relations.   9. Texas—Economic conditions.
I. Conrad, James H.   II. Title.   III. Series.
E185.93.T4S47   2004
333.33'5'089960730794—dc22   2004009477

Black people had carved their autonomy from "free spaces," weak points in a white power structure that whites had not shored up yet, places where whites were not looking, sites that had not yet become important enough to the preservation of privilege that whites cared what Blacks did there.

— DEBORAH J. HOSKINS

Then it dawned upon me with a certain suddenness that I was different from the others; or like, mayhap, in heart and life and longing, but shut out from their world by a vast veil. I had thereafter no desire to tear down that veil, to creep through; I held all beyond it in common contempt, and lived above it in a region of blue sky and great wandering shadows.

— W. E. B. DU BOIS

Contents

CHAPTER ONE

Introduction

Freedmen's settlements were independent rural communities of African American landowners (and land squatters) that formed in the South in the years after Emancipation. These "freedom colonies," as blacks sometimes called them, were to a degree anomalies in a postwar South where white power elites rapidly resumed social, economic, and political control and the agricultural system of sharecropping came to dominate.

Beginning as early as 1866, southern whites swiftly assimilated their former slaves into a pattern of cotton rent farming that maintained as many of the social controls of slavery as landowners, local officials, and state governments could devise. Dreams of land and independence ended early for most former slaves. Generalizing about the two decades after 1870, historian Loren Schweninger noted that freedmen

struggled against oppressive white landlords, the debilitating effects of the crop lien system, discrimination in wage rates, seemingly endless debt, and an increasingly hostile racial climate. Even the most diligent, persistent, frugal, and industrious blacks were often unable to overcome the ironlike grip of whites on the land, or the low wages. Most observers of blacks in the rural Deep South during these decades were struck by the continuity with the prewar era: Negroes laboring in the fields on white-owned plantations in much the same manner as they had during slavery. They were also struck by the deplorable living conditions. After observing the circumstances of black sharecroppers in the South, W. E. Du Bois wrote in his classic 1903 study, *The Souls of Black Folk:* "The size and arrangements of a people's homes are no unfair index of their condition. All over the face of the land is the one-room cabin, — now standing in the shadow of the Big House, now staring at the dusty road, now rising dark and somber among the green of the cotton fields."

Schweninger continued, "The 'cabin,' built with rough-hewn lumber, was nearly always dark, dingy, and dilapidated, without windows, light, or proper ventilation. It smelled of must, eating, and sleeping. Containing eight to ten people, it stood as a silent symbol of the degradation of landless blacks in the Deep South."[1]

So compelling to historians has been this dark image of the "degradation of landless blacks"—of the rise of sharecropping, "debt slavery," the "neo-plantation," and Jim Crow apartheid—that they often failed to notice a counter-movement. From 1870 to 1890, at the same time that what historian Pete Daniel called "the shadow of slavery" tightened its hold on most black farmers in the South, nearly one-fourth of them got their own land. Landownership rose more precipitously in Texas than in any other southern state. In 1870 only 1.8 percent of the state's black farmers owned land, but by 1890 an astonishing 26 percent of them did. Just after the turn of the century, black Texas landownership peaked at 31 percent.[2]

In their focus on the dark side of the New South, historians commonly have dismissed the phenomenon of black landownership as a glass three-fourths empty. Leon Litwack generalized in his 1998 history of African Americans in the Jim Crow South: "Examples of black economic success and landownership existed but failed to proliferate. The great mass of laboring black families, whether they rented lands or worked for wages or shares, remained farmers without land, agricultural workers who comprised a rural proletariat."[3]

"Farmers without land," the phrase of C. Vann Woodward echoed by Litwack, has come to sum up the circumstances of southern black agriculturalists after Emancipation and serves as a chapter title in Neil R. McMillan's history of African Americans in Mississippi.[4] In perspective, however, this dismissal of black landownership seems a strange judgment. That so many former slaves, usually illiterate and disadvantaged in many ways, often beginning with nothing, got their own land surely was a remarkable achievement.

Many—perhaps most—of these new black Texas landowners resided in freedmen's settlements, informal communities of black farmers and stockmen scattered across the eastern half of Texas. These were dispersed communities—"settlements," Southerners called them—places unplatted and unincorporated, individually unified only by church and school and residents' collective belief that a community existed. Up in the sand hills, down in the creek and river bottoms, and along county lines, several hundred Texas freedmen's settlements came into being between 1870 and 1890. Most established themselves on pockets of wilderness, cheap land, or neglected land previously untouched by cotton agriculture.

Southern historians have ignored freedmen's settlements, and data are scanty, but similar communities seem to have formed all across the South. Former slaves determined to get their own "40 acres and a mule," after the federal government failed to provide this, moved from plantation districts to wilderness areas of cheap land. Freedmen pioneered independent landowner and squatter communities in north Florida, the Pine Barrens of western South Carolina, southwest Georgia, the Red Hills of Alabama and Mississippi, and other places.[5]

Focused as they were on the triumph of sharecropping and the accompanying "degradation of blacks in the Deep South," historians neglected the counter-current of black landowner settlements. No account of them had appeared in the *Journal of Southern History* by 2003. Likewise, the scholarly journal of the Texas State Historical Association, the *Southwestern Historical Quarterly,* still had not published a single article about black landowner communities by 2003, although the association's six-volume reference work, the *New Handbook of Texas,* listed over two hundred such places. Historians of the black experience after Emancipation focused instead upon the rise of sharecropping as a replacement for slavery, the move of some Texas blacks into segregated "quarters" adjacent to white market towns, the development of Jim Crow segregation, and the "exodus" of a few thousand Texas freedmen to black developer towns in Kansas and Oklahoma during the 1870s and 1880s.

The desperate migration of freedmen to Kansas and Oklahoma around 1879 resulted from blacks' abiding land hunger and as an avoidance response after white Southerners' resumption of political power at "Redemption."[6] Historians largely missed the similar and more general response of the freedmen's settlements, where ex-slaves remained in the South to establish all-black landowner communities as far away from white authority as possible. Numbers are difficult to estimate, but this ubiquitous, unremarked internal "exodus" to local "freedom colonies" must have dwarfed the famous move north.

Other factors perhaps also contributed to historians' neglect of southern black landowner communities. Most of them never developed past the "settlement" level of organization, remaining dispersed, poorly focused places where a passing stranger might not see a community at all, only scattered farmsteads with perhaps a remote church or school. At the grassroots level, the southern countryside of whites and blacks was organized into these dispersed settlements, but historians have overlooked such places as they have overlooked most of the folk-ideational reality, the "natives'" perspectives, on the now-vanished rural world. Scholars failed to note freedmen's settlements because they failed to note *any* settlements.[7]

Furthermore, freedmen's settlements long remained especially remote, informal, and unofficial—defensive black communities that went almost as unnoticed by white contemporaries in the courthouse towns as by latter-day historians. Courthouse land and tax records (and even the federal censuses) often poorly recorded freedmen's settlements, and for traditional historians no documents meant no history. (Local historians, conducting marker file research for Peyton's Colony in Blanco County, once returned home from days of work at the courthouse with all of their data in a single coffee can.) Only in the living memories of elderly community residents did the vein of information run deep, but many researchers and many interviewees felt uncomfortable with the practice of oral history across racial and cultural lines. Quite understandably, social awkwardness and lingering suspicions often haunted such interactions. The elderly African Americans whose memories embodied the historical knowledge had lived half their lives under the full force of Jim Crow.

Another reason for the scholarly neglect of freedmen's settlements may have been the decidedly counter-current (even "politically incorrect") aspects of their story. For one thing, a good many Texas landowner settlements began with the aid of former slaveholders, some of them blood-related to the freedmen they helped. For another, freedmen's settlements were communities of avoidance and self-segregation, where black people adapted to Jim Crow restrictions not by fighting back or moving north, but by withdrawing from whites and by maintaining what Deborah J. Hoskins called "a culture of dissemblance."[8] Freedmen's settlement residents watched what they said, carefully managed their interactions with whites, and stayed to themselves. In keeping with these inclinations, during the 1960s freedmen's settlements often fought school integration to the end, sometimes in strange political alliances with white segregationists in town. Some blacks did not want to integrate and most simply placed the greatest priority on maintaining their own independent community schools. Finally, the conventional story of African Americans fleeing the hated countryside for the city does not fit the freedmen's settlements. People there were black ruralists, committed followers of the subsistence lifestyle of "living on the place." They had practiced Booker T. Washington's austerities of landownership, hard work, independence, neighborly cooperation, subsistence farming, and avoidance of debt for decades before Washington began to preach these strategies for black advancement. Many residents stayed on their land until the bitter end, and some of them reside there today.

Because of the general neglect of freedmen's settlements across Texas and the South, the authors of this book found few scholarly shoulders to stand on. There are several studies of such famous "black towns" as Mound Bayou, Mississippi, Boley and Langston City, Oklahoma, and Nicodemus, Kansas, but these developer towns are of limited relevance.[9] They were the atypical tip of the iceberg of black landowner communities. Only two book-length studies focus on true freedmen's settlements, and neither of these is about Texas. They are Elizabeth Bethel's *Promiseland: A Century of Life in a Negro Community* (1981) and William Montell's *The Saga of Coe Ridge: A Study in Oral History* (1970). Bethel's detailed account of a South Carolina landowner community is by far the most important of the two. Patterns of life and history in Bethel's *Promiseland* coincide in many respects with those of Texas settlements.

Among scholarly Texas sources, two master's theses stand out—Ronald D. Traylor's study of Barrett in Harris County and Michelle M. Mears's account of black neighborhoods and freedmen's settlements in the vicinity of Austin.[10] Perhaps even more important, however, are recent dissertations by Deborah J. Hoskins about certain black landowner communities of Gregg County and by Debra Ann Reid about the "Colored County Agents" of the Texas Agricultural Extension Service.[11] These agents did much of their work at freedmen's settlements. Published memoirs of black rural Texans are few and far between but very important—especially the oral autobiography of Reverend C. C. White, which contains information on several freedmen's settlements in Shelby and Nacogdoches counties.[12]

In our attempt to research Texas freedmen's settlements for a reasonable overview of the phenomenon, we resorted to a strategy of utilizing every available source of information, primary and secondary. Instead of concentrating on one community, or a small group of communities, we sought information from all across Texas and watched for patterning in the data. As fragmentary information accumulated from many different sources about hundreds of different places, strong repetitive patterns of community origins and evolution emerged.

The project from the beginning has had a unique relationship to a unique reference work, the *New Handbook of Texas*. The remarkable six-volume *NHT* contained information on many communities at a time when scholarly journals failed to acknowledge their existence. Another important source of secondary information was the marker files of the Texas Historical Commission. In recent decades, the THC strongly encouraged county historical commissions to seek historical markers for their important black communities, churches, and schools, and the research supporting marker requests ended up at the THC library. Some of this local research proved very useful, especially that of the remarkable Houston County Historical Commission, headed for many years by Eliza Bishop. Another rarely used source of information has been the reports of "cultural resource management" professionals, employed to conduct "mitigation" research before important historical evidence was destroyed by dam, highway, or reservoir.[13] (Only in such cases do historians, anthropologists, and archeologists turn out to study remote "settlements!") We also examined many obscure theses and dissertations, and a few of these added important information to the story. Finally, in a real grasping at straws, we searched various Texas newspaper files for the weeks before the Emancipation holiday of June 19 in hopes of locating feature articles about freedmen's settlements.

We located some unpublished primary sources—often memoirs—in the files of county historical commissions by a survey mailed to every commission chairperson, and several local collections of relevant oral history tapes were discovered by this same process. We found other important oral history materials at the Center for American History at the University of Texas, the Institute for Oral History at Baylor University, the archives of Texas A&M–Commerce, and elsewhere.

Another important source of interview data was the multivolume Texas Slave Narratives, personal accounts written down somewhat as spoken by mostly white researchers during the 1930s. We made the reasonable assumption that these several thousand interviews of elderly ex-slaves would also contain useful information about the decades after slavery, and that turned out to be the case.[14]

For help in interpreting our oral histories and primary accounts, we learned much from two perceptive eyewitnesses of the Jim Crow South at Sunflower County, Mississippi, during the 1930s—anthropologist Hortense Powdermaker and psychologist John Dollard.[15] This was not eastern Texas, but the southern society that Powdermaker and Dollard described from life seemed uncannily the same.

Dollard wrote in 1936: "The significant, the truly explanatory, data on the South is hidden behind great sets of defensive habits. Much of the relevant material can appear only in intimate relations where fear is reduced. The relationship of friendship is such a one."[16] The primary accounts born of friendship and trust between black informants and white researchers proved most important for the interpretations in our book. These include the interviews of Richard Orton with old acquaintances at County Line, those of Glen Alyn with Mance Lipscomb and other of Alyn's friends, that of Ada M. Holland with Reverend C. C. White, and those of Thad Sitton with the friends—and fellow local historians—of Eliza Bishop in Houston County.[17]

Wesley Taylor Fobbs of Houston County's Wheeler Springs community was one of the latter. Interviewed in 2001, Fobbs had sought out the history of her community from the time many decades before when she first spoke with elderly women about their slave days and recorded the recollections on brown wrapping paper that she kept under her bed.[18] Some African Americans have not cared to look back at their trials and tribulations in the Jim Crow countryside, but residents and former residents of freedmen's settlements often had different attitudes. They were proud of their communities and proud of the parents or grandparents who went forth from slavery with only the clothes on their backs and ended up as community leaders with hundreds of acres of land.

In Texas, as in Mississippi, the life of African Americans in the Jim Crow countryside truly was a *Dark Journey*, as Neil R. McMillan titled his book about black Southerners. Its main story is that of discrimination, disadvantage, and economic exploitation, maintained by an ever-present threat of violence. This focus on black Southerners as victims, however, must not blind us to their achievements against long odds, such as their acquisition of land and establishment of independent rural communities, "freedom colonies."[19] To many ex-slaves, nothing had mattered so much as getting their own land, which brought the only true freedom. A black representative to the 1868 South Carolina Constitutional Convention, speaking in support of that state's land redistribution program, said of his fellow freedmen, "Night and day they dream of owning their own land—it is their all in all."[20]

"Don't ever sell your land, the land will take care of you," Andy Patterson of Houston County told his grandchildren just before World War II, and some of the grandchildren listened.[21] The story of the Texas freedmen's settlements contains many things often left out of our general accounts of southern history, among them the story of the freedmen land accumulators like Patterson, who acquired hundreds of acres to divide among his children, passing down a precious landhold into the twentieth century. Blood told, and at the freedmen's settlements the truncated families of slave times developed almost clanlike solidarity and complexity, based always on the land. Booker T. Washington's programs of black advancement through land-ownership, hard work, and self-sufficiency came together at the freedmen's settlements, where the Colored County Agents of the Texas Extension Service, the Jeanes School Supervisors, and the Rosenwald Fund and Slater Fund administrators found their natural constituencies and revitalized rural communities. The Great Depression, World War II, and the civil rights era had an impact on Texas freedmen's settlements, but many of them demonstrated a stubborn persistence during the decades when rural whites from very similar communities scattered to the four winds, Dallas, and Houston.

CHAPTER TWO

A Terrible Freedom

On June 19, 1865, General Gordon Granger landed at Galveston with a token force of 1,800 federal troops and proclaimed that all slaves held in Texas now were free. Word of this emancipation spread slowly northward at horseback speed from Galveston. As the bumper cotton crop of 1865 progressed toward "laid by" time, after which no further cultivation would be needed until harvest, many former slave owners delayed imparting the disruptive news to their laboring field hands.

However, just north of Galveston, in rural Harris County, the great news arrived early. Harrison Barrett, age fifteen, was chopping weeds from cotton with other slaves in his master's field on the day that someone told them they were free. Most threw down their cotton hoes and began to dance and sing in jubilation, but young Annie Jones, age eleven, also present in the field, recalled that Harrison did not join them. He said, "I don't feel like dancing until I get Ma and get my Pa and all my brothers and sisters, and then I'll dance." By a few years later, Barrett not only had gathered his lost family members around him but had established an independent freedmen's settlement along the banks of the San Jacinto River.[1]

At some point during the summer of 1865, thousands of Texas slave owners called their bondsmen together to tell them they were free. Most begged the former slaves to stay on their farms at least until the year's cotton crop had been picked, and they offered various inducements of money, food, and continued support. Some even offered the ex-slaves their own land to farm.

What happened next depended upon whether the freed persons were young or old and upon their opinions of the former master. Older freedmen tended to stay on for a while; younger freedmen tended to go. To both young and old, the pleas and offers of truly harsh masters fell on deaf ears.

It was a time of jubilation and terror. Felix Haywood recalled: "Everyone was singing. We were all walking on golden clouds. Hallelujah! Everybody went wild. We all felt like heroes, and nobody had made us that way but ourselves. We were free. Just like that, we were free. Nobody took our homes, but right off colored folks started on the move. They seemed to want to get closer to freedom, so they knew what it was—like it was a place or a city."[2] Jeff Calhoun's Freestone County master had been hard on his slaves, so nobody heeded the man's offer of ten acres and a mule to each family to stay on his place. "It was just like throwing a stick among a bunch of chickens, niggers going every direction, and nowhere to go," Calhoun recalled.[3] The brutal master of Richard Carruthers offered no inducements to stay, probably knowing they would be useless. The master called his slaves up to the house and said, " 'All you niggers are freed.' We so glad, we scattered just like partridges. God knows where I went. I was a fiddler. Everywhere we had a ball, I set there all night and played for the folks to dance."[4]

Some young men took to the road, then had second thoughts. Smith Austin's master, Rance Davis, told him he was free to leave and gave him a horse, but after a while Austin turned his horse around. He told Davis, "I don't want to be free, cause I couldn't make no living. I'd rather be a slave." Davis told him there were no more slaves, but he could stay on to work for his food, housing, and clothes. Austin explained, "I worked there long time. By-me-by I bought little piece of land near Irene, right on the line between Navarro and Hill Counties."[5]

Many older family men stayed on for a while because of a lack of resources—a poor living on the old place seemed a better alternative than that of "being turned loose like a bunch of wild hogs." Hannah Jameson of Harrison County recalled: "When surrender broke, you could tie all a nigger family had in a bedsheet. They had nothing cept a house full of niggers and no where to go."[6]

Often a poor offer seemed better than none. Cato Carter's master returned penniless, "wore-out and ragged" from the war, called all the people together in the front yard, and told them: "Mens and womens, you are today as free as I am. You are free to do as you like, cause the damn Yankees done decreed that you are. But there ain't a nigger on my place, that was born here or ever lived here, that can't stay here and work and eat to the end of his days, as long as this old place will raise peas and goobers. Go if you wants, or stay if you wants." Carter reported that some left, some stayed on.[7]

Rather quickly it became obvious that official U.S. Army policy was that former slaves should stay on, the better to harvest the cotton crop of 1865 and the ones thereafter. In July of 1865, only a month after he had freed

Texas slaves, General Granger issued General Order No. 3, advising freedmen to remain with their old masters and sign labor contracts. He warned that he would not allow blacks to collect at army posts, nor would he support them in idleness. Furthermore, he forbade freedmen to travel without passes from their employers.[8]

Perhaps emboldened by such policies, landowners in parts of Texas used violence and the threat of violence to maintain de facto slave conditions into 1866, with or without labor contracts. Months after slaves in nearby Harrison County had been freed, African Americans across the Sabine River in Rusk County labored in servitude under the threat of death. Their white masters hanged or shot any black caught fleeing north to Harrison County and freedom. Late in 1865 and even beyond, some Rusk County slaves attained freedom only at gunpoint. "Government men" forced Susan Merritt's master to gather his people together so that they could be informed of their freedom. "The man read that paper telling us we were free, but Massa made us work several months after that. He said we got 20 acres land and a mule, but we didn't get it."[9]

Likewise, half by enticement, half by threat, James Green stayed on after Emancipation at a big cotton plantation near Columbus, Colorado County, where work conditions closely resembled slavery. During the next year or so, "No great change come about in the way we went on. We had the same houses, only we all got credit from the store and bought our own food. We got shoes and what clothes we needed, too. Some of us got whipped just the same, but nobody got nailed to the tree by his ears. The white men in the habit of having Negro girls still goes on having them. I don't know how much they paid them for it, but they got treated better."[10]

Impoverished by loss of their human property, but with lands, homes, plantations, and market towns largely intact, Texas cotton farmers struggled to survive. The state's agricultural lands had declined in value by over 25 percent, since land without labor to work it was of diminished value, and the work force had been emancipated. Many doubted if blacks could be made to do adequate farm work short of the controls of slavery.[11] As at the Colorado County plantation where James Green labored, landowners commonly tried to maintain as many slavelike conditions as socially and legally possible.

As elsewhere across the defeated South, two related strategies soon sought to intimidate, segregate, and economically subjugate Texas freedmen, one official and legal and one informal and extralegal. These were the "Black Codes," passed by the Texas Legislature and other southern legislatures in 1866, and a wave of white-on-black violence and terrorism that

threatened to engulf Texas "in a race war in which Negroes and their protectors suffered a great loss of life."[12]

Various labor laws passed in 1866 tried to "freeze freedmen into a system of indentured servitude" with a set of interrelated statutes that "gave
local authorities and landowners the ability to coerce free labor with the
threat of forced labor."[13] Many whites feared that blacks would work only
if compelled; hence, the infamous Black Codes of that year. Lawmakers
incorporated many of the army's policies toward the ex-slaves, then went
far beyond them, clearly violating the 1866 Civil Rights Act.[14] One law required all able-bodied blacks to work or else be charged with "vagrancy"
and sentenced to hard labor. Labor contracts proving employment had to be
filed with the county clerks. A man's signature or mark on such a document
obligated his entire family to work, under strong penalties for breach of contract, malingering, disobedience, or even absence caused by illness. Those
unattached to a landowner easily ran afoul of stringent "vagrancy" codes
that first trapped them into county jails, then placed minors into forced
"apprenticeships" and adults into convict-labor gangs, both of which much
resembled slavery.[15]

Other laws of 1866 tried to establish firm barriers between the races that
anticipated much of the Jim Crow legislation decades later. Black codes forbade freedmen from voting, holding political office, serving on juries, or
testifying against whites in court. Marriage between the races was forbidden. The state required railroads to provide separate cars for blacks, thus
setting the pattern for segregation of all public facilities.[16]

Authorities concerned with enticing or coercing black labor into white
cotton fields often disapproved of freedmen who set out to obtain their own
land to farm. Aware of white public opinion, the Eleventh Legislature in
1866 passed a homestead law granting up to 160 acres of free public land to
white persons only, blocking this route to black landownership. According
to Texas Reconstruction historian James Smallwood, "As much as any other
factor, this land act explained why more blacks did not become independent yeomen, but instead remained tied to white landlords. As late as 1871,
not one in a hundred Negroes owned land." In many locales, feeling ran
strongly against whites who dared to sell land to blacks. The editor of the
Harrison Flag denounced this practice as "treasonable." In Travis County,
"night riders" attacked black landowners, hoping to force them out of the
community.[17]

Night riders had impact far beyond Travis County. By late in 1867, the
Texas Black Codes had run afoul of the national Civil Rights Amendment
and the arrival of Republican leadership and "Congressional Reconstruc-

tion," but many of their sentiments and segregationist tactics remained informally in effect, enforced by a rising tide of white violence and terrorism.

Some violence began immediately after Emancipation, triggered by bitterness over loss of the war and the sight of blacks rejoicing. Armstead Barrett personally witnessed the knife murder of a black woman crying "I's free! I's free!" by a white man on a horse, and Annie Row saw her master drop dead of a stroke while rushing with a gun to kill his field hands.[18] Many acts of violence went unreported in the chaotic early days of Freedom, as blacks roamed the roads, visited the towns they had never seen, and searched for lost relatives. A rumor circulated that fanatic whites had wiped out entire black plantation communities by poisoning wells.

Texas officials and newspaper editors had little to say about violence to freedmen during the first years after Emancipation, but the reports of Freedmen's Bureau subagents, army garrison commanders, and the American Missionary Society told a different story.[19] After lengthy study of such records, historian Barry Crouch generalized:

Violence surrounded all aspects of a former slave's life, from work to school, from politics to social relations. In the labor arena violence continually surfaced from signing of the contract to the division of the crop. Whether attending religious meetings harassed or broken up by disgruntled whites, or school where white assailants attacked the children, blacks found mundane activities dangerous. Transgression of established white mores led to physical conflict, and political participation by blacks intensified white racial attitudes, engendering more violence.[20]

Whites required a slavelike deference after Emancipation, and until the social system of segregation sorted itself out, a perceived lack of deference often evoked a violent response. Whites killed blacks for making a display of their freedom, for refusing to remove their hats when whites passed, for refusing to be whipped, for improperly addressing a white man, and "to see them kick." The sheriff of DeWitt County shot a black man for whistling "Yankee Doodle," and Charles Hodges, a member of the Bill Bateman gang, which operated in Harrison County, shot a black youth because the boy had his hands in his pockets and would not stand at attention when Hodges rode by. A Freedmen's Bureau agent in Red River County wrote that whites killed blacks locally "for the pure love of killing."[21]

The Bureau of Refugees, Freedmen, and Abandoned Lands began to function in Texas during December of 1865 and passed out of existence early in 1870. The Freedmen's Bureau had no confiscated or abandoned lands to redistribute to blacks in Texas, and the agency's fifty-nine subassistant commissioners and ten assistant subagents largely confined themselves to supervising labor contracts, aiding the desperately indigent, establishing black schools, and attempting to defend blacks from violent attack. Many agents tried hard to accomplish these things, but their numbers were inadequate, as was their support from federal troops. By the late 1860s, federal troops in Texas had been reduced to 3,700 men, only 1,292 of them manning the nineteen interior garrisons away from the Mexican border and the southwestern frontier.[22] Federal "occupation" of Texas had become almost a farce.

Freedmen's Bureau agents and army garrison commanders repeatedly complained in letters that local whites behaved with great arrogance, as if they had not been defeated. Even at the citadels of federal power, blacks and unionists faced deadly opposition. By late 1868, six bureau agents had been murdered, including the intrepid William G. Kirkman, who had been shot at three times before the evening Cullin Baker's gang called him outside his Boston, Texas, office and killed him. Tyler, Texas, served as headquarters of the 13th subdistrict of the Freedmen's Bureau, and four companies of U.S. troops, 179 men in all, were stationed there, but one morning in 1867 early risers in Tyler found several black soldiers hanging from the limb of an oak tree.[23]

Worse things happened in the remote countryside where most freedmen lived—probably much, much worse. We will never know how many black people died during the 1860s, but during its first three years of operation, the Freedmen's Bureau compiled a list of 2,225 cases of shootings, assaults, whippings, and hangings, and agents believed that large numbers went unreported. Subagent Gregory Barrett complained in 1868 that "they shoot, cut, and maltreat them when they feel like it, and in some portions of this subdistrict a perfect reign of terror exists." During that same year, agent Henry Sweeney of Jefferson wrote of the local terror tactics of the Knights of the Rising Sun: "Whipping the freedmen, robbing them of their arms, driving them off plantations, and murdering whole families are of daily, and nightly occurrence, all done by disguised parties whom no one can testify to. The civil authorities never budge an inch to try and discover these midnight marauders and apparently a perfect apathy exists throughout the whole community regarding the general state of society. Nothing but *martial law* can save this section."[24]

The death toll rose into the low thousands, Barry Crouch believes, calculating that one percent of Texas's black male population between fifteen and forty-nine years of age died violently during the first three years of Reconstruction.[25] Certain communities took especially stunning losses.

Freedmen's Bureau agent Stephen McCreecy reported: "Sulphur Springs, Hopkins County, Texas, is a place of this character. In that place there are now twenty widows and seventy-five orphan children, whose husbands and fathers have been murdered since the close of war."[26]

In very truth, human monsters stalked the land in many parts of Texas where black people lived—terrifying fleshly manifestations of the black folk specter "Old Raw Hide and Bloody Bones." To avenge the South, a Limestone County white identified only as "Dixie" killed all the black men and women he could catch along remote country roads. Outlaws like John Wesley Hardin, Sam Grant, Benjamin Bickerstaff, and Bob "The Man Eater" Lee gained reputations as indiscriminate "nigger killers" and murdered hundreds of blacks.[27]

White terrorist societies began to organize early in 1866, loosely affiliated with the Ku Klux Klan, first founded in Tennessee in 1865. The Pale Faces, White Brotherhood, Knights of the White Camelia, Teutonic Knights, Sons of Washington, and Knights of the Rising Sun rode by night to search black homes for weapons, frighten blacks from their farms to steal their crops, harass independent black squatters and landowners, and to otherwise enforce white supremacy and black subjugation. Night raids on black farmsteads became so common in some areas that families in Bastrop, Limestone, Hopkins, Harrison, and other counties began sleeping in the woods.[28]

Bears, "panthers," and other wilderness varmints seemed little to fear compared to the "white cappers" that came by night. Alex Humphrey of the Hughes Spring community, Harrison County, recalled: "I heard folk say he [Cullen Baker] killed niggers like they was dogs, and if you want to put my folks on the run just say, 'Cullen Baker was seen in a neighborhood community last night.' They'd hide out for two days."[29]

No wonder, then, that many freedmen chose to remain under the protection of their former masters partly because of fear of the KKK-like groups that rode by night and the gangs of freedmen-killers that terrorized whole regions of the state. Hannah Jameson recalled the Klan's beating and killing people. "That's the reason Ma and my step-pa stayed with my old Master. He protect them."[30]

By the middle 1870s, when white Democrats resumed control of Texas government and bureau agents and occupying Union garrisons were no more, most freedmen who had left their old masters now found it expedient to establish subservient economic relationships with new ones. It was still dangerous out there in the countryside, and being somebody's field hand seemed safer for one's self and one's family. In a way, the white terror tactics had done their job. Most Texas freedmen worked as renters on cotton farms, with a minority residing in satellite "quarters" at white-approved locations near market towns and county seats. The Texas contract law was not repealed until 1871, when the Republicans still controlled the legislature, but by that time whites and blacks had reached a wary truce. Blacks had stayed on the land and proven more reliable and efficient laborers as freedmen than many landowners had expected. By 1871, as Robert Calvert noted, "Texas, as well as the South, was forced into choosing the share-crop system as a way to join the labor and the land."[31]

On the surface, sharecropping was a simple agreement, usually informal and verbal, between landowner and freedman farmer, regarding crops, labor, and land. The black family received a plot of land, seed, work stock, farming equipment, a house to live in, and support—"furnishing"—for the year. They paid their landlord with their labor and half of the value of their money crop, which was usually cotton, less his furnishing costs. Freedmen initially preferred sharecropping, since it seemed less like slavery than contract labor, with its threatening and usually indecipherable documents backed up by the local sheriff. White landowners liked the share-crop system because it required no cash payments, avoided putting anything in writing, and allowed excellent control and exploitation of black labor. As historian Leon F. Litwack aptly noted, they had discovered that "a slavery of debt worked almost as effectively as the old slavery of legal ownership."[32]

Sharecropping comprised various relationships as, in fact, slavery had done. In his travels about the South before the Civil War, Frederick Law Olmstead had often observed small slave owners laboring beside their slaves in the field—dressed just the same, living in similar crude log houses sometimes side by side at the edge of the field. Likewise, the black experience of being "on halves" depended on the whites you were on halves with and a good bit upon their scale of operations.

Some cropper-landowner relationships were face-to-face, personal, friendly, and fair. As under slavery, whites controlled social and economic circumstances and dispensed with, or strongly enforced, harsh rules and customs as they wished, but on the big plantations coming back into existence during the 1870s and afterward, conditions closely resembled those of slave times. In the cotton plantation counties of northeastern Texas and along the Brazos and Trinity rivers, freedmen lived in regimented cropper-farm communities, rural "quarters."

Just as they had done in slave days, black people rose in the dark at the sound of the big plantation bells (often recycled from slave times), caught their mules in the dark by lantern light, and worked long days from "can't see to can't see" under the hard eyes of pistol-carrying white "pushers," who closely resembled slave overseers. Technically, each cropper family rented its own land, operated its own farm, and made its own profits, but this was seldom the case. Private farmsteads became mostly fictive at the larger operations. Family members often labored in work gangs on the "through and through" system, plowing or chopping weeds through every family's twenty- or thirty-acre plots with no attention to property lines. A family's cotton profits for the season also had a fictive quality. Black pickers saw the precious cotton from their twenty or thirty acres roll off toward the gin in wagons, but that was the last they had to do with it until the landowner informed them how they had "come out" for the crop year—how much they had cleared over and above their furnishing costs. Rather often they learned they had cleared little or nothing, perhaps even that they remained in the landowner's debt. It was take it or leave it, freedmen knew, and if they remained in debt, even leaving was out of the question. They must stay on that landowner's farm for another year to work off what they owed him. Landowners rarely offered any records or cotton sale receipts to support their accountings of the crop year, and black share renters had little or no recourse. By custom, they could not dispute a white man's word, and appeal to local officers and courts was normally both useless and dangerous.[33]

For most Texas blacks, sharecropping proved the bitter reality that quickly followed the joy of freedom, and some thought this debt slavery without paternalism to be worse than conditions before 1865. Disillusionment came swiftly for some freedmen. Felix Haywood recalled, "We knew freedom was on us, but we didn't know what would come with it. We thought we were going to get rich like the white folks. We thought we were going to be richer than the white folks, because we were stronger and knew how to work, and the whites didn't, and we didn't have to work for them no more. But it didn't turn out that way. We soon found out that freedom could make folks proud but it didn't make them rich."[34]

"You talk about slavery, it never began until after we was supposed to be free," Dave Byrd of Houston County said. "We had to work farms on the halves, very little to eat, and no clothes except what we begged. Then after we got a crop made, it would take every bit of it to pay our debts. We had no doctors when we got sick, and from the day we was turned loose, we had to shoulder the whole load. Taxes to pay, groceries to buy, and what did we get? Nothing."[35] When Eli Coleman's master informed his slaves that they were free, he told them they could stay on as sharecroppers if they wished. Coleman stayed with most of the others and came to bitterly regret his decision. "I was sharecropper, and Mr. White Man, that was really when slavery began. For when we got our crop made, he took every bit of it to pay our debts and had nothing left to buy winter clothes or pay doctor bills. And Masser he never owned us anymore. He didn't care what become of us, as he wouldn't lose nothing then if we got sick or died, and it never mattered cause he could get another slave without it costing him anything."[36] All across Texas and the cotton South, a cynical postwar saying summed up this new work relationship: "Kill a mule, buy another'n; kill a nigger, hire another'n."

By the late 1870s, sharecropper farms that in some measure subscribed to this harsh dictum dominated economic life on the better cotton soils across the eastern half of Texas. More fortunate freedmen lived on smaller cropper farms in more humane circumstances, and some had accumulated enough property in work stock and farming equipment to become tenants, "thirds-and-fourths renters," usually selling their own crops and paying their landlords with a third of the corn and a fourth of the cotton. Sometimes such families lived in dispersed farmsteads. Sharecroppers on larger farms, however, usually lived in villages of small board-and-batten houses, virtually wooden tents, gathered together in parts of their plantations.[37] Large farms might have several of these "quarters," the rural counterpart of the segregated black neighborhoods that had grown up adjacent to white market towns and county seats. White names, often derogatory, labeled the latter places—at Lockhart in Caldwell County, "Cocklebur"; at Kountz in Hardin County, "Fly Blow"; and at a great many other places, simply "Niggertown."

However, another sort of black community might occasionally be encountered by travelers in the remote countryside, and these squatter and landowner settlements had withdrawn from whites and named themselves. During 1872, a wagon train of freedmen from Webberville on the Colorado River led by preacher John Wynne founded St. John Colony in a wilderness of post-oak sand hills along the Caldwell-Bastrop county line. White contemporaries only casually noted such places, if at all, and then often dismissively. One traveler crossed the Trinity River valley about this time and wrote to his wife. "All the improvements worth noting are on the prairie, but a free nigger patch, with demoralized log-hut, occasionally appears in the low wooded bottoms, where that class usually lives."[38]

At the end of remote roads, along county lines, and down in the river bottoms, few such places had been incorporated, or platted, or even properly listed on county maps. These were unofficial places by their very nature, some so much so that the sheriff or the census taker only rarely intruded on their affairs. In truth, the casual traveler might pass through one of these rural communities without even noticing that a community was there. Infrastructure was slight, and it might be scattered about at different locations in the dispersed community. Almost always there was a church, or churches, and a school; almost always there was a gristmill and a cane mill to produce the community's survival staples of corn meal and cane syrup; sometimes there was a small steam-powered cotton gin, often of the multiple-use variety that also ground corn and sawed lumber.[39]

Communities often renamed themselves for internal reasons or used more than one name at the same time. In Cherokee County, Hog Jaw became Sweet Union and Andy became Cuney. In Goliad County one community became successively known as the Colony, Perdido, Centerville, Ira, and Cologne, the name that finally stuck. Several of the state's Bethlehems were such freedmen's communities, as were all three of its Nazareths. Scattered across the eastern half of Texas were Green Hill, Yellow Prairie, Red Branch, Black Branch, Weeping Mary, Board Bottom, Jerusalem, Freedmen's Ridge, Egypt, Frog, Elm Slough, Lost Ball, and several hundred other places.[40]

Certain patterns showed up in the names of these black communities. The common use of place-names from the Bible and the word "chapel" emphasized how many settlements began with establishment of rural churches. The words "sand," "creek," "branch," "slough," and "bottom" were common components of settlement place-names, suggesting locations on less-than-ideal cotton soils in sand hills and flood-prone creek and river bottoms. As at St. John Colony in Caldwell County, the word "colony" commonly occurred in community place-names, implying a colonizing move by freedmen pioneers into a wooded wilderness surrounded by unpredictable whites.[41]

Some such freedmen's settlements had their origins on the very day that certain masters told slaves of their freedom. More paternalistic owners sometimes tried to provide for their former slaves. Slavery had been many different experiences for the bondsmen, depending always on the attitudes and policies of the slave holders, who in truth held even the powers of life and death over their human property. Some owners chose to operate their plantations as sadistic death camps; others ran them as interracial Christian families; slave holders had the power, and the choice was theirs. Generalizing about Bastrop County, freedman Robert Prout reported the failed rumor of 1865 that every family would get forty acres and a mule from the government, then added, "A lot of masters was good enough to help their ex-slaves get a start by giving them some land, horses, and milk cows."[42] Amy Else had been enslaved on a plantation near Marshall, and she recalled that the master and the missus had come out on the porch to tell their slaves they were free. Both whites were crying. The former slaves could go or stay, as they wished, and those who wanted could buy land on the plantation. "Most of the old generation stayed on and bought farms from him. He let them pay them out by the year."[43]

Freedman John Sneed reported a festive "freedom day" on his master's farm in Travis County, with reassurances from the former owner.

> We had a tearing-down dinner, and the niggers bellowed and cried and didn't want to leave Marse Doctor. He talked to us and said as long as he lived we would be cared for, and we was. There was lots of springs on his place, and the married niggers picked out a spring and Marse Doctor gave them stuff to put up a cabin by the spring. And they took what they had in the slave quarters to the new house. They wanted to move from the nigger quarters, but not too far from Master. They would come back to the big house for flour, meal, or meat up to Marse Doctor died.[44]

Sneed's master willed every slave something. Most got a cow, a horse, a pair of hogs, and some chickens. Sneed's mother received a pair of horses, a wagon, and seventy acres of land.

Rare owners went beyond this. In Houston County, slaveholders John and Anna Jane Smith formally deeded portions of their Trinity River valley plantation to their slaves, house servants and field hands alike, even before the Civil War ended. This became the Cedar Branch settlement, named for the brush arbor, then church, erected on land donated by the Smiths. The family built their bondsmen a church, then gave them a big plantation bell to hang in its bell tower, where (in a successor structure) it yet resides.[45] A few miles to the south of the Smiths, a family named Hall sold land on easy terms to its former slaves and to others coming from afar for decades. The Halls' large plantation thus gave rise to the linked freedmen's settlements of Hall's Bluff, Wheeler Springs, and Dixon-Hopewell, which stretched southward for miles along the wooded bluffs overlooking the Trinity River valley.[46]

Even before Emancipation, some slaves had fled to the woods for self-granted freedom. Runaways eked out a subsistence living in wilderness areas adjacent to many big plantations. Historian Abigail Curlee wrote, "Some left impulsively; others established a camp in the woods when the roasting ears and wild plums were ripe; still others timed their departures from the cotton fields by the purpling grapes, the silvering cane, and the dropping of the pecans." After two or three weeks, most of these short-range runaways returned, took their punishments, and returned to work, though "a few planters had Negroes in the woods all the time, particularly the woods around 'Peach Point' in the lower part of Brazoria County."[47] Jack Little of Cherokee County was such a woodsman, and by the time Little learned of Emancipation he had already made himself free. Preely Coleman remembered: "Jack Little was almost a wild man. I think he came from Africa. Caused a world of trouble, wouldn't work, finally ran off and lived in the woods two years. Somebody slipped a frying pan to him, and he had his gun, just lived on wild turkeys and rabbits. He was staying in the woods when freedom came."[48]

Likewise, after word of Emancipation, a good many black people "took themselves and their freedom to the woods," as William Owen wrote of former slaves in the vicinity of his home community of Pin Hook.[49] The first impulse of some was to leave their former masters and to get as far from white people as they could, and in a good many cases these woods squatters would in time give rise to freedmen's settlements. Few newly emancipated slaves could afford to buy land, but some squatted on unworked land and, using sticks as tools, planted crops. They supplemented their diet by fishing and by hunting with bows and arrows and made clothes from animal skins. One freedman said, "If the woods were not full of wild game, all us Negroes would have starved to death."[50]

Other squatters moved off into the woods after the wonderful rumor of a government-provided "forty acres and a mule" ended in dashed hopes at Christmas 1865. Certain wartime land-redistribution policies of General William T. Sherman in South Carolina had launched this dream of forty acres and a mule, but after the war Reconstruction politics and President Andrew Johnson's adamant opposition soon quashed the idea of land reparations for slavery. Meanwhile, however, the rumor spread across the conquered South like wildfire. In Texas, as elsewhere, blacks waited for the dream of landed independence to come to pass, and whites feared it might turn out to be true, but both hopes and fears died at Christmas 1865. The great gift did not come. Former slaves now realized that if they wanted the real freedom that only land could bring, they would have to get it for themselves.[51]

Few former slaveholders were as helpful as the Smith and Hall families of Houston County, although the rare whites that did assist former slaves in getting land helped to create many freedmen's settlements. Blacks had few resources after slavery, and formal land acquisition required money or credit, whites willing to sell to freedmen, and white neighbors willing to allow this to happen—necessities that rarely came together.[52] In fact, in Harrison, Collin, Grimes, and other plantation counties, white landowners often joined forces to prevent land sales to blacks; the freedmen work force belonged in their cotton fields, they believed. No wonder that only 1.8 percent of Texas freedmen farmers owned their own land by 1870.[53]

However, squatting on land was another matter, and a considerable number of Texas freedmen gained informal landholds by this means of possession common on the southern frontier. Harrison Barrett of Harris County was one of these supposedly landless freedmen, and he listed himself as "agricultural laborer" in the U.S. Census of 1870, but Barrett already had full use of his lands along the San Jacinto River—property that he would not formally purchase until 1889. Probably Barrett squatted on wooded wilderness lands along the river with full permission of his likely former owner, a man named White, who finally sold him the property in 1889. With little doubt, already by 1870 Harrison Barrett's determination to reassemble his family, his leadership ability, and his white friends had created a land-holding freedmen's community known locally as Barrett's settlement or simply Barrett.[54]

Evidence suggests that there were many more just like it. No federal census men or county tax collector enumerated squatters, but oral traditions attest that many black squatter communities existed in the eastern half of Texas by 1870. Again and again, people told how their ancestors pioneered the wilderness, cleared the big woods, built brush arbors and log churches, and formed backwoods communities many years before seeking formal land titles by purchase, preemption, or the "law of adverse possession"—the law of "squatter's rights" on "lost land."[55]

Whether composed of squatters or of landowners, most freedmen's settlements began in wilderness areas previously untouched by ante-bellum cotton agriculture. As historian Edward Ayers aptly noted, the blacks took the "backbone and spareribs" that the whites did not want.[56] Settlements took root in post-oak sand hills, pine barrens, creek and river bottoms, and other places previously uncleared for agriculture. Much remains conjectural about the origins of Texas freedmen's settlements, but where they located may still be seen.

Seldom has the move to the wilderness been recorded in direct testimony, but in a 1938 interview Eddie McAdams told of going to ground in the remote Trinity River bottoms of Madison County at the end of Reconstruction. Fearful of local "paddyrollers," McAdams worked for a white man for a time, then:

> I come to Madison County on the Trinity River on what they called the Island and started to farming for myself. I built me a house here, first out of poles that I cut and stood them up on ends, fastened together at

the top, cleared me some land, got me two oxen that I raised to plow that land with, and started to farming.

For a number of years, all I had to eat was corn parched green and meat that I killed out of the woods. And I eat lots of that raw, as we did not have a very easy way of starting a fire. Yes, and fish that I could catch out of the river. Then, after I got three or four children big enough to help me, I cut poles and built me a four room house out of logs, and split out boards to cover it with.[57]

Wilderness sand hills and wooded uplands also attracted many freedmen seeking land and isolation, as at Sand Hill in Nacogdoches County, Nettleridge in Shelby County, and Germany in Houston County. Cotton farmers did not value these sandy soils, but they worked well for the frontier survival crops of sweet potatoes, peas, peanuts, "greens," and corn. Sandy-land farmers rarely starved, no matter what happened to the cotton. Their semi-feral cattle survived on the sparse grasses and forbs that grew under the widely spaced virgin pines, and "rooter hogs," the chief southern meat animal, fattened themselves on the fall mast of acorns, hickory nuts, and wild fruits. Sand hills and swampy bottoms often remained as free range well into the twentieth century, long after fence laws had been established in areas with fertile soils. Free-range customs allowed not only cooperative use of unenclosed lands as commons for the ranging of semi-feral hogs and cattle but other traditional privileges. Free range also meant the rights to trespass, hunt, fish, gather nuts and plant foods, and collect fuel wood on other people's land. Slightly stretched, such traditions allowed production of minor money crops such as railroad ties, barrel staves, animal pelts, and cypress shingles.[58]

Free-range customs, legal and extralegal, often lasted longest in the bottoms. Bottomland locations were environmentally richer but chancier. Edge-of-the-bottom homesites had been favored by whites since the first European settlement of Texas, but the bottoms themselves were usually avoided. The virgin hardwoods that grew there required backbreaking labor to clear the land for agriculture. Once cleared, bottomland soils produced profusely, but creeks or rivers might flood and destroy promising crops one year in three. In addition, bottomland homesites risked the killer fevers presumed to be caused by the "miasmas" of decaying vegetation. According to one old folk dictum, if you built your home in the bottoms, "you better get on a big bluff where you get the breeze both ways and away from that old green water." No one understood the relationships between stagnant water, swampland, mosquitoes, and deadly fevers in 1870, but they did know that

Clear Lake near the Angelina River. Traditional site of picnics and baptisms for the County Line community of Nacogdoches County. (Richard Orton)

fevers and chills plagued such locations. However, the freedmen, with few or no resources, had to go somewhere for their landholds, and as ecologist Dan Lay observed, "the bottoms attracted the people who had nothing."[59]

Since large creeks and rivers often formed county lines in the eastern half of Texas, a remarkable number of freedmen's settlements ended up in those locations, as in the case of aptly named County Line, Nacogdoches County, just east of the Angelina River. Perhaps other factors motivated people to settle near county boundaries. Property values generally declined with distance from centrally located county seat towns, and county lines were as far from townsmen landowners and centers of white authority as freedmen could get.

Again and again, perhaps in most cases with at least tacit permission from nearby whites, freedmen established squatter communities in the bottoms. A mixture of motives for white acquiescence may be assumed, though few sources directly commented on this. Texas had much wilderness land in 1870, and most agriculturalists viewed the heavily wooded and flood-prone bottomlands as of little value. As in the case of the traveler across the Trinity River valley, "free nigger patches" in the swampy bottoms drew hardly a notice. Some former slaveholders felt concern for their former bondsmen, and willingly allowed them to form squatters' communities on their land in nearby bottoms. Such locations afforded good hunting, fishing, foraging, and subsistence farming (assuming no big floods drowned the fields), and freedmen there required little support from their former patrons, who nonetheless kept them close by and available for employment as sharecroppers and wage hands.

Early land sales to freedmen often involved some of the same considerations, as unwanted, poor, or dangerous land changed hands for not much money. Local traditions hold that whites in northeastern Cherokee County got together after Emancipation and decided that squatting would be allowed, then lands would be sold, in a certain agreed-upon area. This policy segregated former bondsmen on poor wilderness land well away from white communities but close enough to be drawn upon for agricultural labor. Thus, presumably, did the Black Ankle (later Woodville) community begin.[60]

In south-central Texas, plantation owner Seabourne Lewis and other landowners allowed their former bondsmen to move into the wooded wilderness of the nearby San Antonio River bottoms and establish a line of squatter communities that lasted until World War II. Lewis's Bend, Sprigg's Bend, and others sprang up—a riverside freedmen's district collectively known as "The Bends." Subject to floods, the San Antonio River bottom had been left in heavy woods and uncultivated by Lewis. From time to time, the San Antonio River flooded the bottom and people rode out on wagons through the backwater. Then the river went down, and people drove wagons back in and cleaned up, scraping alluvial mud from their house floors with cotton hoes. Here, as at a lot of other places, bottomland dwellers had the process down to a drill.

Similar settlements grew up upstream and downstream of Lewis's Bend. One man recalled: "There were a lot of tiny communities all up and down the San'tone River. There was the Dalton bottom near DuPont. The Linnville boys were bootleggers there. Then there was the Joshua bottom where the Joshuas lived and inside that community was a bunch of Mexican shacks called 'the Palmettos.' There was also Sand Bayou and Black Bayou along the river. People were allowed to roam and squat up and down that river."[61]

Eugene Tillman had been born at Lewis's Bend in 1902. Of the first settlers, he noted: "They farmed along the river. Pecans, peaches, and grapes were everywhere. There were hackberries, mulberries, and anaqua. The ground had wild greens and wild onions and chinquapins. . . . The river was important, you see. . . . When these people come in here to settle, they had to be near water. . . . Lewis's Bend was a crossin' spot. . . . We never used a doctor in that river bottom. We used lots of natural medicines and herbs."[62]

At some back-of-beyond locations, freedmen and poor whites moved into the same wilderness bottomlands to establish adjacent settlements and uneasy cooperation during the era of Jim Crow. The freedmen's squatter settlement of Evergreen and the white squatter settlement of Sugar Hill formed after 1865 in that part of Titus County known as "Between the Creeks," a stretch of bottomlands, cross-cutting sloughs, tangled hardwoods, bad roads, and poor soils between White Oak Creek and the Sulphur River. The area settled just after the war and remained outside the mainstream history of Titus County until very late. Historians Deborah Brown and Katharine Gust wrote: "Until the 1940s the changes of the twentieth century passed on either side of the rivers, seldom touching the lives of those between. The few roads into the area became a sea of mud when it rained, forcing the people to rely on themselves. Local women acted as midwifes, since it sometimes took hours for a town doctor to cross the rivers. The 'law' rarely came between the creeks, finding it difficult to penetrate both the thickets and the defenses of the people. Left to themselves, they developed their own code, based on their unwillingness 'to let people run over em.' "[63]

Blacks in Evergreen and whites in nearby Sugar Hill shared a hardscrabble existence, dictated by environmental circumstances. Most relied on cotton as a cash crop, though soils between the creeks were sandy and poor. They also raised subsistence crops of corn, field peas, sweet potatoes, and peanuts. Most important, probably, was the stockraising of hogs and cattle on the free range, which lasted very late. Many old-timers interviewed in the mid-1970s recalled that the area long remained uncleared and unfenced. One man described it this way: "It was a free part of the world at that time, free. You'd start in here, ride plumb to Avery horseback and never cross a fence, never cross nothing." Black or white, everybody hunted and fished and lived off the open range. Most families squatted on their land, ran hogs and cattle in the unfenced woods, chopped railroad ties, made white oak barrel staves, and distilled moonshine whiskey.[64]

As at Lewis's Bend and other places, people often saw no good reason to formally own the land. One old-timer from Between the Creeks explained the obvious to an interviewer: "I can't tell you how long we used that land for nothing. That's the reason we didn't own none of it—we didn't have to buy it, we already had it! We didn't want to pay taxes on it, when we already had it."[65]

A little more cautious than others, freedmen Green Logan and Moses Price took care to preempt land within a decade of moving in after Emancipation to form the Evergreen settlement. (Green Logan had named the community for himself in hopes that it would last forever.) They prospered, became successful farmers, then invited other people on their lands as sharecroppers. A black community of landowners, rent farmers, and squatters grew up and spread out, with squatters on the periphery. Log houses scattered down a dirt road, their chimneys built of mud and straw, with a pole nearby for toppling them away from the house if they caught fire. No stone was available locally, and bricks cost money the freedmen did not have. After a while, Evergreen had a church, a school, and a small store run by Mose Price. Evergreen and Sugar Hill were segregated, but blacks and whites worked together in the bottoms, cutting timber, hacking ties, making whiskey, or helping each other with their stock. Ear-marked and branded, "rooter hogs and woods cattle" mixed and merged on the open range, and stockmen had to cooperate for the system to work. Strict Jim Crow segregation did not make sense on the free range. Mose Price kept a "traveler's bed" where white folks stayed when they were trapped by darkness or had business at Evergreen.[66]

In the two decades after 1870, many freedmen squatters such as Mose Price, Green Logan, and Harrison Barrett took legal steps to establish clear title to their lands, and census takers soon recorded an astonishing increase in the numbers of black landowners. Many obstacles stood in the way of black landownership, but the percentage of black Texas landowners increased almost fourteen times between 1870 and 1890, growing from 1.8 percent to 26 percent. Black landownership in Texas peaked at 31 percent in 1900, a year in which only Florida among states of the Lower South had a higher percentage of black owner-operators. The Lower South, including Texas, averaged 20 percent in 1900, the Upper South 41 percent, and the South as a whole 24 percent.[67] Even more remarkable, the great increase in African American landowners in Texas went against the general trend, which saw overall tenancy rates in the state rise from just over one-third in 1880 to one-half in 1910. Blacks attained land in the same decades that whites—for complicated economic reasons—lost it and passed into renter status.

By the middle 1870s in Texas and the South, Congressional Reconstruction drew to a close, and Democratic "Redemption" loomed on the horizon. Many freedmen feared a complete loss of liberties after resumption of political power by white Democrats. The threat seemed very real, triggering the "Exodus of 1879" by several thousand black Texans in search of cheap or free land in Kansas.[68] To the freedmen, land and freedom seemed almost the same thing; only land could protect them against total white control. It seems reasonable to assume that during these same years many Texas squatter-farmers, who already had land after a fashion, now took the initiative to firm up their landholds by means of formal purchase, preemption, or the law of adverse possession.

At many Texas freedmen's settlements, squatters like Harrison Barrett negotiated with white landowners, many of them their former owners, and purchased lands they had lived on for a decade or more. Whites took the lead in other land sales. Whether motivated by altruism or simply strapped for cash, a good many whites gave up on postbellum agriculture and broke up their large landholdings into small plots for sale on credit to blacks. William E. Kendall followed this policy at Fort Bend County, establishing the community of Kendleton.[69] Colonel George Washington Grant, prominent white leader at Huntsville, Walker County, marketed several thousand acres of hilly woods in ten- and twenty-acre tracts to freedmen. Grant also donated land for a church and school at this place that became known as Harmony or Grant's Colony.[70] The Alexander family of Wharton County, the Billingsleys of Fall County, and the Hodges of Limestone County did the same. In fact, historian Lawrence D. Rice documented over a hundred such estate subdivisions and sell-offs to freedmen.[71]

Most land purchases came at the end of a long period of hard work and frugality by a black family of which there is little record, but the "cashbook" of Daniel Trotter of Natchitoches Parish, Louisiana, offers a rare look at how a black family pieced together enough for a farm. This document demonstrated the long struggle to accumulate cash for a land purchase at the dollars and cents level. Trotter's wife sold eggs, a dozen at a time, and sewed for others. The family sold a few pigs and picked cotton for whites after their own crop was in. Trotter, adept at mechanics, repaired milling machinery, clocks, and firearms. Finally, in 1900, enough dollars and cents had accumulated that the Trotters bought "a plantation" for an undisclosed sum.[72]

Other freedmen settled so far back in the hills and bottoms that they homesteaded on "government land," land claimed by no one. Usually after a decade or two of use and improvement of this free land, they braved the white officials at the county courthouse to preempt it. Preemption converted government no-man's land to legal ownership, but preemption was a tedious, prolonged, and bureaucratic process, requiring the usually illiterate freedman to repeatedly deal with white authorities at the county courthouse. The applicant had to establish a residence on the land for at least three years, hire a professional surveyor to survey the land and file field notes on it, file an applicant's affidavit of three-year occupancy with two supporting affidavits, and wait for the state land office to issue a patent for 160 acres.[73]

Most families waited longer than the three years of required occupation before they put themselves through this ordeal, and some could never bear to do it and lived as squatters until abandoning the countryside after World War II. Still, at Peyton Colony in Blanco County, Germany in Houston County, and many other freedmen's settlements across Texas, black pioneers gained clear title to 160 acres by preemption. Research in Houston County land records, for example, showed the freedmen families at the Germany settlement, in the pine hills north of the Old San Antonio Road, passing through the stages of preemption during the 1870s and 1880s. At the same time, beginning in 1871, the isolated German family that gave the community its name also bestirred itself to preempt, having squatted in the virgin pines for no less than forty years.[74]

Most unimproved wilderness — "lost land," people called it — had been neglected by private landowners, not the State of Texas. Many freedmen squatters, the ones without permission, moved onto this land, which abounded in the pineywood counties of eastern Texas after the Civil War. Pine barrens and bottomland swamps had little value for decades, and absentee owners, many of them out of state, paid small attention to squatters on their lands. This set the stage for acquiring "lost land" by way of "squatter's right." Brown Wiggins of the Big Thicket accurately explained: "If you went and settled on a place and went to living there, anywhere in these woods, if you paid taxes on it and they didn't bother you for ten years, the court would give you a title to 160 acres. Some of these squatters would get 160 acres off most any big land owner before he would know it."[75]

Numerous freedmen and poor whites founded wilderness settlements and attained land by squatter's right, otherwise known as the "law of adverse possession." As historian Stephen Reich noted, "under this statute, any settler without evidence of title — a naked trespasser — could occupy and claim land held in title by someone else, and through continuous possession that is open, visible, and hostile by constructive acts of ownership, could acquire legal title to 640 acres if the titleholder failed to act to recover possession within ten years." East Texas wilderness woodlands were vast, unpopulated, and worth little until the big lumber companies began to arrive in the 1880s, and occupation and improvement of just a few acres might get the squatter 640 acres until 1879, at which time the Texas Legislature limited "lost land" acquisitions to 160 acres. However, this avenue to land ownership remained open, and a good many freedmen in Newton, Jasper, Polk, and other counties took advantage of it.[76]

In one way or another, several hundred Texas freedmen's settlements came into existence between 1865 and 1900, and the full stories of most of their fascinating origins are forever lost. At Barrett, County Line, Easton,

and one or two other places, researchers followed the difficult documentary trail of deeds and wills and tax records backward only to find them
stop short before a period of mysterious origin.[77] The reason seems clear.
Most freedmen's settlements existed as informal communities for years before courthouse records began to register their existence in land deeds and
other legal transactions. Even thereafter, records are sparse and incomplete
—partly because of Jim Crow neglect, partly because of black suspicions
of the white courthouse. Lands often changed hands without deeds being
recorded, people died intestate, and property fragmented. "The problem
of collecting data for this study has been difficult," a Prairie View A&M
graduate student complained about his research in Shelby County during
the 1940s. "Negroes in rural areas live and die without leaving any records
of any kind about themselves."[78]

To a degree, oral history and oral traditional history (accounts passed
down from others) reach back before the documents and fill gaps in the
records to reveal the patterns of community formation and development.
Family ties mattered at the settlements, and family ties survived across the
generations and with them the fragmentary stories of communities' origins.
This much seems clear: at the freedmen's settlements, African American
families shattered and truncated by slavery reformed, extended, and attained
almost clanlike complexity. These places represented a triumph of family
and of the ties of kinship, even of the ties of kinship across race.[79]

Rather often stories told of a band of siblings joining forces at the origins
of a settlement. Typically, they pooled their resources after several years of
working for whites, then squatted on unclaimed land, or purchased squatter's rights from earlier pioneers, or bought the land outright.[80]

At County Line in Nacogdoches County, Guss, Jim, and Felix Upshaw
formed an excellent team of leaders and backwoods pioneers at this community along the eastern edge of the Angelina River bottoms. Felix was an
excellent farmer, but Guss and Jim were jacks-of-all trades who could hunt,
fish, farm, operate steam-powered gristmills and sawmills, and do blacksmith and carpentry work. The Upshaw brothers also maintained good relationships with whites in the nearby Douglass community, to which their
family had been brought as slaves.[81]

Often, as at Jones Colony and Barrett, one sibling took the lead and
others followed. Harrison Barrett at Harris County established the landhold, then over a decade he gathered brothers, sister, parents, and a half-
brother around him.

Another common pattern of community origin involved a preacher leader
and his assembled congregation colonizing the wilderness. After Emanci-

Jim Upshaw of County Line, Nacogdoches County. Brothers Jim, Guss, and Felix
Upshaw founded the community around 1870. (Richard Orton)

pation, some freedmen felt the call to preach and gradually drew congregations of believers around them, worshiping in private homes or in brush
arbors. After a few years of accumulating resources, the ministers located
cheap or unclaimed land and white neighbors willing to allow black people
to settle, and the congregation pulled up rent-farm roots and followed their
"Moses" into the wilderness. This exact scenario unfolded for sharecrop-

per John Wynn's congregation at Hog Eye (Webberville) in Travis County. After Wynn found an unoccupied sand-hill wilderness along the Bastrop-Caldwell county line and whites willing to sell it cheaply, Wynn and most of his congregation launched a wagon train to the promised land one day in the 1870s. This place became known as Wynn's Colony and later St. John Colony.[82]

Sometimes freedmen's settlements and white settlements developed as linked communities in a kind of symbiotic relationship, as in the case of Evergreen and Sugar Hill in Titus County. Certainly many Texas freedmen's settlements ended up with special relationships, delicate linkages of obligation and friendship, to certain nearby white settlements. Jim Crow segregation might be suspended to a degree between such linked communities, and whites felt free to enter the black settlements to recruit day labor and sometimes regarded themselves as protectors of the nearby blacks.[83]

Most such special relationships between settlements began soon after Emancipation. Former slaves of whites at the Klondike community in Delta County moved a few miles south to the Sulphur River bottoms along the Hopkins County line after 1865. Klondike whites sold them land to establish the Friendship settlement, then sold land to other freedmen moving in from the Deep South (often with their former owners). Friendship blacks maintained a cordial relationship with the small market town of Klondike for a half century—working for Klondike whites, selling their cotton in town, and trading in the community's mercantile store, which in later years "ran a chicken peddler" into the Friendship community.[84]

At Hopkins County to the south, black Sand Field and white Reilly Springs had a similar relationship. Sand Field's pioneer families once had been the bondsmen of Reilly Springs' whites, and many of their family names were the same. Cad Ford, who operated a Sand Field syrup mill frequented by cane growers from both communities, came from a family of slaves owned by Allen Ford, the Reilly Springs pioneer. Some of the old intimacy of slavery times persisted between the two settlements. Free-range hog raisers worked together in late winter to separate and earmark the wide-ranging hogs, which sought fallen acorns with no respect for property lines or race. Sand Field and Reilly Springs neighbors of both races occasionally attended each others' churches and customarily played baseball at end-of-school celebrations, usually followed with a "famous Hopkins County stew" (although the two groups ate outside and sat somewhat apart). Blacks and whites freely moved back and forth between the linked communities on business of various sorts, and familiar anomalies were accepted, as in the case of mulatto Henry Durham, who looked entirely white, lived with his black wife in Sand Field, and commuted to cut white men's hair in a Reilly Springs barbershop.[85]

Some freedmen's settlements originated not along county lines in the remote countryside but just beyond white market towns—close enough for residents to walk in for "public work," should they so desire, but far enough out to be independent. Cross Hogs Branch outside of Brenham, Washington County, and Clarksville, just outside of Austin, were such communities. Virtually every county-seat town in the eastern half of Texas had one or two "Clarksvilles."[86]

Clarksville began soon after Emancipation in a wildernesslike setting just west of white Austin. Poor dirt roads linked Clarksville to town, and the place long remained isolated. Despite their closeness to the state capital, Clarksville residents operated their independent community much like a freedmen's settlement. They grew small patches of cotton and the usual subsistence crops, ran hogs in the woods, kept chickens and cows, and upon occasion shot rabbits, squirrels, and deer from their front porches. They cultivated large gardens and dried, canned, and stored most of the food they ate. Hog-killing time occurred in the late fall, as at settlements in the backwoods. At Clarksville, partly because of Jim Crow–era neglect by the Austin city fathers and partly because of community independence, rain barrels sufficed for drinking water, kerosene lamps for light, and outdoor toilets for sewers well into the early twentieth century.[87]

Clarksville's location maximized opportunities for its residents, who might choose to operate small farms, to commute out to the countryside for day work and rent farming, or to travel into the white town to work for whites as laborers, domestic servants, janitors, hostlers, carpenters, porters, and a wide variety of skilled and semiskilled blue-collar trades. Various Austin "quarters," including Wheatsville, Horst's Pasture, Ryna Branch, Gregorytown, Red River Street, and others, established themselves closer to the city center than Clarksville, and the independent freedmen's settlements of Kinchionville and Burdett's Prairie located farther out.[88] Houston and Dallas originally seem to have had this same complex array of black emancipation communities—independent freedmen's settlements on the far perimeters, black quarters downtown, and intermediate forms like Clarksville in between.[89]

Other anomalous black landowner communities emerged in the late nineteenth-century countryside, settled by freedmen and the sons and daughters of freedmen. At Littig in Travis County, Harvard Switch in Camp County, Hufsmith in Harris County, and other places black communities sprang up along the new railroads.[90] Harvard Switch seems to have begun around a house along the Texas and St. Louis Railroad built by a black railroad section foreman named Hard Ivory. Near Ratcliff in Houston County, the Allen Chapel community had another sort of industrial origin at the abandoned "Dago quarter" of the big Four-C Sawmill that "cut out" and left the place in 1918. Houses of the company's now-departed Italian workers sold for little or nothing to Ratcliff blacks, former company employees who had come to work for the Four-C from nearby Pine Springs and other freedmen's settlements.[91]

Older freedmen's settlements continued to spawn new settlements even after World War I. Communities typically ended up with a few thousand acres of land surrounded by whites reluctant to sell them more. By the second generation after the freedmen pioneers settled, family lands had fragmented to the point that younger sons often had no place to go. Sometimes they moved into town, but sometimes they located land a few miles away and began a new black landowner community. At Lee County around 1890, "twelve founding families" from the old community of Antioch migrated to establish Sweet Home settlement, and the first-generation community of Post Oak also spawned new settlements.[92]

Sometimes black districts composed of multiple communities formed (as in western Houston County), and sometimes these black districts developed names. People called the area along the San Antonio River "The Bends" and a part of San Augustine County "The Preemption."[93]

This same hiving-off process happened all across Texas, although land squatting had become difficult, if not impossible, at most places after 1890. By then an African American farmer needed good credit or hard cash to get increasingly expensive land. Between 1890 and 1900, as the acquisition of real property became more difficult, the precipitous rise of black landownership in Texas slackened, increasing only from 26 to 31 percent, the ultimate high-water mark.[94]

At a handful of locations, mostly after 1900, black entrepreneurs established market towns in the pattern of Boley, Oklahoma—black crossroads communities with businesses, banks, gins, and stores—in areas formally occupied by freedmen's settlements. In this way Center Point in Camp County, developed from the old O'Center settlement just before 1900. Ambitious locals built a new road to connect with the county seat of Pittsburgh, ten miles away, established a "Union Company" in 1898 to help blacks buy more land and improve their homes and farms, and modernized the local school. In 1916 a better-schools campaign resulted in a successful bond issue that built a new five-classroom school, which expanded to a fine rural high school with Rosenwald Fund assistance in 1927.[95]

Black promoters established Easton in Gregg County as a black residential community and market town in 1928, drawing residents from several freedmen's settlements in the vicinity.[96] Cuney developed from the old Andy settlement along the Neches River in Cherokee County around 1917, after Palestine banker H. L. Price moved to the community, bought land, set up the Andy Real Estate Company, and promoted the area as a commercial and agricultural center for blacks. He renamed the place Cuney after his son Cuney Price, who had been named in turn for prominent black politician Norris Wright Cuney. Like other such places in the era of Jim Crow (including famous Mound Bayou, Mississippi, much celebrated by Booker T. Washington), Price and his developer town finally fell on hard times, but not before growing into a considerable crossroads village. Cuney never incorporated and never had municipal water or sewers, but in its heyday this black community accumulated churches, stores, gins, sawmills, railroad station, hotel, telephone system, high school, and semi-pro baseball team.[97]

Some anomalous freedmen's settlements had unpredictable origins only marginally linked to railroads and the New South's modern industrial age. The story of Ames settlement, Liberty County, may stand as an example. A group of freedmen Creole families had migrated from Iberia, Louisiana, to the Republic of Mexico in search of a better life. Disillusioned by 1890, they gave up on Mexico and headed home by railroad, departing the train to stretch their legs at a stop in Liberty, Texas. Sylvester Wickliff and Terrance Trehan told their story to a sympathetic local white and learned of a large tract of land for sale cheap four miles out of town at the edge of the Big Thicket. They looked the land over, liked it, and purchased it for $3.75 an acre. Thus began the black Roman Catholic settlement of Ames, a community in time ministered to at Our Mother of Mercy Church by Josephite priests from Houston.[98]

From 1865 to 1900, freedmen's settlements rather often began with the arrival of a single black man or black family with mysterious resources allowing the purchase of land. Inquiries were made, whites were found willing to sell, with neighbors willing to allow the sale, and a black landhold was established. Then, rather quickly, other black families appeared to work as sharecroppers or to buy plots from the original settler, who often encouraged community formation by donations of land for church, school, and cemetery. Altruism and racial solidarity doubtless explained some of this generosity, but it was lonely out there in the white countryside. Soon, where once a single family had landhold, a black community formed.

Where they survived, settlement stories often raised more questions about the mysterious community founders than they answered. Soon after

Emancipation, a freedman named Abram Betts came from Virginia to Fayette County, then purchased land in nearby Lee County and founded the freedmen's settlement of Betts' Chapel. But how had Betts the Virginian come by his resources to buy this Texas land immediately after Freedom? And how had another Virginian freedman, Anderson Willis, purchased 3,000 acres of Freestone County in 1868?[99] Likewise, in 1870, Nacogdoches County freedman Edwin Arnold Wynn arrived in the county seat of Canton, Van Zandt County, with money in hand, purchased 300 acres of land, then offered a free acre to any black family that moved on his place and helped with his large farming operation. The Wynn settlement soon developed, an all-black community with two churches, a school, and its own water system.[100]

At about the same time, the West Chapel community of Camp County took root under the strong leadership of Richard A. Caldwell, who somehow obtained 400 acres of land in the area just after Emancipation. Active in church and school affairs, Caldwell ran a syrup mill, conducted agricultural experiments with peach trees, fathered eighteen children, and in 1885 purchased an 800-pound bell to proudly announce his community from the belfry of a combined church and school building.[101]

As in these examples, the handed-down accounts often remained silent about the sources of the money allowing land purchase. Sometimes, however, stories do admit that the mysterious resources derived from the social intimacies of slave times. Ugly as it was, brutal as it could be, slavery had been a time of great intimacy between the races, and some of the relationships begun during slavery did not shatter after Emancipation and segregation. The Birch Creek–Pleasant Hill community of Hopkins County, for example, began when a white man named George Wynn deeded acreage at Emancipation to each of his three children by a half-Indian, half-black freedwoman.[102]

In another case, Reverend James B. Sadler founded Rock Springs settlement, also known as "The Colony," in Bosque County. Descendants tell that the light-skinned Sadler was the son of the white Dr. Sadler, who relocated to Bosque County soon after the Civil War. James Sadler had been educated along with his master's white son and had been treated as a member of the family. He married an ex-slave of the Sadler household and began to preach and form a congregation. In 1878 he used family resources to purchase 545 acres and form a black community. After a few years, Reverend Sadler's Rock Springs Cumberland Presbyterian Church had a huge bell (not unlike Richard Caldwell's) "that could be heard throughout the area."[103] This church community became the focal point for African

American social and religious life in Bosque County, which had many more sharecropper quarters than freedmen's settlements.

Descendants of black families from Garland's Colony, Bowie County, told a somewhat similar story. John Calhoun Garland came to the area from Tennessee around 1850 with twenty-seven slaves. By all accounts, Garland treated his slaves well, taught many of them to read and write, and took care to keep families together. One of the twenty-seven was Ruth Garland, his daughter by a woman of Indian blood, who married another slave (also named Garland). Traditions suggest that John Garland also had other children among his twenty-seven bondsmen, and he certainly acted as if his slaves were blood-related. Garland emancipated all of them in 1862, went away to the Civil War, then returned to divide his 1,195-acre plantation among the twenty-five family heads, deeding the land outright or selling for minimal sums. Garland's body servant during the Civil War received 500 acres. John Garland then moved fifteen miles away, but he kept a close watch over his black community, helping to set up an early school with black trustees and white missionary society teachers.[104]

Very occasionally the story of blood relationship comes from close at hand. According to his daughter, French Taylor's white father recognized him as his son, accompanied him to Texas after the Civil War, and helped the young man purchase several hundred acres of land in the Hall's Bluff community of Houston County. During the 1880s, French Taylor became the key founder of the Wheeler Springs community, just to the north.[105]

Annie Mae Hunt of Washington County also had close personal knowledge of the white connections. Hunt's grandmother, Matilda Boozie, called "Tildy," a teenaged house slave, had become a sexual target of opportunity for the eldest son of the Boozie family Matilda lived with near Brenham. After a while, learning of her pregnancy, the "Old Mistress" swore Matilda to secrecy and arranged for her marriage with a black man named Eli Randon. Then, as Hunt recounted, "After Tildy was freed, they gave her this 1,500 acres of land down there in Washington County, 14 miles out in the country, on account of this illegitimate baby that my grandmother had by this young master." The Randons' large acreage seems to have been the origin of the freedmen's settlement of Mill Creek.[106]

Sometimes the tie with helpful whites had been a personal relationship, not kinship. At about the same time that French Taylor first arrived in Houston County, some miles to the south an older man named Josh Houston bought 200 acres to help begin the Hall's Bluff community. Josh Houston had served as Sam Houston's body servant from 1840 until Houston's death in 1863. The next year, the black Houston migrated to Houston County with $3,000 in cash and his Irish-Indian wife to help found a freedmen's settlement.[107]

Josh Houston had begun his life in Africa, and it was no accident that he took his light-skinned wife and mulatto children to a freedmen's settlement. Jim Upshaw, one of the brothers who founded the County Line community of Nacogdoches County, also had a wife who "looked like a white woman." Couples like the Upshaws and Houstons probably could not have lived in their county-seat towns of Nacogdoches and Crockett. The Texas Black Codes of 1866 included a law against interracial marriage, and Jim Crow laws later emphatically restated this racist rule.

More often than not, however, it was the men in the relationship who were white or looked white, requiring them to establish homeplaces in remote freedmen's settlements. As previously noted, gray-eyed, brown-haired Henry Durham, part African American on his mother's side, lived with his black wife in the black Sand Field settlement of Hopkins County. Durham worked as a barber in the nearby white community of Reilly Springs, but the Durhams probably could not have moved there to live. Certainly the notoriously racist county seat of Sulphur Springs would not have accepted them as man and wife. In violent, racist frontier Texas, mixed-race families had to act with great discretion. Around 1840, for example, Henry's father, Zach Durham, had migrated to Texas with his mulatto slave Daisy and a wagon full of light-skinned children, and Zach had avoided dangerous encounters with disapproving whites by riding in the woods just out of sight of the wagon.[108]

The remote Boykin, Bibles Hill, and Wilson Creek settlements all began with white-led, mixed-race families—families that probably could not have lived together at any place but a freedmen's settlement. Frenchman Antoine Deadrick and mulatto wife Mary Washington founded the Wilson Creek settlement in 1882, after the red-haired Frenchman purchased 196 acres along the creek bottom from the family of Shanghai Pierce in Matagorda County.[109]

The Boykin and Bibles Hill communities both began before Emancipation. Johnny Bibles settled on the Middle Fork of the Bosque River in Bosque County in 1855 with four Indian wives and several mulatto slaves, by whom he also fathered children. Bibles seems to have been of mixed race himself, though contemporaries thought he looked more Indian than anything else. Bibles avoided contact with white people, for whom he had great distaste, and in time a mixed-race clan of Bibles grew up along the remote Bosque. Ada Davis, who knew the settlement well, wrote in the 1930s: "The

Bibles negroes of the middle Bosque are his [Johnny Bibles'] descendents. They are a fiery set, with prominent characteristics of white, Indian, and negro races. They are defiant and zealous of their rights."[110]

People said similar things about other freedmen's settlements. The Boykin community in the remote longleaf forests of southeastern Angelina County also mixed white, Indian, and African American racial stocks, representing the successive wives and offspring of white pioneer Sterling Boykin (1800–1871). Doubtless, few locals challenged the six-foot-eleven, 375-pound Boykin about his mixed-race children or his predilections for teaching them to read and write. After a generation or so, the Boykin settlement (like other similar ones) presented a confusing face to whites in nearby Zavalla or distant Lufkin. One might encounter all-white Boykins, black Boykins, black Boykins that looked white, and various Indian-white-black Boykins.[111]

While white friends and white blood relatives may have helped many land purchasers of the 1860s, so soon out of slavery and so strapped for resources, by a decade later freedmen had had time to accumulate their own funds by the sort of hard work, frugality, skilled employment, and shrewd dealing evidenced in the Trotter family's "cashbook."

Some began this process even before Freedom. James Smith of Lee County, Nelson Sneed of Cherokee County, and "Free Jim" Brigham of Hunt County all had been permitted by their owners to work for others before 1865 and to accumulate money for self-emancipation and later land purchase. Each of them founded a black community. The Stocktons purchased James Smith in Virginia at age eleven. Generous masters, they later allowed Smith to "give suppers, sell apples, candy, and etc." and keep the profits. According to family tradition, Smith had $500 accumulated by Emancipation, moved to Lee County, and (as his granddaughter described): "With this money he purchased a farm consisting of more than a thousand acres. He built a two-room log cabin from the trees on this land."[112] His granddaughter did not mention the name of the freedmen's settlement founded by Smith, but Nelson Sneed joined Andy Bragg in founding Andy in Cherokee County, and James Brigham began Neylandville in Hunt County soon after Emancipation.[113]

Like Daniel Trotter, some freedmen bought precious land and founded settlements only after a decade or more of hard labor. Aaron Nunn's father, a slave blacksmith on the Wilson farm near Brenham, stayed on with his former master after Emancipation and continued to run his blacksmith shop. People came from miles around to have horses shod and plows fixed, and blacksmith Nunn pocketed a portion of their payments. He made additional money by hauling charcoal into Brenham to sell for fifteen cents a bushel and by the manufacture and sale of shuck mattresses, treenware trays, and a variety of split-cottonwood baskets used to pick cotton and gather corn. After years of hard work and saving, Nunn purchased 200 acres in Lee County and founded the community of Nunnsville. His grandson told this story, but from the perspective of people around Nunnsville Grandfather Nunn may have arrived on the scene as a mysterious outsider with a pocketful of cash.[114]

Only occasionally did oral accounts survive about the first hard days of settling the wilderness at the Nunnsvilles of Texas. Descendants of the pioneers at the Pelham community in Navarro County passed down stories of the time when their grandparents and great-grandparents had attacked the giant hardwoods of the Ash Creek bottoms with axes and teams of mules. The huge trees of the virgin wilderness haunted people's recollections at Pelham and elsewhere. Lines in the Pelham school song, written by Sarah Douglas in 1915, mentioned this. "Amid the scenes of hard times, they had their ups and downs. / They cut some terrible trees upon this old famous ground." Pelham pioneers worked together as they felled the terrible trees, piled and burned brush, and pulled up stumps on the rich bottomland that eventually made large harvests of cotton and corn. While the hard labor went on, "We'd grow a field of sweet potatoes that would feed the whole community," J. B Porter recalled, using the collective "we" from his grandparent's stories. Pelham had its own legendary pioneers from the epic first days—for example, "Bear Dave" Henry, who lived during three centuries (1790–1905) and once killed an attacking bruin with his bare hands.[115]

Origin stories about Peyton Colony in Blanco County told of a helpful Caldwell County master who agreed to outfit his former bondsmen with the bare necessities of the farming life in return for their labor with the crops of 1865. After the former master's cotton had been picked, men and boys headed west to locate free "government land" in distant Blanco County, well inside the Hill Country. Here freedmen led by Peyton Roberts discovered an unfamiliar wilderness of limestone hills wooded in mountain juniper and "shinnery" oak. Wolves howled and Tonkawa Indians prowled by night. Somewhat dubious about the locale, the Caldwell County freedmen nonetheless chose land for their families and helped each other build dirt-floored, one-room log huts, chinked with caliche mud, their roofs thatched with straw. Then the men returned to their old Caldwell County plantation for the winter. In early spring, the old master presented each family head with wagon, mule, plow, cow, hog, chickens, and dog, just as he had promised—the basic essentials of the farming life—and Peyton Roberts and the other freedmen headed west with wives and children. Upon arrival, as they topped the last hill and their new cabins came into view, the pioneers were shocked to see that the caliche mud used for filling the cracks between the logs had all washed away and the straw roofs had fallen in. Now, they realized that "you can't caulk with caliche," as local people already knew. Freedmen at Peyton Colony would have many other surprises, both pleasant and unpleasant, before they adjusted to free life in the arid blue hills of "the shinnery."[116]

St. John Colony began with another wagon train, but this one moving into Caldwell County, not away from it. Reverend John Wynn, a part-time Baptist minister and full-time sharecropper at the Hog Eye (Webberville) community in Travis County, discovered whites willing to sell land around 1871. The place was a remote wooded area in Caldwell County owned by Abner D. Cardwell and others. After Wynn "stirred the minds" of his congregation, the heads of sixteen families became interested, and one great day they rode horseback from Hog Eye on the Colorado to the Caldwell County woods. All afternoon long they "stepped across it," crossing and recrossing the area, looking for the plots they wanted for their families, trying to decide how much they could afford to buy. Then they told Wynn their choices, and he consummated the deal.

Not long afterward, in 1872, the Hog Eye families moved out by wagon, on horseback, and on foot to settle the new land. Reverend S. L. Davis's family took acreage that had an old house on it, and they spent the first night sheltering under its fallen roof, which leaned against a big elm tree, while other families slept in and under wagons. In the days that followed, men worked together to build temporary one-room log huts for each family, chinked with mud, each with one window and one door. People used the cabins tent-fashion, as sleeping shelters at night, but cooked and ate outside. With no matches, settlers kindled a fire with flint and steel and kept it perpetually burning in stumps and logs. "Grease lamps" and open fires provided light. People lived on wild game from the woods and corn obtained from nearby farmers until their own first crops came in. They purchased a cow for collective use. Men cooperated in the hard work of building rail fences around fields and gardens, and after a while they built a brush arbor for community worship. Bitterly hard labor to clear the forest trees continued for a generation.[117]

As at hundreds of other freedmen's settlements across Texas, the black frontiersmen of St. John Colony took great pride in their achievement of taming the wilderness. Whites had allowed them to buy land and to live there, but no one helped them to homestead the big woods or to survive as a community across the era of Jim Crow. Born in a log house at St. John in 1888, Reverend Davis emphasized his pioneer ancestors' great accomplishment to an interviewer in 1977: "These people colonized themselves!"[118]

CHAPTER THREE

Making Do, Getting By

Farming at the freedmen's settlements often began as hoe agriculture in a ghost forest of girdled and leafless trees, which people gradually felled by slow fires burning at the trunks. Soon, with hammer and anvil, freedmen fashioned wooden plows tipped with iron scavenged from the worn-out parts of old implements or from scrap metal gathered from here and there. They built crude wagons and carts, made horse collars by plaiting corn shucks, fashioned harnesses from hickory saplings with ax and drawing knife, and made traces and other parts of the harness from old pieces of chain or home-tanned leather. Many implements were made entirely of wood. In Navarro County, Mollie Dawson recalled, "Our harrows and scratchers was made of oak with hickory pegs sharpened and drove in holes bored in this piece of wood."[1]

As the decades passed at St. John Colony and other freedmen's settlements, wooden harrows, dogwood plows, oxen, and other old ways of doing things tended to persist due to continued isolation, avoidance of whites, and a certain lack of ready cash. At the Possum Trot community of Shelby County around 1900, C. C. White's uncle, Ossie Cartwright, still made and used a kind of dogwood and iron plow called a "wooden foot," and C. C. learned to plow with that homemade implement, working behind an ox. People at Possum Trot kept communal fires burning in stumps and logs as backups, just as at St. John in settlement times. Matches still cost money that many did not have. Families banked their household fires at bedtime to preserve glowing coals for the next day, but sometimes the fires died out, requiring a child to be sent to the community's burning stump to ignite a "fat pine" splinter or to borrow fire from a neighbor.[2]

The fire rekindled, a woman often prepared her family's morning meal in the fireplace. Fireplace cooking by winter, and cooking over an open fire under a brush arbor by summer, were frontier practices often surviving at the freedmen's settlements, where women long remained masters of the three-legged, cast-iron cooking utensil known as the "dutch oven." The daily cornbread and even special pies and Christmas cakes could be prepared in the Dutch oven, assuming the cook skillfully manipulated her fire and hot coals.[3]

Much cooking went on directly in the hot ashes. People roasted sweet potatoes beneath ashes or baked them under cone-shaped metal "wagon thimbles." Still in its shucks, sweet corn might be roasted under ashes, and small piles of dry corn might be buried under ashes to parch. To make "hoecake," people spread thick cornmeal batter on a big cotton hoe and held the hoe just over the fireplace coals, taking care not to ignite the wooden handle. Interviewed in 1977, Bubba Bowser of Washington County recalled preparing "ashcake" by sweeping off the ashes from his stone fireplace hearth, pouring cornmeal batter directly on the hot surface, then covering the batter with a layer of hot ashes. After a time, Bowser dug up the cornbread, dusted off the ashes, and ate it.[4]

Other old ways persisted at the freedmen's settlements. After her return to Peyton Colony in the 1950s, one woman found some elderly residents still living in one- and two-pen log houses, with wooden-shuttered windows and dirt floors swept impeccably clean.[5] To guard against snakes and wildfires, bare-dirt yards surrounded most houses, surrounded in turn by rived-board picket fences that kept out large domestic livestock. Just as women maintained mastery of the dutch oven, many men retained competence with the "poor man's sawmill," the froe-and-maul, quickly splitting off short lengths of board for fence pickets, roof shingles, and a score of other useful things, including the "pieux board" fences produced around Nigton, Trinity County, well into the twentieth century.

White landowner James Womack occasionally ventured into Nigton to hire rived-board gate builders for his place long after the skills to do this had been lost by Womack and other whites.[6] Others did the same. Blacks of freedmen settlements still used certain nineteenth-century technologies and techniques, including the employment of oxen as plow stock, the construction and repair of split-rail fences, and the building of corner-notched log structures. Old-time craft persons also persisted at black landowner communities—people capable of making ox yokes, leather harnesses, tool handles, wooden plows, treenware, animal traps, board "eating tables," common household furniture, corn-shuck mule collars, pine-straw or palmetto palm-leaf hats, gray-moss saddle blankets, gourd utensils, bark baskets, and clothing from fiber to finished product (spinning, weaving, dyeing, and tailoring).

Traditional basket maker at the Deadwood settlement,
Panola County. (Thad Sitton)

As in the case of the excellent pieux-board gates, many of these folk products retained their utility long after most people forgot how to make them. Bark-basket makers remained in demand to produce functional "shuck baskets" and ornamental sewing baskets for decades after baskets for cotton picking had been replaced by ducking sacks.[7] Zig-zag rail fencing kept hogs from cultivated fields better than anything but expensive hog wire, and the raw materials came directly from the farmer's land or from the free range. Rail fencing cost nothing but the hard labor to build and maintain it. Herbal cures still worked better than patent medicines or medical doctors, some country people believed, but the masterful herbal curers and "root doctors" were a rare and declining specialty by 1900. (Likewise, so were the other "doctors" who dealt with problems caused by malicious magic.)

Isolation, poverty, and a reluctance to endure the Jim Crow realities of white market towns kept such skills and practices alive. Rural white families in very similar communities stepped to the same drummer, trying to live off their places, avoid debt, and practice a waste-not, want-not lifestyle of subsistence agriculture, frugality, and recycling, but freedmen's settlement families in the era of Jim Crow did this with greater intensity.[8] Crafting shoes from wild-cow hide, reprocessing salt from the smokehouse floor, sewing children's jackets from old cotton sacks, and making cane knives and butcher knives from worn-out crosscut saws kept a family out of debt and out of the white town.

Many interviewees commented on these austerities. Interviewed during 1990, Grover Williams recalled with amusement remarkable frugalities and recyclings of his early life at the Flat Prairie settlement in Washington County. During cold weather, Williams and his brothers wore "jumper jackets" made of old cotton sack material fastened with baling wire instead of buttons. Baling wire also functioned as all-purpose repair material for the family's Model T Ford and farming equipment. Williams fashioned turkey bells for their hen turkeys from snuff cans with little rocks inside. Family members wore every item of clothing until it had patches on its patches, then women salvaged every square inch of sound fabric to be made into "britches quilts," rough quilts suitable for use on the floor. Williams's brother Cecil went a step too far with his improvisation on one occasion when he recycled his grandmother's plum jelly as hair pomade. At the rural school the brothers attended, a cloud of flies soon made Cecil a laughingstock.[9]

In freedmen's settlements like Flat Prairie, people pursued the ideal of subsistence farming, of living on the place, with pride, determination, and efficiency. Sandy hills or moist bottoms might be poor for cotton, but they often worked well for the subsistence survival crops of sweet potatoes, peas, peanuts, corn, and syrup cane. A resident of the settlement of East Caney, Hopkins County, proclaimed his subsistence credo to an interviewer: "You can't hardly ever starve a black man out, especially if he lives in the country. He knows how to make a garden, stretch his side bacon, ham hocks and turnip greens to last a lifetime. Just give him a few seeds, a little barnyard manure and a gooseneck hoe, and he can make a crop."[10]

At Boykin settlement, using an old folk technique, Jim Runnels of Angelina County cleverly rotated his garden with his cow lot every few years, thus manuring the vegetable rows by a natural process.[11] Extensive gardens accompanied the homes of most landowners and renter families, and beyond the gardens, with their many vegetables, lay specialized "patches" or "lands" of sweet potatoes, melons, cabbages, and syrup cane. Still farther away, subsistence field crops of peas and peanuts grew beside the cash crop of cotton or interspersed in the master crop of corn.

Cane did best in moist bottomlands, and many farmers not only produced large quantities of syrup for home use but sold or bartered the excess. A large family might think it needed at least fifty gallons of the substance slaves had called "long sweetening" to consume during the year. Cane loved creek bottoms but rapidly depleted soil fertility. Consequently, farmers often cleared new ground for their cane patch every few years and sometimes "blocked a branch" for midseason irrigation. Cane liked a good wetting. At Grover Williams's homeplace, Yegua Creek might rise to drown the cotton, but this watery disaster only invigorated the syrup cane. Likewise, drought perennially reduced the yields of sandy-land cotton, but peanuts, peas, melons, and sweet potatoes rarely failed to make a crop.

The poorer the family, the more likely it was to make heavy use of field peas—purple-hull, black-eyed, crowder, whippoorwill, and all the rest. The names mixed and merged, as did the peas in the field; rather often, the farm family did not know exactly what it grew. Interspersed every third or fourth row in the corn field or planted in the furrows during the last cultivation of the corn, peas almost always prospered and produced, even on poor soils in seasons of little rain. (Only the very worst of soils might be dismissed with the exaggeration, "that land's too poor to sprout nameless peas.")

Peas sprouted in the furrows and twined up the nearby corn stalks, drawing water and nutrients from the soil at a time when the corn had "made" and no longer needed them, its kernels hardening on the ears. People consumed peas at the green "snap pea" stage and gathered large quantities at

A Colored County Agent and two Limestone County farmers examine a row of field peas interspersed in the corn, 1949. (Courtesy of Texas Cooperative Extension)

maturity. They separated cotton-sack loads of field-dried peas from their shells by a folk-threshing method reported all across Texas and the South. Family members, usually the children, "pea thrashed" by jumping on the cotton sack and pummeling it with sticks until—by its limpness—they could tell that most of the peas had been shattered from their dried shells. Then, on a day of high wind, someone stood on a wagon bed and carefully poured the liberated peas down to a ground cloth, while the shell fragments blew away to the side. Pearl Gregory of the Sand Hill community, Nacogdoches County, summed this up, "Let the Lord do the separating, call that pea thrashing." [12] Then it remained only to store the dried peas in five-gallon metal lard cans or large pottery crocks, perhaps with a silver spoon, handful of snuff, or sprinkling of chinaberry leaves to keep the weevils away. For most families peas were a relished survival food, usually cooked with a generous seasoning of salt pork. If an excess of peas grew in the field, they were recycled for pork after the field was "hogged out" by the family's swine following corn harvest or plowed under to restore nitrogen to the soil. [13]

Peanuts were another sandy-land crop that doubled as food for swine. Peanuts matured underground, were turned over to dry in shocks in the field, then were removed by the wagonload to store in cribs at the barn. People fed vines and all to cows as a fodder crop after picking off all the kernels they wanted for home consumption. A Hopkins County man recalled a large pan of peanuts always roasting on the back of his family's wood stove, ready for hungry children home from school and on their way to field work. At the Lake Creek community, on the Houston-Trinity county line, one elderly farmer grew two sorts of peanuts, a small, good-tasting Spanish peanut and a larger, coarser peanut known as "hog goobers." The farmer dug, dried, and stored his Spanish peanuts in the barn, making them available to any neighbors who chose to pick them off the vine for a payment of one gallon for every four gallons picked. His family dug and consumed some hog goobers, but most remained buried in the ground until the farmer fattened his hogs there a few weeks before hog-killing time. Turned into the field, the doomed swine greedily rooted up their own peanuts. [14]

Sweet potatoes also matured underground, but if hogs got to them, a disaster had occurred. At most places, and especially on sandy-land farms, where they grew well, sweet potatoes served as an important subsistence crop — tasty, nutritious, and producing abundantly on a small area of ground. Pearl Lee Gregory recalled coming home from Sand Hill School to partake of the large pan of sweet potatoes kept on the back of the stove. Every time her mother cooked on the stove, she put in some tubers to roast, then added them to the pan. Pearl's family had few luxury foods, but she had all the peanuts and sweet potatoes she could eat. People might become tired of the same foods, but with sweet potatoes in the "bank," corn in the crib, pork in the smokehouse, peas in the can, and a generous supply of syrup, at least nobody would go hungry. [15]

Sweet potatoes were relatively easy to grow. People carefully preserved small tubers over the cold season, then sprouted them in a hotbed liberally

Henry Easter and son tend hotbeds on their farm. Sweet potatoes grow at bottom left.
(Courtesy of Texas Cooperative Extension)

laced with manure. Gardeners planted sprouts in raised beds and let them grow, watching for the telltale cracking of the earth that signaled tuber development in midsummer.

Sweet potatoes might be harvested right along, but all had to be dug in early autumn. At some communities with restricted free-range rights, only in fall were gates lowered and hogs released from pens to scavenge the fields for crop residues and the woods for "mast"—acorns, hickory nuts, and fall fruits. Hog owners depended on this limited autumn free range for a no-cost fattening of their animals, but hogs in the sweet potato patch before harvest was something families could not afford.[16]

Sweet potatoes might be stored in sand under the house, but many chose to "bank" them, using an old (and probably Native American) method of food preservation also sometimes used for turnips, cabbages, beets, and Irish potatoes. Considerable attention to detail was needed for successful banking, as for so many other subsistence techniques of rural life. Mollie Dawson of Navarro County recalled that her family often had several banks scattered around their back yard to preserve cabbage, beets, sweet potatoes, and even tomatoes "to run us till vegetables comes in again." First, they piled up a low mound of dirt in a circular shape a few inches above the ground surface; then, they added three or four inches of sand on top of the earth. This completed the foundation mound of the bank. Field hay and dried corn stalks were then hauled in and piled to the side. Dawson's family placed sweet potatoes or other vegetables on the foundation mound—lightly embedded in the sand, close but not quite touching—then a built a "teepee" of corn stalks over the mound, leaving a small hole on the south side for access to the vegetables. Hay and then insulating dirt were placed over the corn stalks, thick enough so that winter rains would not wash the dirt off and seep through. Finally, they tightly fitted a board or piece of elm bark to the south-side hole, completing the bank.[17]

Beyond the home gardens and cane and potato patches of the family farm lay its main fields, and at most freedmen's settlements the crops that grew there were cotton and corn. Cotton brought in the necessary cash for the yearly round, or, if it did not, necessitated day labor for more fortunate farmers or else "public work"—temporary salaried employment by timber crews, sawmills, railroads, construction gangs, or town whites. Cotton was the gambler's crop, with the outcome of each season always up to chance—the saving rains that fell or did not fall, the bottomland field that flooded or did not flood, how bad the boll weevils were that year, and the final price of ginned cotton, determined by the world market, ranging from five to forty cents a pound. No wonder that family work discipline peaked in the cotton field, as kind and doting parents became harsh taskmasters. Near Kaufman in the 1930s, Willie Johnson's father disliked having his daughters plow the land, but chopping and picking cotton was another matter. He insisted that they work hard and steady, girls and boys alike. Once, as Johnson told an interviewer, her father saw one of his daughters "looking at birds just flying around, and he said, 'I didn't bring you out here to count them damned birds! Go to work!' She said, 'My back is hurting!' He said, 'You don't have no damned back! Get to work!'"[18]

Family cotton and corn farming required child labor, and it began early. One man's first memory was the day in 1874 when his father cut off the end of a hoe handle, put the stub-handled hoe in his son's hands, and took him to the field to show him how to chop cotton.[19] Much hung in the balance at the first thinning pass through the cotton or corn, and at Hall's Bluff, Houston County, Vivian Lovelady's father invariably took all his children out for a refresher course in how to chop, no matter that the older ones already had spent many hundreds of hours wielding hoes. This man distrusted his hoe hands to do things right, but he had to use them. "My daddy had his own way of doing things," Lovelady remembered. "He didn't have too much team, but he had a lot of children."[20]

Desperate necessities always hung over the cotton and corn fields. Vivian Lovelady's father always planted two grains of corn in every hill to make sure at least one germinated, no matter that his children had to stoop over and pull up the extra corn sprout by hand. Born at Lincolnville, Coryell County, Deola Mayberry Adams recalled that her father "didn't believe in going to the fields at sun up—he went as soon as he could see and stayed there as long as he could see. We didn't work like people today. It's hard, you go out there, your arms so sore you can't hardly use them, and chop all day. You give out. He'd say, 'Deola, we have to go to work early if we're going to make anything.' And he raised good crops, I mean good ones."[21]

Failure of the cotton crop might bring much hardship to a family, but failure of the corn crop could force them off their farm and into town. Farmers at the freedmen's settlements often emphasized subsistence crops over cash crops, and in this hardscrabble system of agriculture, maize, or Indian corn, held a special place. Maturing rapidly in the wet spring and early summer, corn provided critical human food from the "milk ears" of June to the hard dry "flint corn" ears of October. Dry corn served as "fuel" to power mules and horses in hard field labor, and corn sustained a menagerie of domestic animals intended for human food—hogs, chickens, turkeys, ducks, guinea hens, and geese.

Black farm families prided themselves on consuming "all of the hog but his squeal," but their use of field corn rivaled that. They not only roasted or boiled the "milk ears" of early summer but also grated soft corn for a moist bread and processed the field-dried autumn corn for lye hominy, grits, parched corn, mush, pudding, porridge, ashcake, johnnycake, hoe-cake, pone, or dodgers.[22]

People at freedmen's settlements ground hard corn for bread by a variety of methods, often beginning with the Indian mortar-and pestle technique. After freedman Gus Weatherby moved into the Leon River bottom soon after Emancipation, he hoed a small field out of the woods, planted corn, survived on small game and berries while it grew, then beat the corn into meal in a hollow stump with a heavy tree limb.[23] At Lincolnville, Barrett, and other places, the hand-cranked (and appropriately named) Armstrong Mill followed the stump-and-branch, and by the late nineteenth century a variety of mule-, steam-, and water-powered mills ground communities' corn. Vivian Lovelady's family at Hall's Bluff, Houston County, took their corn to be ground at the water mill of the community's most affluent farmer,

A Brazos County farmer examines his tall corn, 1954.
(Courtesy of Texas Cooperative Extension)

and she recalled a common sight of the turn-of-the-century countryside—
boys passing on the road every Saturday morning with sacks of shelled corn
behind their saddles, destined for the mill. Millers ground each family's
weekly corn for a toll, usually one-fourth or one-eighth.[24]

Corn also served as a cash crop—if the farm family believed it had any
corn to spare. Often it did not; farmers tended to be conservative about
their corn. Even more than pork in the smokehouse, corn in the crib meant
family security. Every farming season was a gamble, another roll of the dice,
and the poorer lands of black landowners embodied greater risk, so farmers

breathed a huge sigh of relief each year that enough corn matured in the field so they would make a crop. This was almost as true during the 1930s as it had been just after Emancipation, when more than one freedman testified that raising corn had been a matter of life and death.

Rare seasons when corn did not "make" brought disaster, as for the freedmen's settlements of Lee, Washington, Fayette, and adjacent counties in 1925. In autumn of that terrible drought year, during which little or no corn grew, Colored County Agents toured their counties showing black families how to process starving milk cows and work stock into canned meat, the better to survive the coming winter.[25]

Many families preferred to eat hogs and other domestic animals that had been "cleaned out" with corn for a week or so before butchering. However, as a general principle, animals for most of their lives were fed just enough corn to domesticate them to some extent, keep them close by, and force them to forage for most of their food in barnyard, fields, and woods. To varying degrees, chickens, ducks, geese, guineas, turkeys, and hogs all remained at least semi-feral. Minimal doles of corn tied animals to the farmstead, but they hustled for the rest of what they needed on their own.

"Yard chickens" stayed closest to home, but even they scavenged the farmyard and nearby fields for seeds, insects, and worms. Turkeys, raised by many families both for home consumption and as a money crop, ranged much farther afield. Virtually every farmer had some "grasshopper turkeys," which returned for a dole of corn in the later afternoons and roosted in trees near the farmhouse at night, then departed at first light to roam for miles across pastures and woodlands, scavenging for grasshoppers in the spring and summer and fattening on natural mast—acorns, pecans, and fall fruits—in the autumn. Grover Williams's household at Flat Prairie, Washington County, lay in prime turkey habitat, near prairies and the wooded Yegua Creek bottoms, and Williams recalled that turkeys were marked and fended mostly for themselves. "We had the black ones and Mrs. Amanda Perkins, she had brown turkeys," he explained. "Everybody else had the black turkeys with the psychedelic colors on their wings. Everybody had domestic turkeys, and had long lines of turkeys going back and forth. They didn't mix—if they mixed, then they went to fighting."[26]

Turkey raisers cooperated with each other, feeding each other's birds when they found them mixed up with theirs, notifying other turkey raisers about the whereabouts of their flocks, and scrupulously separating the marked birds as the holidays approached. Mercantile stores and market towns served as collection points for turkeys just before Thanksgiving and Christmas. Turkeys, like hogs or cattle, could even be driven to market

A black farmer and son proudly pose with domestic flock and state-of-the-art chicken house. (Courtesy of Texas Cooperative Extension)

A boy and his flock of turkeys. Such turkeys often ranged long distances from the farmstead to scavenge most of their own food. (Courtesy of Texas Cooperative Extension)

for considerable distances.[27] Despite all the neighborly cooperation, turkeys wandering remote woods sometimes proved too great a temptation for poor black families in need of meat on the table, as county jail logs attest.[28]

Stock laws had little to say about turkeys, and laws forcing hog and cattle owners to confine their animals arrived late at many locales with black landowner settlements. Down in the bottoms and up in the hills, free-range customs survived well into the twentieth century, and black families often ranged semi-feral hogs and cattle in much the same way as they did turkeys. Stockmen kept hogs tame enough to be worked with stock dogs by doles of corn and cattle by doles of salt. In free-range counties like Lee, Freestone, Limestone, Jasper, Polk, Hardin, and Newton, hogs and cattle wandered, ear-marked and branded, across any man's property into the 1940s and 1950s. Fence-them-out fences protected cultivated fields from these roaming "rooter hogs and woods cattle," but nobody erected perimeter fences around their land. To do so would have been unneighborly, an affront to the customs of the free range. Other men's hogs and cattle trespassed on your land to eat your acorns, grass, and switchcane, but so did your animals on theirs. That you had fifty acres and your neighbor five hundred was not supposed to matter.[29]

Where they were allowed to fully benefit from it, free-range rights to run stock greatly profited poor black farmers. At Boykin in the remote long-leaf forests of southern Angelina County, for example, community pioneers Jim Boykin and Jim Runnels owned only a few hundred acres apiece, but they ranged thousands of hogs and cattle across many square miles. At other places where white stockmen operated closer by, evidence suggests that whites expected their black counterparts to make more modest uses of the Jim Crow free range. Retired sheriff Aubrey Cole of Jasper County recalled that blacks at Holly Springs and other freedmen's settlements all had "little bunches of cattle and hogs" around their homeplaces, and that was regarded as permissible, but none had dared to possess large herds like those of Boykin and Runnels. Stockmen often patrolled the free range, checking on their animals, and too many sightings of hogs with a black man's ear mark might goad a white competitor to "cut his britches off" by calculated hog theft, with the black stockman having—as usual—little recourse in the local courts.[30]

Evidence also suggests that blacks at freedmen's settlements exercised other customary free-range rights—rights to trespass, hunt, trap, fish, cut firewood, collect pine knots, gather wild plant foods or herbs, and even to hack ties and make barrel staves—on other people's land, but that those customary rights became problematic outside the area owned by settlement blacks. Beyond the edge of black-owned property, a hunter might feel that he needed to ask the white landowner's permission or perhaps to operate in stealth and by night.[31]

Since slavery times, African Americans had specialized in nocturnal, silent, no-gun hunting methods, and they ate some small animals that some whites would not eat. This hunting remained a form of a male recreation at the freedmen's settlements, but it also served as an important way to put meat on the "eating table."[32]

Boys everywhere went out on all-night possum-hunting excursions, re-turning at first light with several live possums in a sack. Hunters sought possums along creeks and at known feeding areas. They caught them by hand on the ground, or, if possums treed, they climbed for them and shook them out. Guns were unnecessary. Many persons enjoyed baked possum with sweet potatoes, though some insisted on feeding the animals a con-trolled diet under a washtub for a certain number of days before butchering and baking. Possums ate almost anything, and upon occasion people found them feeding inside decaying horse or cow carcasses. Possum cooks divided into two quarreling camps, those who skinned the animal and those who only singed it. Those who hung it up for a few days to "taint" and become more flavorful formed a minority third faction.

African Americans also ate a lot of rabbits, an animal less often consumed by whites. Boys hunted cottontail or swamp rabbits in daylight in grassy fields, bramble thickets, and fence corners. Rabbits instinctively crouched in their "forms," hoping to escape detection until the last moment, and if slowly approached and spotted beforehand they could be killed with sticks, thrown rocks, or slingshots. Some boys specialized in chasing rabbits to ex-haustion across open fields, or by using dogs to run them to hollow trees where they might be extracted by hand or "twisted out" with a stick. Others used highly effective box traps or snares. Recreational groups of adult males sometimes hunted rabbits in competitive excursions using greyhounds, with betting on the side.

Close knowledge of local landscapes guided many hunters, who often killed game directly for the pot. At Collin County, for example, young Eddie Stimpson "knowed every hole where I could go and pull out a rabbit and every tree hollow where I could pull out a possum in a stretch about seven mile long and about three mile wide."[33] N. E. Upshaw of County Line, Nacogdoches County, often departed at the first gray light of day, returning in time to provide a breakfast fare of possums, squirrels, or ar-madillo meat field-dressed in a flour sack. Upshaw hunted with a shotgun and was good with it. His son sometimes saw him jump-shoot rabbits and quail from the hip while moving through the woods. Upshaw also took an occasional deer, sometimes by night. Hunting season began "when my gun is loaded," Upshaw liked to say, but he took care to kill only what he needed and to waste nothing, as well as not to get caught.[34] The white game warden usually was no black man's friend. At Holly Springs in Jasper County and many other places, blacks specialized in fire-hunting deer, though they took care whose land they fire-hunted upon.[35] Rich pine splinters burned in a torch holder or wrought-iron firepan while the hunter slipped through the woods, looking for deer's eyes reflecting light. At a distance the eyes appeared as a single bright point of light, and the hunter carefully approached until the bright point parted into two eyes. Then he shot. With a bright firepan, this was good shotgun range, about forty yards away. After the firepan era, night hunters used head-mounted carbide lights or battery-powered flashlights. Fire hunters announced their presence by lights and gunshots but were hard to catch. At the least suspicion of trouble, the hunters simply extinguished their lights and slipped away in the dark.

Blacks of freedmen's settlements rarely seem to have hunted deer in broad daylight in deer drives using long-range hounds and hunters on stands in the method preferred by many southern whites. An occasional African American doubtless took part in these white-directed affairs, but in general dog hunts for deer covered too much territory, were too out in the open, and seemed too likely to evoke a Jim Crow response from disapproving whites. African Americans often preferred using short-range dogs to help them hunt, not long-winded Walker hounds capable of chasing deer or fox into the next county. Although they might be mixed breeds, dogs received specialized training. In the Shawnee Hills of Nacogdoches County, freedman "Big Charlie" White had different dogs for every purpose—stock, coons, possums, squirrels, deer, and even snakes.[36]

Perhaps because it was also a "stealth" method, animal trapping seemed a black specialty. Special trapping techniques had been passed down in the Upshaw family, as in many others. Some specialized in steel traps for fur-bearing animals. Others took white-tailed deer by way of snares and "deer stakes," the latter often positioned to skewer the animal when it jumped the fence into the family garden. Various sorts of clever rived-board traps caught ground-feeding birds—bobwhite quail and even wild turkeys. Deadfall traps triggered from a blind by a pulled string killed blackbirds, robins, and other small birds, which were eaten in pies. One man recalled his father using the heavy tailgate from a cotton wagon for this purpose.[37] During the winter, communally roosting birds such as robins also were taken at night in "bird thrashings" (also called "bird blindings"), semi-social affairs that involved confusing low-roosting birds with torches while thrashing them out with long poles.[38]

African Americans' fishing had commonalties with their hunting, and sometimes the two mixed and merged, as when Holly Springs blacks waded Jasper County creeks with fat pine torch, gig, and .22. Fish, bullfrogs, and soft-shelled turtles might be gigged by men and boys wading slowly down the clear creeks, with an occasional possum or coon shot on the bank.[39] Fish also might be "light-hunted" in river backwaters and taken with gig or club. At Boykin, the children of Jim Runnels often prowled the edges of an old oxbow lake by night, watching for fish on the surface and dispatching them with a long, narrow club made from a straightened buggy wheel.[40] As in the case of the young Runnels children, fishermen were ingenious and opportunistic. They "grappled" catfish by hand from under logs and holes in the bank, "doodle-socked" for bass and grennel using cheap spinner lures on cane poles, and "mud-poisoned" small creek and slough pools with feet and cotton hoes to drive fish to the surface. Other poisonings occasionally were used—most commonly, immature black walnuts crushed in their green shells.[41]

Like N. E. Upshaw's morning hunts, this sort of fishing was based on detailed local knowledge of nearby creeks and ponds. Most settlements were near some place where hand-held poles and single-line "bank sets" caught as many fish as people could process and consume in the days before iceboxes and freezers. When Lake Creek blacks in Houston County went down to check their overnight bank sets at the creek, they sometimes saw live fish on the hooks with several fish heads above each one, testifying to the abundance of both fish and fish-eating turtles.[42] As in hunting, traps often came into use, ranging from a simple hollow-gum-log or basket trap for catfish, through a range of larger mesh and wire baited traps to the V-shaped, cross-river fish weir Guss Upshaw built on the Angelina River. Constructed of vertical rived boards anchored in rock rubble laboriously placed on the river bottom, the County Line fish weir blocked river flow enough to create an artificial rapid that washed unwary river fish down onto a fish-catching sieve of wooden "fingers."[43]

Fishing occasionally turned into a community social event. When County Line blacks needed a large supply of fish for Juneteenth celebrations, men often turned out in numbers for a festive seining of the nearby Angelina River. Wading bank to bank, they pulled a long chicken-wire seine down a river pool, collecting fish in front of it. Then, at a signal, men at one bank stood fast while fishermen at the other end of the seine rapidly swung around to the same bank. This trapped large quantities of fish in shallow water next to the bank, where fishermen grappled for them by hand, often going entirely under the water to catch them. To show off, N. E. Upshaw once surfaced with a big buffalo fish in each hand and a third in his mouth.[44]

In this case, as in the case of the rather common fall hickory-nut gatherings, hunting, fishing, or foraging on the free range occasionally rose to the level of community social event, but families normally did these things to collect resources for home consumption. Wild plant and animal foods often were considerable in the back-of-beyond locations to which freedmen had gone to set up their communities. With several hundred acres of land and five black rent farmers on their place, French Taylor's family at Wheeler Springs, Houston County, nonetheless filled a whole crib in their barn with wild hickory nuts. Others did the same, collecting in season spring "greens" (pokeweed, or "poke salad," lamb's-quarters, watercress, wild onions, and others), dewberries and blackberries, mayhaws, high-bush blueberries, persimmons, black haws, plums, various grapes, and the edible "mast" of autumn—hickory nuts of several species, native pecans, and the miniature sand-hill chestnut known as the chinquapin. Nearly everyone knew these plant resources, but until World War II times, most freedmen's settlements contained a few individuals, often older women, who had knowledge far beyond that. As repositories of folk medicine derived from Indian, African, and Anglo sources, these "herb curers" and "root doctors" knew many more helpful plants.[45] Their traditional practices survived longest at the freedmen's settlements, as did many other folk practices, skills, and beliefs.

Isolation, independence, landownership, and avoidance of whites defined the special nature of the freedmen's settlements, which resembled similar white rural communities in many ways but displayed greater degrees of social "tightness" and mobilized mutual help more often. Ties of familiarity—by blood relation, marriage, or life-long, face-to-face interaction—knitted black settlements closely together internally, as they did the white, but in external relationships there was a difference. Black settlements were islands in the Jim Crow sea of the white-dominated countryside, and not all the whites were friendly. Whites often displayed ambivalent attitudes to their nearby black landowner communities, which elicited varying degrees of increased respect, envy, and suspicion. Some whites thought blacks in such places had land and property they were not supposed to have, and suspected them of inappropriately "uppity" attitudes to go along with these things.[46]

Often the suspicions were correct. Black people in the independent settlements might be careful to dress like field hands when they went into town, maintain unpainted homes, and be secretive about any valuable property they possessed, but their children grew to maturity in communities where Jim Crow's dictums did not rule.[47] Nobody had to get off the sidewalk to let a white man pass in a freedmen's settlement, or be careful not to look directly at a white woman. White people rarely entered such communities, and some of them had embarrassing experiences when they did. If locals did not know you and what you were up to, your inquiries about the whereabouts of someone probably would not be fruitful, even if the man's house stood just down the road. Other experiences also were possible. As Jim Boykin's descendants like to tell, two white men in a buggy once pulled up in front of Boykin's house and inquired (omitting the "mister," as was the invariable practice), "Where can we find Jim Boykin?" Boykin identified himself from his porch, but the men said, "No, we want the nigger Jim Boykin." Laughing, the light-skinned Boykin told them, "Here's your nigger! Come on up and set a spell."[48]

Relatively secure in their isolated, all-black communities, people felt more free to do as they pleased without reference to Jim Crow rules and customs. No wonder that the railroad station at Cologne failed to provide the usual segregated waiting areas, or that one eccentric old man (who admired certain white outlaws) might get drunk at night, shoot off his pistol, and cry, "John Wesley Hardin!" or that another old man in Houston County often rose at first light to play cow-horn reviles for his Wheeler Springs neighbors. Black persons probably could not get away with such things in the Jim Crow "quarter" of a white town or on some white man's cotton plantation. Freedmen settlement blacks were "uppity," and consequently they were more inclined to fight back. At County Line, hunter and fisherman N. E. Upshaw, one of the many offspring of community founder Guss Upshaw, acquired such a reputation among certain neighboring white stockmen with whom he exchanged threats. According to Upshaw's son, whites feared N. E. Upshaw and excused themselves from their Jim Crow duty of confronting him for his defiance by saying, "Oh, he's just a crazy nigger."[49]

Especially in the decades before 1900, blacks in freedmen's settlements kept to themselves, ran their mostly subsistence farms, made do with what they had, limited their interactions with whites, and helped each other out. Rural whites also practiced these helpful "habits of mutuality," as one historian has called them, but blacks in freedmen settlements had additional reasons for social solidarity and assisted each other with greater intensity.[50] Rural people themselves commonly described these complicated practices of communitywide work events, food sharing, barter, work swapping, and borrowing as "helping out" or "just being neighborly."

Neighborliness involved many things. Community work occasions like fish seinings, hickory-nut gatherings, and (in early days) salt makings profited all participants and at the same time offered a chance to socialize. People had to have salt, and every year or so several families might travel for miles to a salt spring or "saline" to camp out for days and process salt in the big black iron kettles also commonly used for cooking syrup from cane juice. Other work events profited a single family but set up reciprocities not to be shirked. If neighbors came over to help clear your land in a "log rolling," replace your mudcat chimney, put a new roof on your house, build a split-rail fence around your "new ground," or even to bury the dead, by accepting their help you obligated yourself to do the same for them. And without fail—upon the risk of shunning and ostracism.

Individual acts of neighborliness also set up reciprocal obligations, which collectively formed the community's only social support. Families gave excess food from field and garden to their neighbors, expecting that in time the favor would be returned. Neighbors freely borrowed from each other—food, goods, farming equipment, coals of fire from the hearth, and even children to assist in child-size tasks for which additional hands were needed. Much economic cooperation also took place, mostly outside of the cash economy. Farmers "swapped work" with each other on a day-for-a-day basis, and they bartered a wide variety of goods and services for other goods and services. The midwife might go home from her stay with a family with the customary two or three dollars in payment, but she was more likely to leave with a few chickens, a shoat, a few gallons of syrup, or the promise of a small blacksmithing job. People so commonly swapped chickens and gallon cans of syrup for goods and services that these commodities attained the status of informal currency.

In time, disasters fell on every family, and neighbors rushed to their assistance. People died, houses and barns burned, and farmers fell ill just as the corn needed to go in the ground or the cotton needed to be chopped or picked. At most places, such an event triggered a prolonged ringing of the community's church bell. The bells, sometimes recycled from slave plantations, each had distinctive peals that carried for long distances across the countryside. Larry Leonard of Cedar Branch community in Houston County recalled that their bell "had a clapper big as your fist, and when you ring that bell on a still day, twenty-five or thirty miles wasn't nothing."[51]

People like Leonard identified with their community bell and easily distinguished its sound from the bells of nearby settlements. At the first ring, listeners paused to see if the bell rang for the dead or signaled an emergency requiring immediate response. Bells "tolled" for the dead at their

Late-autumn hog butchering at County Line, Nacogdoches County.
(Richard Orton)

Mrs. D. H. Roland outside her smokehouse in the countryside a few miles from
Beaumont. (Courtesy of Texas Cooperative Extension)

passing, with one measured peal for each year of life, and listeners carefully counted the tolls to determine who had died. Most knew which community members lay seriously ill. If the bell rang continuously, families sent a child runner or some other family member to the church to find out what had happened and who needed help.[52]

Wesley Fobbs of Wheeler Springs community well recalled her father French Taylor returning home in the middle of the day to gather his sons, equipment, and cotton seed to go plant a sick man's field at a nearby community, or to carry a wagonload of shingles to help roof a neighbor's storm-damaged house. In every poor black community, better-off landowners like French Taylor of Wheeler Springs or Andy Patterson of Vistula (twenty miles to the south) shouldered special burdens of neighborliness, since they had resources most community residents did not have. As in the case of Patterson and Taylor, it was these men who had donated land for the church, school, and cemetery and who served as church deacons, school trustees, and—very often—as mediators and intermediaries between residents and white authorities. Most gave generously of the time, skills, and resources, relishing their informal role as community "patron." The literate Taylor often interpreted letters and legal documents for his illiterate neighbors, and when he had time he skillfully split piles of free shingles for people to use in roof repairs. Taylor had five black families on his large farm, and he treated them as many black landlords (but not all) treated their renters. Taylor's wife did little field work, but she maintained milk cows and gardens well beyond the needs of her family. On a daily basis, their renter families drew milk, butter, and garden vegetables from the Taylors' home garden, and the Taylors assisted them in other ways as well. Of a certainty, the renters had full free-range rights for stockraising, hunting, fishing, and foraging on Taylor's several hundred acres of land, and his daughter recalled that he may have offered them a larger share of the crops than usual. Renters walked up from the Trinity River bottom every day to catch mules from Taylor's home corral, for they had brought no work stock and farming equipment to the deal, but Wesley Taylor Fobbs believed that her father took only one-third of their corn and one-fourth of their cotton, not one-half of everything, as was customary with sharecroppers.[53]

French Taylor and Andy Patterson also performed other philanthropies for their respective communities. They bought school shoes for the children of poor families in the autumn, and they made small cash loans to neighbors that some never repaid. Such men often disguised their philanthropies in requests for assistance with monumental hog killings and syrup makings. Patterson would rise in his Vistula church to announce such occa-

*Landowner Mrs. M. L. Allen of the Harrison community, McClennan County, stands
beside her Colored County Agent after a hog-butchering demonstration on the Allen farm.
Mrs. Allen provided free meat for her cotton tenants. The can contains fine white lard.
(Courtesy of Texas Cooperative Extension)*

sions and ask for help, though in truth he had all the hands he needed in
his own sons and daughters. After the hog slaughtering or syrup making,
many neighbors went home with wagonloads of meat and molasses, two of
the "three M's" (meat, molasses, and meal) that tided families over the winter.[54] Nelson Jones, the wealthiest landowner in Sweet Union community
of Cherokee County, did the same, often contributing fifty gallons of syrup
for each family that helped him process his cane into syrup.[55] Jones, French
Taylor, Andy Patterson, and many similar community patrons all went to
their graves with many people owing them money. In his last years, Patterson liked to tour the Houston County countryside in a car driven by his
grandson, and he often remarked in passing about which families owned
him money, and how much. It did not matter to him, he said, he "had been
blessed in his life," but the unpaid debts still rankled this shrewd old man,
born a slave, illiterate, but with a memory that forgot nothing.[56]

The Givenses of Givens's Hill settlement, Houston County, demonstrated the degree to which one founding family could sustain a community.

The son and daughter of freedmen, Solomon and Lula Burleson Givens bought land a few miles south of the county seat of Crockett in 1892. They prospered, and a black community soon grew up around them, assisted by the four sons and one daughter who chose to live on the family farm all of their lives. Solomon and Lula helped found Pine Grove Baptist Church, where Solomon served for fifty years as superintendent of the Sunday school, church clerk, chairman of the deacon board, and president of the Home Mission Society. Lula taught in the Sunday school from the 1890s until her death in 1954 and played hostess to the long procession of visiting ministers who stayed in the Givenses' big eight-room farmhouse.

The Givens family helped their community in other ways. Solomon and his sons founded a local chapter of the Grand Lodge of Pythius, and Solomon served for many years as trustee of the nearby Reed's Opening School. A "storm house" on the Givenses' place, complete with bedding, food, and lamps, served as emergency shelter for the needy. Solomon, a skilled carpenter, assisted his neighbors whenever needed, while Lula Givens, her daughters, and her daughters-in-law made quilts and mattresses for the poor. Solomon and Lula helped their neighbors for a half century with generous gifts of garden vegetables, pork, eggs, milk products, firewood, and well water, and Solomon even built a small store and barber shop to serve his namesake community.[57]

At County Line in Nacogdoches County, the Upshaw brothers—Guss, Jim, and Felix—had pioneered the community, and down through the years they served as community supporters and patrons in much the same way as Solomon and Lula Givens, Andy Patterson, and French Taylor. Felix chiefly farmed, but Guss and Jim Upshaw had specialized skills that provided the community with necessary services not otherwise obtainable short of the small white market town of Douglass, some miles to the south. Jim Upshaw ran a small steam-powered multipurpose sawmill, gristmill, and cotton gin that served County Line and adjacent communities, and both Jim and Guss operated syrup mills in the fall and winter. To some degree, gristmills and syrup mills were neutral ground in the Jim Crow countryside, often serving both blacks and whites, but residents of freedmen's settlements still preferred to get the subsistence necessities of life from one of their own. As noted, millers and syrup makers took a toll for their services, and in one of the informal dictums of Jim Crow, a black person was not supposed to dispute a white person's word about anything—not even the amount of meal his corn yielded.

Guss Upshaw also served the County Line community as blacksmith, carpenter, wagon maker, harness maker, and basket maker—as one of those multitalented jacks-of-all-trades who could build or repair anything he turned his hand to. Upshaw's neighbors doubted there was anything he could not do. He carved hickory tool handles, singletrees, and ox yokes and could craft replacements for any broken wagon part. He performed necessary blacksmithing for farmers desperate to repair broken agricultural equipment or reshoe work stock in crop season. He did leatherwork, including human footwear, ox whips, and mule harnesses. After a good look at a white man's elaborate cross-river fish weir upstream on the Angelina River, Guss Upshaw returned to County Line and built his own. Some of what he did bordered on the uncanny—for example, the wonderful split-hickory-bark baskets woven so tightly that they held water.[58]

Every isolated freedmen's settlement needed someone like Guss Upshaw, though not all of them had such a person. At Flat Prairie in Washington County, Grover Williams's grandfather tried to fix riding planter, middle-buster plow, and Ford Model T with desperate applications of the same baling wire that "buttoned" his grandchildren's homemade jackets, but at some point he gave up and sought a blacksmith. Truly professional blackmithy was not always necessary, but someone had to be found with the charcoal forge, tools, and skills to pound the plow point back straight or to fit shoes to the mule. One or two part-time blacksmiths at Flat Prairie possessed "government balls" that they used as makeshift anvils—round iron weights with telltale ankle cuffs left over from the county chain gang.[59]

Blacksmiths, midwifes, and gristmill and syrup mill operators provided the most critical part-time services for their communities. Jim Upshaw's light-skinned wife served as community midwife in the early days at County Line, and "Captain Houston," Sam Houston's former body servant, performed blacksmith duties for residents of Hall's Bluff, where another early resident and large landowner operated a water-powered gristmill and French Taylor had a syrup mill. Usually, at any one time two or three persons in a community ran seasonal syrup mills—in early days cooking the cane juice in three or four large black iron pots, then, by the late nineteenth century, in a flat, compartmented, copper "syrup pan." Black or white, rural people consumed astonishing amounts of sorghum or ribbon cane syrup, and an open one-gallon container of the high-calorie survival fare usually stood on every table at every meal.

At Sand Hill, Nacogdoches County, Chester Gregory's father operated a syrup mill from September through December for decades. Gregory made both sorghum and ribbon cane syrup for people in the community, taking every third can as his toll for processing the syrup from cane to can. Neighbors cut cane in their fields, stripped it of leaves, hauled it to Gregory, and

A young man feeds cane into the cane mill to produce juice for syrup at Deadwood, Panola County. (Thad Sitton)

piled it in his yard beside all the other piles. People grew many different sorts of syrup cane—"gooseneck," "orange top," "September sorghum," and all the rest—and the syrup maker constantly had to adjust his cooking process to the various cane juices. Some cane produced syrups that were light-colored and relatively light-tasting, others that were dark and strong. Final taste also varied with the soil in which the cane had been grown. People's preferences differed, but all the syrup consumers had clear ideas of how their cane syrups should taste at the end, and they readily detected "sour" product canned too soon or "burned" product canned too late. All expected Gregory to get things just right.

Young Chester Gregory helped with the family syrup mill at Sand Hill. Such mills required at least three persons to operate it—one to feed the mule-powered mill squeezing juice from the cane, one to manage the cooking fire and to run the "back of the pan," and one to serve as cook, masterminding the "front of the pan" and making the critical decisions about when to can the finished syrup. Chester's father played the latter role. Chester's job was to get to the mill before daylight, hitch up two mules to the cane press, and begin to cram multiple stalks of cane into the mill. His father expected a full barrel of fresh juice ready to begin the run when he arrived, and throughout the day the mule-and-mill hand had to hustle to keep up.

Juice was fed from the barrel through a pipe into the back end of the cook pan, as needed, then was moved from one end of the pan to the other as it cooked. At every stage of cooking, impurities boiled out and were diligently skimmed off the top—the careful process that more than anything else determined the quality of the final product. All the long day Chester watched the mules go around and around and fed the cane into the juice mill, careful that darkness, boredom, and tired inattention did not let his hand or clothing become caught in the grinders. The countryside had more than its share of one-armed men, and not all of them had lost their limbs at cotton gins. Another problem plagued the person running the juice mill, at least in the first month or two of the syrup season. As Chester Gregory recalled: "You have to fight them wasps and yellow-jackets out there when you be feeding that mill, they be swarming—honey bees and yellow-jackets, and wasps."[60]

Other part-time specialists served the needs of their communities, especially during the agricultural downtimes of midsummer and midwinter—after "laid by" and after harvest—when work on their own farms slackened. Carpenters built houses and barns for their neighbors; work stock specialists "broke" horses, mules, or oxen to the plow or wagon; and well diggers, with pick and shovel or post-hole digger, practiced their dangerous trade, often after "witching" with a forked limb to identify the most likely spot

Workers cook cane syrup at Deadwood, Panola County. (Thad Sitton)

to dig. Other people built chimneys, cut people's hair, made furniture, or distilled whiskey, whatever their particular talents.

Besides offering goods and services more cheaply, individuals like these allowed residents of freedmen's settlements to remain in their communities and avoid visits to the segregated market town, and a good many chose to do that. Small community stores, peddlers in the communities, and the arrival of parcel post after 1912 also helped black isolationists avoid white contact.[61]

People still needed a few necessities from the store that they could not grow or produce on their farms, but rather often the store came to them in the form of yet another part-time specialty operated out of some black family's home. Such small community stores commonly sold flour, coffee, salt, matches, soft drinks, candy, and perhaps a few other things.

One of the numerous sons of the community pioneers, Claude Upshaw at County Line operated a small store for decades after 1900. Upshaw stocked basic foodstuffs. His "sacred list" included sugar, flour, meal, salt, baking powder, crackers, canned goods, and a few exotic items that came and went with Claude's whim. Located directly across from County Line Baptist Church, Claude Upshaw's store functioned as community center and secular social "hangout" from the first light of day well into the evening. Entertainment was mostly conversation, though Claude had an old radio. Claude posted no rules, but all knew that he forbade profanity, drinking, and fighting on his premises. Children played in the street in front of Claude's store from daylight to dark, while old men conversed on the "dead pecker bench" on its front porch. Claude had many eccentricities. Kind but somewhat tight-fisted, he often employed nieces or nephews for the pay of cold soda water (but not the adults-only "short Cokes," thought to be dangerously potent). Claude's community store ran mostly on the honor system by day, but by night Claude defended it with shotguns from his rooms in the back. Once a month Claude Upshaw went into Nacogdoches, his back pocket bulging with a thick wallet that was held together by rubber bands and in which he carried all his money. A niece recalled that the eccentric storeowner sometimes executed a strange little dance from front door to pickup truck on these grand occasions.[62]

Occasionally the "soda man" serviced Claude's store, his truck throwing up big clouds of dust on the sandy road. From the 1880s on, certain whites had peddled useful items in freedmen's settlements, and these white people were known and welcome. Peddler James Cartwright of nearby Douglass included the blacks of County Line, Winter's Hill, and other freedmen's settlements on his monthly round of northwestern Nacogdoches County, often bartering needles, thread, ribbon, spices, kitchenware, and other small luxury items for chickens, eggs, or anything people had to swap for his goods.[63] Cartwright's route served as a sideline to his small cotton farm, or perhaps the opposite. He sometimes functioned as middleman, picking up small craft items or commodities and peddling them along his route for a commission. As Cartwright's journals make clear, he was, like most early peddlers, a restless extrovert who purveyed gossip as much as goods. He often sold items on credit to both black and white customers, and sometimes broods in his journals about the "chix" different people owe him. Various latter-day "chicken peddlers" (often the ubiquitous Watkins and Rawleigh men) continued to serve black rural communities until World War II.[64]

Other local specialists performed critical services in the area of health care. Midwifes helped neighbors with their birthings year round and often functioned as herbal healers after people's home remedies had failed. Every family had such remedies—watermelon tea and catnip teas to soothe babies; sage, sassafras, mullein, pine leaf, or pine root teas for fevers and chills; pepper and corn-shuck teas for various ailments; and peppermint tea for common indigestion. Some of these things worked well, and some did not. People recalled that they occasionally did not report childhood fevers because of remedies their mothers preferred—for example, "sweating out" the fevers under wet sheets covered by piles of quilts augmented by hot bricks, or the dreaded "chip" teas concocted from the droppings of cows, horses, sheep, or chickens. One man recalled being made to pursue the family's horse around the pasture until it produced "fresh," then being compelled to drink a tea made from this. Another remembered gathering the chief ingredient of "chicken pip" tea from the hen house.[65]

As in rural white homes, other common remedies were concocted from whiskey, honey, butter, and the familiar household substances of turpentine, kerosene, and bluing, all mixed and merged in various ways. People took whiskey, honey, and butter preparations for colds and made cough syrups of honey, whiskey, and lemon juice. Less palatable alternative cough syrups included, for example, turpentine (or hot pine resin) mixed with whiskey, honey, and onions. Prophylactic folk medicine ran heavily to laxatives, thought necessary to "clean out" or "purify the blood" of children in the spring. Pepper grass, pokeberries, senna leaves, mayapple roots, and the inner bark of ash trees, alone or in combination, emphatically did their job. Chewing-tobacco poultices drew the poison from insect bites, insect stings, and even poisonous snake bites, which were also treated with milkweed poultices, half a fresh-killed chicken applied to the wound, or even half the snake that had done the deed. Salve from elderberry flowers stewed in hog lard brought relief from red bugs and ticks. People used kerosene on minor cuts and an application of soot and spiderwebs to stop the bleeding on major ones.[66]

As family remedies failed to work, both blacks and whites often turned first to part-time community healers. Some persons had herbal knowledge far beyond the ken of ordinary housewives, and others (or the same ones) brought magical or religious powers to bear on the problem. Severe bleeding could be stopped by the right Bible verse repeated by a person with special power to use it, some believed. Preachers sometimes visited to pray over the sick, and some did double duty as faith healers. One man recalled a Reverend Alfred telling him to tie a string to the branch of a dooryard fig tree, to tie a knot in it every time he had a chill, and each time to walk away from it without looking back. Soon, he claimed, the chills ceased.[67] Concerned relatives sometimes summoned Reverend Troy Taylor of Matagorda County to childbirths gone wrong and desperate sickbed situations. On one occasion, after being asked to attend a seriously ill person, Taylor took hymn book and Bible (and pistol) into the woods to pray for several hours to "have the spiritual feeling of having the Father, the Son, and the Holy Ghost with him" before praying over the sick person, who subsequently improved.[68]

Scoffed at by some, beliefs about "conjur" or "hoodoo," malevolent magic practiced by one's enemies, persisted at many communities well into the twentieth century, and people sometimes asked preachers to counteract evil spells with biblical power. Conjur spells could cause bad luck, incapacity, or illnesses of the most horrible kind, including cancers, blocked bowels, or live vermin (worms, snakes, and scorpions) crawling around inside one's body. Many persons wore "jacks," "mojos," or "hands"—small bags of magical ingredients—to serve as a first line of defense against conjur attacks. In Fort Bend County, Patsy Moses's grandfather was a "hard-shelled Baptist preacher" who knew all about hoodoo and conjuring, though he did not practice these things himself. People often came to him and asked him to break spells laid on them by practitioners of these dark arts, and he often did so, successfully pitting good against evil.[69]

Blacks living in the numerous freedmen's settlements of Limestone County knew of a succession of powerful healers, risen from among them. Born under slavery, Alex Dancer practiced into the twentieth century. A local woman wrote of Dancer, "It was claimed that cold sweat came from the palms of his hands at all times, and he would rub the bellies of the little boys and thereby drive out all the symptoms of malaria which they had acquired by eating green peaches and wild mustang grapes. He enjoyed a great practice in his lifetime."[70] Another such man was John Jefferson, born in 1877, a prosperous "native herb doctor, Baptist preacher, and advisor, who would conjure away but would not conjure up people." Jefferson operated an office in Mexia, filling the void created by the absence of any black physicians until 1956. Jefferson removed "hinders," malicious spells placed on people, and he also used an "Indian herb book" until his death in 1958.[71] Another famous healer was the remarkable Annie Buchanan, "born [in 1892] with the gift to tell fortunes and to heal," a seventh child of a seventh son, who developed a major practice extending far beyond her home county. Blacks, whites, and Hispanics mingled in Buchanan's Mexia waiting room, despite the rigid segregation customary elsewhere in Mexia. She could remove hinders and conjurs, tell fortunes, and "could heal some diseases and 'conditions' with a touch of her hands." Other cases required a special liquid medication, concocted with muttered incantation. Buchanan owned several houses, drove a succession of new Pontiacs, and married eight men in turn, setting each one up in his chosen business. A devout woman who believed her power came from God, Annie Buchanan used her considerable resources to build seven Primitive Baptist churches, some of them in Limestone County freedmen's settlements.[72]

Modern medical practitioners sometimes attended seriously ill people at freedmen's settlements, and sometimes they did not. Many rural blacks only reluctantly consulted white doctors, and sometimes doctors virtually refused to treat them, even when they showed up in town. A doctor at Burton in Washington County not only refused to make house calls at Flat Prairie and other communities, but he dismissed black patients at his office with a handful of aspirin, even if they had serious injuries. Grover Williams remembered one man whose broken leg healed crookedly because of this and another whose arm ended up withered and useless as a result of a severe knife cut.[73] Conversely, white physician Stony Rabb of Gatesville often drove out to deliver babies at Lincolnville, Coryell County, and Dr. Fred William Cariker of Cushing, Nacogdoches County, "never turned down a call no matter race, color, creed, or financial condition." He rode horseback and went by buggy for decades, even swimming creeks and rivers with his saddle horse when that was the only way to get there. Cariker wore out fourteen buggies and several Model T Fords during his medical career, after 1914 buying a new car every year.[74]

Despite the occasional doctors like Cariker, the dedicated midwives, and the sometimes effectiveness of homegrown healers, health care at the freedmen's settlements left much to be desired. People at Peyton Colony and many other places often just sickened and died, with no one knowing why.[75] That things were worse in remote rural communities than in urban areas, however, is not certain; overall black death rates remained high during the era of Jim Crow. Statewide, annual mortality rates per 100,000 population in 1935 stood at 961.5 for whites, 1,321.3 for blacks. Whites suffered 33.2 stillbirths per 1,000 births, blacks suffered 73.4. White mothers died in childbirth at a rate of 6.3 per thousand, black mothers at a rate of 14.3.[76]

At the freedmen's settlements, independence and isolation exacted a certain price, but residents chose to pay it. Children there grew to adulthood with their self-esteem intact, protected from the "death of a thousand cuts" inflicted upon black people by the laws and customs of Jim Crow in the white-dominated towns outside. Sometime after 1890, the settlements reached a high-water mark of geographical expansion, independence, and population, as the aging freedmen founders of the communities approached the end of decades of land accumulation, and while their many offspring remained in the communities waiting to inherit. For a grandfather of Helen Darden's husband, the goal had been 1,000 acres owned free and clear of debt, and just before the man's death he attained it.[77]

Others had done the same. By 1900, Jacob White of the Omen settlement in Smith County owned several farms totaling over 600 acres and worth about $20,000. White, who had ten families and more than sixty individuals renting from him, had helped create a community of forty-five black landowner families occupying over 12,000 acres of land. Some distance away in the Starrville community of Smith County, John Wheeler had accumulated 788 acres of good land, "from which he gave all of his children homes."[78]

Just before 1900, most settlements included at their core a small number of major landowners like Jacob White of Omen, French Taylor of Wheeler Springs, and Andy Patterson of Vistula, men risen from slavery to buy land and never sell. "Don't ever sell your land, the land will take care of you," Patterson liked to say.[79] Such men accumulated their precious acres against long odds, somehow negotiating the dangers of Reconstruction and those of the decades of segregation and discrimination that came after it. Profoundly disadvantaged by educational and social circumstances in the time of Jim Crow, they nonetheless prospered. Some whites always envied and disapproved of such black prosperity. At Nate Shaw's Alabama community, a white neighbor passing on the road at hog-killing time glanced at Nate's freshly butchered pork spread out in preparation for the smokehouse and told him, "I ain't never seen that much meat that no one nigger owned it."[80] Across several decades, white neighbors, businessmen, and bankers looked at these men's large acreage and fertile fields with the same disapproving, envious eyes.

Jealous white enemies might be assumed, men ready to rob with you with a fountain pen if they had half a chance, no matter how they bided their time and smiled. The cultivation of prominent white friends and protectors provided the best defense, especially important at a time when local courts often failed to protect black people and a white man's word could not be easily disputed. Andy Patterson was especially careful to remain friends with Lloyd Murray, owner of the huge sharecropper plantation just across the Trinity River from Vistula, once selling him upon request a thin slice of his own land so Murray could complete a levee. Murray had huge social clout. The sheriff customarily called him to ask permission to come on his land to look for someone, and a call from Murray in the other direction instantly released a black sharecropper jailed for a minor offense. Patterson also took other precautions. He dressed like a field hand when he went into town and remained humble and deferential in his interactions with whites. Despite all this deference, Patterson had "some of the white man in him," his grandson surmised; he just did what he needed to do to get what he wanted. In town for a bank loan and asked how he was doing, Patterson might reply, hat in hand, "Fine, white folks, I'm doing good, I just need a little money to raise my crops." Patterson never failed to get his loan, and he never failed to repay it.[81] Wealthy landowner Jacob White of the Omen community of Smith County took even fewer chances than Patterson. His rule was to never owe anyone a debt.[82]

Elderly freedmen landowners such as Andy Patterson had their personal eccentricities, but they all were shrewd, careful, diligent farmers who ran their farms with discipline, organization, and energy. Most of them could not read or write but made up for this terrible disadvantage by possessing sharp memories and trusted friends, usually white, who checked every important document for them before they signed it. Black landowners who did not take this precaution often lived to regret it.

Freedmen land accumulators also often accumulated many children by a succession of wives, as in the case of W. C. Williams's father, Emanuel Williams at Smith Grove, Houston County. W. C. was the sixteenth of Emanuel's seventeen children, born when his father was fifty-six. Emanuel had been taught to read, write, and figure after Emancipation by his first wife. The former slave had gradually accumulated over 300 acres, on which he raised cotton, corn, sugar cane, and "high gear" (hegari, a grain sorghum) while running cattle and hogs on the adjacent free range. Upwardly mobile, he bought a green Chevrolet in 1920, though he never learned to drive and left this task to his sons. W. C. Williams experienced his elderly father as hardworking, distant, and somewhat stern—a man who insisted that his children work hard in the field and never sit down to rest. W. C., who already planned some career other than farming, sometimes had to be warned by his mother to get to his feet before his father caught him. Emanuel Williams supervised every detail of his farm and was something of an efficiency expert. W. C.'s first chore of the day, for example, was to feed corn to the hogs in complete darkness so the chickens would not get any of the hog's corn. Far from challenging this stern father, old enough to be his grandfather, W. C. nonetheless practiced some mild rebellions when Emanuel left the farm on business. W. C. sometimes cut cane in the cane patch, ate some, then thrust the truncated stalk back in the ground to cover his crime. He also killed and fried the occasional yard chicken, taking care to bury the leavings so his father would not know.[83]

The best portrait of a first-generation Texas landowner comes from another son of a freedman, Reverend C. C. White. C. C. visited "Big Charlie" White, the father he had never met, about 1906. By that time Big Charlie owned "593 acres and a bunch of tenant houses" near the Shawnee Hills about seven miles south of the county seat of Nacogdoches in Nacogdoches County. After C. C. identified himself to the farmhouse, Big Charlie and all his wives and children came outside to greet the visitor. (C. C. White never actually admitted this, but he seems to have been Big Charlie's "outside son" by a previous relationship.) The landowner's two current wives lived in domestic harmony with him in the house, along with their combined work force of sixteen children. Big Charlie was a huge black man over six feet tall and weighing 385 pounds, as C. C. described, "the biggest blackest man I'd ever seen." Big Charlie was so pleased to see his lost son that he offered him sixteen dollars a month and room and board to stay around—a very generous offer, it turned out, since all Big Charlie's other children worked for him for what amounted to room and board and tobacco.[84]

As the days went by, C. C. White found this strange man and his strange family hard to fathom. Big Charlie had regimented and organized his large household as he saw fit. He himself wakened the household every morning with cries of, "Get up! Get out them beds, everybody! It's time to get up!" C. C. explained, "He never let daylight catch him in bed, and when he was up couldn't nobody get more sleep."[85] Thereafter, family members performed their daily chores to a sequence of loud handbells rung by the older wife, Roxie, who seemed to be second in command. Roxie bossed the girls in outside work, second wife Nancy ran the kitchen and the inside girls, and Roxie's son Peevy directed the boys in field work. Big Charlie rode around the farm on his horse and supervised all operations.

Big Charlie did not work, but he took pains to demonstrate to his wondering son that he *could* work. One day, on a whim, for his own amusement, he got down from his horse and outpicked teenaged C. C. down a row of cotton. Of his farm he told C. C.: "I worked for every bit of it. I sweat for it. I learned a long time ago if you want to keep ahead of the other feller you gotta work harder and longer and think faster than him. That's how I operate."[86]

Everything ran like clockwork on Big Charlie's farm; he had everything organized, even the dogs, who were specialized for deer, hogs, squirrels, coons, and rabbits. At first light, Roxie and several girls marched to the barn, each girl carrying a calf rope. Cows came in from the woods, and each girl waited until her assigned calf found its mother and began to nurse. Then the girls tied it to the fence, "milked three tits," then turned its calf loose to suck the fourth. "We let the calf have all of one tit and let him strip the others, so he gets most of the cream. That makes good calves," Big Charlie explained.[87] Every detail of farm operations had such a fixed and precise routine.

Business ran by clock and handbell on Big Charlie's farm, with Saturdays always the same. Right after breakfast the big boys hitched six mules to three wagons, drove to the bottoms, cut enough ash trees to make three wagonloads of stovewood, returned for a noon meal, then took the three wagonloads to sell in Nacogdoches, with Big Charlie leading the way in a buggy. Big Charlie ordered liquor by the case from Louisiana and usually drank a full bottle on the way home from town, with the older boys sometimes getting a little. The next day, however, Big Charlie always led a serious home prayer meeting, sometimes with tears streaming down his face, before the women and most children departed the farm for Sunday school and church.

Big Charlie handled all the money in this household, though others could request some for special purposes. They might or might not get it; Big Charlie was very tightfisted with the cash, except for C. C.'s monthly sixteen dollars. Food was another matter, however. Under Nancy's preparation, the family enjoyed fried food for breakfast, boiled meals for lunch and dinner, and plenty for everybody all the time. Raised in poverty and occasional real hunger, young C. C. White had never seen food like this: all you could eat; meat with every meal, butchered from the farm's hogs, cattle, sheep, goats, chickens, ducks, and turkeys; eight pounds of butter churned at a time; plenty of vegetables from an enormous garden; and a "syrup house" filled with gleaming cans stacked to the ceiling.

After a while, C. C. White quarreled with his father and departed the farm, though all had been forgotten a year or so later when C. C. returned

Mrs. O. M. Polk of Harris County gathers eggs in her hen house.
(Courtesy of Texas Cooperative Extension)

for a visit with his new wife and child. Nor did he comment further on the fate of Big Charlie White's fine farm on the edge of the Shawnee Hills. Probably, as in the case of so many other landowners' properties, after Big Charlie's death the farm fragmented into the hands of his many children to become a kind of family compound. Perhaps, before his passing or thereafter, like John Wheeler of Smith County, Big Charlie White had given all of his children homes.

Subdivision of the large farms of freedmen among their big families must explain some of the astonishing increase in the numbers of black landowners between 1890 and 1910, by which latter date three out of ten black Texas farmers owned their own land. While the landowners had increased, average farm size declined.[88] As in the case of Jim Runnels of Boykin, some large landowners braved courthouses and white lawyers to make careful arrangements for the division of their family lands before their deaths, but many others died intestate. Runnels' neighbor, Jim Boykin, passed on without a will, fragmenting his land among his many children.[89]

In one way or another, most of the large farms of the turn of the century disappeared, but a precious landhold had been handed down to the next generation. A child's inheritance from the family farm might be inadequate for a complete living, but it could serve as a new family's subsistence base, while family members rented additional land to grow cash crops or spent part of the year in public work. A homeplace yet remained for many freedmen settlement families at a time when more and more white families lost their land and declined into tenancy.[90] In the era of Jim Crow, many black persons still believed that owning land in their own communities brought the only real escape from white domination—"a kind of concrete freedom, a daily practical reality of being at liberty"—replaceable by nothing else.[91]

One man tried to put this into words when he explained: "I ain't never been to heaven but I'd rather have this here outside of anything I know. I can do anything I want to. All of it's mine. Nothing can be more enjoyable. Chickens crowing, get the eggs, eat the eggs, kill the chickens and eat the chickens and go on according to the year."[92]

CHAPTER FOUR

Saturday Nights and Sunday Mornings

C. White inherited no land from his eccentric father, but in 1914 White and his wife Lucille managed to purchase 27 ½ acres from a black farmer named Ben Richardson at the Richardson settlement, a few miles out of Nacogdoches. The Whites paid $350 for the land, which had "a little old house on it." Owning land made a big difference, as White explained:

> The house wasn't much more than a shack. It had three rooms, and wood shutters for windows. But Lucille never complained. And the children was too little to care.
>
> Lucille and me always had worked hard, both of us. We hadn't ever minded work. But looked like when we got some land that belonged to us it just set us on fire. We didn't seem to get half as tired, or if we did we didn't notice it. One day when we was cleaning up a field Lucille said, "You know, Charlie, even the rocks look pretty."[1]

The Richardson community was a freedmen's settlement in decline, with neither church nor school in 1914, and C. C. White soon turned his land-owner's zeal to community rejuvenation. To White, as to so many others before him, a community without a church at its core seemed no community at all. Acting on an old urge to preach, White built a brush arbor on the farm of the widow of the community's founder and began holding Sunday school. White's neighbors turned out, and after a while he advised the Baptists in Nacogdoches that he wanted a license to preach. Following the usual procedure, a committee of several Baptist ministers came out to attend White's services, approved of his preaching, and issued him a license. Then, as White explained:

> I got a regular church organized. I guess I just liked to preach. I always felt better when I was on good terms with God, and when I was preaching seemed like him and me hit it off awful well.
>
> We held church in people's houses that winter and the next summer I built us a church house. We called it Richardson's Chapel.[2]

Since Emancipation, most freedmen's settlements had begun with establishment of a church. The ex-slaves' dream of landed property was closely linked to their dream of religious freedom, and congregations formed early at many communities. In fact, congregations rather often preceded settlements, as in the case of St. John Colony in Caldwell County and other places. Typically, a man like Charlie White or John Wynn got the call to preach, formed a congregation around him (perhaps meeting in private homes or under a brush arbor), then after a few years led his people to the hoped-for promised land. On rare occasions such pioneering congregations had formed even before Emancipation, as at Cedar Branch in Houston County, where a helpful slaveholder built his bondsmen a frame chapel in 1864, then went on to deed them land and assist them in establishing an independent community.[3]

Cedar Branch was not the norm. Religious worship on the slave plantation depended on the whim of the white landowner and ran the gamut from attempted suppression of all religious observance to compulsory chapel, directed by the slaveholder himself. Slaves did not necessarily see the latter as the more favorable alternative, as at Henry H. Buttler's plantation, where one harsh taskmaster held forth every Sunday to a captive audience of his slaves and those of surrounding plantations. As in this case, whites preached to their bondsmen from mixed motives of Christian zeal and economic self-interest, and their sermons commonly emphasized the need for docility, obedience, honesty, respect for property, and acceptance of the slave's role, justified by certain key biblical texts. A favored quotation came from Paul's epistle to Titus: "Exhort servants to be obedient unto their own masters, and to please them well in all things; not answering again."[4]

Equality of souls in the sight of God and other dangerous Christian ideas usually were not on the master's Sunday school agenda, and when they were, the slaves recognized the hypocrisy. Slaves knew Henry Buttler's owner as a harsh master to his own bondsmen, so when he preached a sermon on the need for Christian kindliness, some slave imprudently laughed out loud. At this point, the kindly minister moved out into his audience to administer "twenty-five hard licks," then and there.[5]

Whites allowed Christian religious worship at most Texas plantations, although slave preachers usually were hand-picked by the owners and expected to confine themselves to a certain range of topics. Masters sometimes allowed, encouraged, or even required slaves to attend white churches, sitting at the back or standing in a balcony. Additional services, more heartfelt but clandestine, often went on later in the slave cabins or down in the woods after dark.[6]

Owners had uneasy feelings that religious freedom might lead to other kinds of freedom, incompatible with slavery. Spontaneous praying, hymn singing, and unauthorized prayer meetings in creek bottoms or thickets were considered dangerous and often forbidden. As one ex-slave remembered, "We weren't allowed to pray cause the Lord might hear us and free us."[7]

Slaves such as freedman John Bates's "Uncle Ben," who read the Bible and served as informal religious leader, could present a problem for owners. One day, "Master Harry" overheard Ben discussing how the Bible affirmed the slaves' coming freedom, and the master made fun of Ben, saying: "Hell, no, you never will be free. You ain't got sense enough to make a living if you was free, no siree. You'll be a slave as long as you live." But the matter was not taken lightly, Bates says: "We always went to church till this happen, and after that we wasn't allowed to go. He even takes Uncle Ben's Bible away from him, saying that book puts bad ideas in our heads." After a while, Uncle Ben got another Bible, though now he kept it out of sight of the master.[8]

After Freedom, African Americans led by the "Uncle Bens" quickly severed their uncertain memberships in the white churches of their former masters. Feelings were mutual; most whites wanted them out, and most blacks wanted to leave "captivity" to organize their own congregations.[9] Some of these new congregations gave rise to freedmen's settlements, and others formed soon after landholding communities took root in the countryside. Many denominational allegiances were observed, but the Colored Methodist Episcopal (CME), African Methodist Episcopal (AME), and Baptists became the most common.[10]

At these settlements, congregations sometimes long predated church buildings.[11] Most freedmen subscribed to the Protestant notion that the real church was the congregation, the community of believers, and that infrastructure was less important. Nor did the new residents immediately have the money to pay for it. Furthermore, overt social organization had been denied to African Americans under slavery, and during the violent decade of Reconstruction many ex-slaves remained cautious about manifesting it. They often chose to keep a low profile in their remote communities, preferring not to announce themselves with fine new churches. For a time—sometimes for years—congregations met in private homes. After a while, people built a brush arbor for outside services in the hot summer months. Later on, perhaps beside the brush arbor, they built a dirt-floored, log church and after that a succession of frame churches, the new ones often partly recycled from the materials of their predecessors.

The cornerstone of Shiloh Missionary Baptist Church in Barrett settlement, Harris County, listed 1879 as the founding date of the church, though community religious worship had begun several years earlier. Barrett residents worshiped in a brush arbor and a one-pen log church before they constructed a frame church on land donated by Harrison Barrett in 1895. Of board-and-batten construction, 12 feet wide by 24 feet long, elevated on cypress or heart pine blocks, with windows not of glass but of hinged board-and-batten, the 1895 Shiloh Missionary Baptist Church closely resembled a thousand other black country churches across Texas.[12] Many other freedmen churches also shared the proud name "Shiloh," taken from the appropriate biblical text of Joshua 18:1: "And the whole congregation of the children of Israel assembled together at Shiloh and set up the tabernacle there, and the land was subdued before them." Like the children of Israel, the chosen people of God, African Americans had passed through the trials of slavery to set up their tabernacles in the wilderness.

Churches remained the core institutions of Texas freedmen's settlements for a century. Community education normally began there—first, as privately funded "subscription schools" in the pioneer log chapels and brush arbors, then as public schools in frame churches like that of Barrett. From the 1880s, white county superintendents and county school boards in the courthouse towns directed rural public education, and black schools rarely were a priority. At many places, the frame churches, with their characteristic low square steeples (or double square steeples, one on each side), served as community schoolhouses well into the twentieth century. Some community residents resented this neglect, but others tacitly approved; the church house remained entirely their institution, and (unlike a public school building) whites had no say about it.

Slowly, other infrastructure developed adjacent to the church—rather often, a small two-story lodge hall where one or more of the many fraternal orders held their secret meetings, a picnic ground, a baseball field, or a primitive brush arbor, still useful for lamp-lit revivals in the hot summertime. Churches often changed locations for two or three decades after Freedom, then they tended to remain fixed, anchored to their developing graveyards. During these same decades, and afterward, new congregations sometimes formed or old congregations split to form additional community churches. Bitter internal conflicts often spawned the new churches, though quarrels usually soon dissolved into the customary cooperation. At Friendship, Delta County, an important landowner's anger at a "dirty Sunday School card" distributed by the Methodists led to the formation of a Baptist church, though in time this matter was forgotten.[13] Baptists themselves were notorious for dividing and then making up, as in the case of the two churches at Shady Grove in Houston County that faced each other across a sandy road.[14]

African Methodist Episcopal and Colored Methodist Episcopal churches stepped to the distant drums of church governance boards, but local Baptist churches had full congregational autonomy. Seven-member "deacon bodies" governed policy at Baptist churches—hiring and firing ministers, regulating Sunday schools, watching over church finances, and deciding thorny issues like the "de-churching" of members of the congregation for wayward behavior. Deacons always were men, although behind the scenes and working through the various clubs and missionary societies women ran most of the day-to-day business of the church. Not surprisingly, men and women of a community's principal landowning families invariably took the lead at church, school, and lodge hall, for which one or more families among them had donated land.

Black churches at freedmen's settlements cooperated to a degree not typical of rural white churches of the same denominations. Across the eastern half of Texas, congregations normally attended each other's churches on "pastoral days," the one Sunday each month when the visiting minister came to preach. Usually there were enough churches within traveling distance that services could be attended at least three Sundays out of four, as at Shankleville in Newton County. Congregations often met at their own church for an abbreviated Sunday school, then traveled together by wagon or Model T to another church in that community or in an adjacent settlement that had a minister that Sunday. Baptist, AME, CME, Presbyterian—the denomination made little difference to people, who often remarked that the services were much the same. Church congregations from different communities cooperated in other ways as well. They attended each other's funerals, fund-raisers, and social events, especially the week-long

Sweet Home Baptist Church at the freedmen's settlement of Sweet Home, Guadalupe County, 1954. The two-steepled architecture characterized many early African American churches in rural Texas. (Courtesy of Texas Cooperative Extension)

A church picnic, often termed "dinner on the ground," follows the service at County Line, Nacogdoches County. (Richard Orton)

midsummer revivals, which communities often held on different dates so that adjoining communities could attend.

The "Holiness Church," the Church of God in Christ, was a partial exception amid all this Christian unity. Black Protestant churches in general emphasized spiritual zeal, but older denominations remained somewhat suspicious of the people some called "holy rollers" and their insistence on profound religious experience at every church meeting and "testimony" about it afterward. At Richardson Chapel in Nacogdoches County, Baptist minister C. C. White began to lose church members to the Holiness church in nearby Nacogdoches, then—at local people's request—he reluctantly agreed to allow Holiness adherents to hold occasional services in his own church. Many locals soon converted to the fervent Holiness faith, including White's wife Lucille, but he hung back. The Church of God in Christ emphasized the need for a powerful conversion experience, a possession by the Holy Ghost, but White's problem was that he thought he had experienced a perfectly good Baptist version of this already. He explained: "So I went to church, and I went to church, and I went to church. And nothing happened. I didn't get the Holy Ghost like the rest of them. I didn't get saved, or nothing." Eventually White realized his sin of pride and reluctance to humble himself at the altar in front of his erstwhile congregation, and "When I finally realized that, I went to the altar and humbled myself, all the way down flat. And then I got the Holy Ghost. The Church of God in Christ people made me a preacher in their church right then. They knowed I could preach."[15] A decade later, in 1928, Reverend White found himself unable to drive his car across a railroad track while an inner voice told him "Jacksonville, Jacksonville, Jacksonville!" Having heard the call, White soon sold his precious farm and moved to the Jacksonville quarter, setting up his ministry on the devil's ground in a notorious red-light district of gamblers, bootleggers, prostitutes, and juke joints.[16]

Most of the part-time ministers who migrated to hold services at freedmen's settlements reported inner voices and conversion experiences that had impelled them to preach the Gospel. The social world of rural black people was bipolar, divided into secular and sacred, flesh and spirit, the activities of Saturday nights and those of Sunday mornings that did not easily mix and merge. It was customary for a believer to recount how he or she had made the turn from darkness to light, and especially so for ministers. Reverend White's story of his first conversion experience to the Baptist faith had been more conventional—that of a sinful teenager who suddenly saw the truth. Most black ministers told the tales of their conversions many times during their preaching careers, and stories often emphasized the depth of their sins and the potency of their sinning before they changed their ways. Lucy Mauchison's father, for example, had been known as the biggest gambler and hell-raiser in all of Jasper County until the night a disapproving internal voice spoke to him during a card game.[17] Likewise, young S. L. Davis was returning by wagon to St. John Colony, his head aching from a night of "spreeing" in Lockhart, when a voice repeatedly asked him a question he could not answer and which haunted him for weeks until he experienced a profound religious conversion. The voice said, "Why do you do as you do?"[18]

Black ministers at freedmen's settlements usually came from rural backgrounds. Sometimes the call to preach came early in life, and sometimes it came late. At the Hall's Bluff community of Houston County, Vivian Lovelady's father was middle-aged before he became a Methodist preacher. Causing his family some hardship, he left their poor sandyland farm twice a month to preach in distant communities.[19]

During a six-day week of eleven-hour work days, Reverend Henry Truvillion labored in the "steel gang" of the company railroad of Wier Longleaf Lumber Company at Wiergate, but on Sundays he preached in the freedmen's settlements of Newton County and Jasper County. Remote communities knew Reverend Truvillion's approach by "his holler and his blow," two long blasts followed by two shorts, done with voice, cow horn, or car horn. Residents also well knew his story of personal conversion and his special sermon, an unforgettable metaphor of Christian redemption. As a boy in Mississippi, returning home cross-country after dark on a moonless night, Truvillion got lost in a dangerous brushy field that contained a deep pond. Fearful of drowning in the pond, he cried for help in the dark, and a distant stranger came out of his house, lit a torch of pitch-pine splinters, and shouted to the boy that he would be safe if he came directly to the light. Truvillion trusted the stranger, did as he was told, and was saved. "Now this Bible I'm holding up here is God's splinters," he told audiences at hundreds of church services, "the Holy Spirit is the fire. My job here is to hold up this light. Now, is there anyone lost here tonight? I invite you to come to the light."[20]

Visiting ministers like Truvillion developed reputations based on preaching performance, and some attained a celebrity status at times resented by community members of a more secular persuasion. In any case, African American folklorist J. Mason Brewer (born and raised in the freedmen's settlement of Cologne), collected many stories about hypocritical, greedy, or sexually indulgent preachers during his field work along the Brazos River valley. In one typical story, a son complained so frequently about visiting preachers hogging the best food at the family's home that his father ban-

Members of the County Line Missionary Baptist Church gather in a circle for a
prayer by pastor James Wickware. (Richard Orton)

ished the son to hell. Returning after a time, people asked him what hell was
like, and he answered that it was just like here, "So many damn preachers
round the fire you can't get to it."[21]

Freedmen's settlements tended to be what rural Southerners called
"church communities," places dominated by Christian values and morali-
ties and somewhat apart from the looser and more secular communities of
sharecropper farms and market towns. Sometimes the contrast was stark
indeed, as in Houston County, where the Vistula community held church-
based Saturday night fund-raisers of chili and ice cream while wild weekend "balls" at the Murray farm, a few miles to the west, featured live
music, dancing, gambling, fighting, and bootleg whiskey. Not that straitlaced freedmen's settlements were immune from the wilder side of things.
Milder forms of secular social life went on all the time, though people might
sneak around to indulge in some of them. Nor were church communities
immune from a degree of hypocrisy. A Vistula man was an adult before he
discovered that certain of the local church deacons had bankrolled community whiskey makers who supplied dances at the Murray farm with recreational refreshments.[22]

County Line settlement in Nacogdoches County typified many black church communities. The County Line Baptist Church dominated community social and moral life, including Claude Upshaw's small store just across the road. Adults and children "hung out" at the store—conversing, sitting on benches outside, listening to the radio, or playing in the street—but all obeyed Upshaw's unspoken prohibitions against profanity, fighting, gambling, or drinking at this location so close to the church.[23]

Claude Upshaw's sister-in-law, Leota Upshaw, wife of Monel Upshaw, and other community leaders took stands championing strict Christian morality at County Line. Leota Upshaw's great-grandmother had instilled in her the idea that "your name always goes ahead of you," and her father had been a church deacon who "always practiced what he taught." Juneteenth celebrations challenged Christian decorum, but Leota's family held the line with a festive but very sober Juneteenth, beginning with church service and culminating with homemade barbecue and treats of ice cream and soda water brought from Nacogdoches. As befitted her position as leader of the church missionary society, Leota Upshaw remained a strict interpretationist about the sporting life. She told a white friend, "Can't nobody tell you they've ever seen me take a drink of whisky, and I don't play games because it turns out to be gambling. I don't play anything." One little bottle of beer or hand of cards prepared a slippery slope to more grievous sins, in Upshaw's view, and she sometimes saw evidence of this process at work at County Line.[24]

Other people, some of them Upshaw's friends and relatives, behaved less strictly. Men sometimes went out in the woods to gamble, usually to shoot dice or play cards. A good many families made home brew, though males with bottles in hand took pains to conceal them from the public view of Leota Upshaw and other church stalwarts. Claudie May Joyce's father brewed beer and always provided some for her Grandmother Ross, a very devout church member who nonetheless liked to drink beer. When Grandmother Ross got some, she liked to drink it and "take off walking," perhaps headed someplace where Leota Upshaw would not see her. Even among the Upshaw family, a few small, home-based "juke joints" operated in County Line, providing loud amplified music and refreshments at private homes, sometimes under brush arbors. Any County Line resident who wanted to find a moonshiner's bootlegger knew how to do this.[25]

Such sporting-life activities of gambling and drinking were disapproved of but to a degree tolerated at County Line, but sexual immorality and violent acts often brought community members before the church deacons. Adultery, property theft, out-of-wedlock pregnancy, and serious in-group violence occasionally happened at County Line, as everywhere else, and these transgressions sometimes led to "de-churchings," which in extreme cases drove people from the community.[26] At Neylandville in Hunt County, residents simply shunned evildoers, withdrawing from all interactions with them, and this severe treatment soon forced them to leave. Others who remained, or were allowed after a time to return to the community, suffered all their lives in a small face-to-face society where everyone knew what they had done. Driven to alcoholism in later years, the Peyton Colony man who had killed another resident in a long-ago fight told his niece that he never looked at a piece of food on his plate that he did not see the ghostly hands of the dead man's children reaching for the food.[27]

At County Line and elsewhere, deacons sometimes disagreed about expelling people from their church, hiring or retaining preachers, and doctrinal matters, and such quarrels sometimes spread to bitterly divide church communities. People's deep beliefs and devotion to religion powered these quarrels, which rather often (and especially among the Baptists) led to congregational splits and new churches.

Church quarrels had a low flashpoint. One Sunday morning, peaceable Harrison Barrett became incensed at something the visiting minister said in the church for which Barrett had given land and which he had helped build. He asked the preacher not to repeat the offensive statement, but the man refused, saying that this was his church, and he would speak as he wished. Barrett told him it was not his church, that he was only a "hired man," and rose to assault the preacher at his pulpit, assisted by two of his brothers.[28] As recalled by the minister's daughter, Vivian Lovelady of Houston County, such unseemly incidents happened more commonly than they should, with the worst conflicts all taking place within congregations. An elderly man once remarked to her that the reason for this was that not all of the people in a church were really Christians. It was like Noah's Ark, the old man told her; not all the animals in the ark were "good animals." There were, for example, "skunks in the ark." And there were skunks in the church, too![29]

Despite the disruptive presence of the occasional "skunk," church business was conducted through the activities of church missionary societies, dedicated to "beautifying" the church, raising money, and helping needy families in the community. Women did most of the work in the missionary societies, of which almost every Protestant church had at least one, though they rallied men to their causes as needed. Missionary societies rarely supported work abroad, but labored within their own church communities. They organized an array of social affairs to raise money—for example, the popular "heaven and hell parties" at Vistula, which served chili and ice cream for a small fee. Great ingenuity manifested itself in these social events. At the time of her 1930s fieldwork in Sunflower County, Mississippi, anthropologist Hortense Powdermaker found missionary societies sponsoring chicken hunts, chitterling suppers, candy pulls, fashion shows, queen contests, brideless weddings (all parts taken by men), biblical plays, and other imaginative affairs. Admission typically cost five cents. Powdermaker was much impressed with the humor, wit, and vitality of these black affairs in comparison to the social events of white churches that she also attended.[30]

Missionary societies all had names—for example, the Willing Workers. They met weekly or biweekly at someone's home to socialize, plan fundraisers, discuss which families in the community needed their help, and make quilts or clothing for the needy. Church missionary societies often functioned as the organizers of community neighborliness when families or individuals got in trouble—when homes burned, farmers became ill in crop season, or housewives fell sick. Elderly persons, isolated in their homes, or poor young women, burdened with many children, often drew the women's help. While unwed mothers might be shunned to a degree during their pregnancies, after the birth things usually changed; no one wanted to disadvantage the innocent child.[31]

An array of fraternal lodges and insurance and burial societies also developed in close association with the churches, sometimes meeting at the church, more often (as in the case of the Colored Benevolent Association of Houston County at Germany) meeting upstairs in a two-story frame structure near by.[32] The Masons, Knights of Pythias, Courts of Calanthe, Odd Fellows, Builders of the Walls of Jerusalem, Daughters of Tabor, United Gospel Aid, Brothers and Sisters of Charity, and all the rest needed a second-floor lodge hall to shield their secret rituals from the public eye. Besides their social activities, the professed purposes of the lodges, mutual aid societies, and insurance societies was much the same—to help the sick, bury the dead, assist needy members, and support widows and orphans.[33]

Perhaps more so than rural whites, black people in freedmen's settlements planned for impressive funerals. Many of the lodges and societies sold burial insurance or included burial assistance with their memberships. People wanted to pass from this world with style and dignity and often advised family and friends about their preferences. The church bell symbolized community identity, and an elderly Hopewell man told Vivian Lovelady and other people that he wanted his death "tolled" from the time the hearse carrying his body came into sight over a certain hill. This was done, with one toll of the bell for each year of the man's life.[34]

Probably this man's passing had been tolled once before, at the time news of his death reached custodians of the church. Tolling of the bell announced a death and summoned neighbors to help the bereaved family. They bathed the body and laid it out on a "cooling board," often a door of the house that had been taken down and positioned across two chairs. Then they closed the corpse's eyes with silver coins, placed a saucer of salt on its chest to help preserve it, and covered it with a sheet. Lamps burned in the house throughout the night after a person passed, and friends and neighbors sat up with the corpse to show their respect for the family and to "keep the cats away." House cats were believed to exhibit an unseemly interest in the recently dead (though perhaps the real danger was rats). The next day after a person died, neighbors removed the body from the cooling board, re-dressed it, placed it in a homemade coffin, and hauled it by wagon to the church or graveyard service.

Church services for an important person in the community might go on for a long time, with some people moved to "shout" and attain exalted religious states, as the end of Sunday service or during a summer revival. Whatever one may have wished in life, the fervor of a person's funeral somewhat depended on his or her status in church and community. One ne'er-do-well sinner at Boykin in Angelina Country died with no provision for his funeral, and Jim Runnels, Runnels's wife, and others pitched in to build a board coffin and arrange a minimal ceremony. The widow ungratefully remarked that her poor husband had been "buried like a hog," to which the insulted Runnels replied, "Well, he lived like a hog, and died like a hog, so we buried him like a hog."[35] At the other extreme, as befitted a godly man's passing over into Glory, the funeral of community leader "Preacher Dunbar" of the Jerusalem community of Freestone County lasted for three days and triggered Juneteenthlike celebrations, complete with food stands and cold drinks.[36]

In some cases, and perhaps famous Reverend Dunbar's, a "second burial" ceremony at the cemetery eulogized the deceased several months after interment. This service may have been as much for the comfort of the living as an expression of respect for the dead. Some African Americans believed that the spirit of dead people tended to hang around after death, passing judgment on the excellence and appropriateness of their funerals, and it was unwise to displease them. Matter-of-fact ghost incidents abound in the Texas slave narratives from the 1930s, many of them set in the recent past, as in the account of a man who often passed his dead wife in the hall at night, sometimes smelled the smoke from the pipes of two deceased old ladies, and once observed dead persons passing from graveyard to church house to hold midnight worship.[37] Old cemeteries at freedmen's settlements testify to African American attitudes about the dead—that spirits "must be placated or might maliciously cause misfortune, pain, or even death." The *Encyclopedia of Southern Culture* notes examples of black funerary customs: "In traditional black graveyards bodies are interred with the objects used by the person in life, and often personal items like razors, lamps, clocks, toys, medicine bottles, glasses, cups, and so forth are clustered on the top of the grave mound. These items are placed there to provide the spirits with material comforts so they might 'rest easy' and not roam outside the community."[38] Remnants of such grave offerings may still be seen adorning older graves at many Texas freedmen's settlements.[39]

In life, many residents of these communities had often done little roaming. For almost a century, people lived and died in their home communities and ended their days lying in coffins at the front of the churches that they had attended so many times.

Sunday services in a community church normally occurred once a month on "pastoral Sunday," the weekend that the visiting minister arrived. Churches in an area normally scheduled their pastoral Sundays in rotating order so that members could attend each other's services, and when they had ministers they tried to make the most of the occasions. As Janice Parker of the Weeping Mary community in Cherokee County explained, "On Sundays when we have a preacher, we stretch it out as much as we can."[40]

Getting ready for Sunday required much effort. For many families, preparations began the Saturday before with cooking, washing, and ironing for the next day. Asked during an interview what she had done for recreation on Saturday nights at Hall's Bluff in Houston County, Vivian Lovelady laughed out loud. This daughter of a Methodist minister invariably spent Saturday nights preparing her Sunday school lessons.[41] Many families prepared only a single morning meal on Sunday, and some did not cook at all on the biblically ordained day of rest.

At Flat Prairie in Washington County, Grover Williams's pastoral Sundays typified the daily round of a strict church-going Baptist family. William's grandparents allowed no cooking, working, laughing, playing, or whistling on Sundays. (Whistling was allowed on other days, but only of religious melodies—no "reels.") A home prayer meeting, during which the younger children recited Bible verses and the older ones offered prayers, preceded the family's long walk to church, shoes in hand to avoid soiling them with dust or mud. The church in sight, they wiped off their feet with a cloth and put on their shoes. After a long day at church the family again removed their Sunday shoes, walked home, and resumed the day of rest and reflection. All prohibitions remained in effect. Williams and his siblings could walk around the pasture for recreation, but that was all. No work occurred, even of an emergency nature; if the cows broke into the corn field or the hogs got into the sweet potato patch on Sunday, it was just too bad.[42]

Beatrice Upshaw Ali recalled similar devout customs of pastoral Sabbaths at County Line Baptist Church in Nacogdoches County. Clothing to wear on Sunday had been prepared on the previous Saturday, since Ali's mother, Leota Upshaw, prohibited washing and ironing on church day and cooked all the food for the day at breakfast, including a big cake for the evening meal. Sunday breakfast served as a special feast, however, often featuring fried chicken, biscuits, and gravy. Afterward, the Upshaw children used halves of biscuits to shine their patent leather shoes for church, since shortening in the biscuits made shoes glisten. The children also shined themselves for church service, rubbing faces, arms, and legs with small amounts of beef tallow.[43]

Church services at County Line resembled those of other black rural churches. Sunday school meetings for adults and children began at midmorning. Secretaries took elaborate minutes at these meetings, which were conducted with discipline and decorum. At County Line the superintendent of Sunday school used an ancient little chrome and black dinner bell to dismiss classes and bring meetings to order. After Sunday school, the main service began, and as Rowena Weatherly Keatts of Lincolnville in Coryell County noted, "Preachers at that time, black preachers, they preached a long time."[44] Church lasted for several hours for most families, and Keatts recalled many occasions of sleeping on a pallet at church when she was small. "Britches quilts," rough quilts intended for floor use, served these "pallet babies," sometimes for two naps during the long day.[45] Families often carried dinner and stayed into the afternoon, attending Baptist Training Union and other meetings, and then perhaps the evening service. At Washington County's Hollow Springs Baptist Church, where Dave Taplin's family attended, Sunday church lasted eight hours for the Taplins, including Sunday school, first service, afternoon service, and evening service. Here and elsewhere, families living some distance from their churches often rode home after dark.[46]

Midday service was the major religious event of pastoral Sundays. Preachers began slowly, then built their long sermons toward a climax, usually choosing themes from a range of topics very familiar to their audiences: the fragility of life in this world, the need for love and compassion, the necessity for Christian redemption for our sins, and the coming glories of heaven. "Hell and brimstone" sermons perhaps occurred less frequently in black rural churches than in white ones, though there were memorable exceptions. One sermon at Emma Jackson Wisdom's church in Lee County so vividly evoked God's destruction of the world by fire that Wisdom dreamed a terrible nightmare of the sun falling from the sky to destroy the earth, which she clearly recalled a half century later.[47]

As an hour or two hours passed and ministers built their sermons toward dramatic conclusions, their audiences urged them on with ever-increasing responses. The ministers—and their congregations—expected a few persons to be overcome with religious feeling and "begin to shout." At Lincolnville, Deola Mayberry Adams's mother might become one of these. "She wasn't showing out," Adams explained, "that was her belief, and she couldn't help herself. When the Lord hit her, well she felt it. She was sincere in what she believed in. That's the way all of them was back in them days. They'd get up and get happy in church, and they'd let the Lord know they was happy."[48]

At Grover Williams's church, women who felt they were about to shout sometimes asked others to hold their purses for them before they lost control. "When they feel it coming on, some didn't want you to hold them when they were shouting, and some they had to hold because they looked like they was going to hurt themselves. They'd jump up and stand up in the seats, and they'd just run all down the aisles. The more they hollered and whooped, the more the preacher would try to make them."[49]

At County Line Baptist Church, religious emotions often overwhelmed the same people, Sunday after Sunday. Beatrice Upshaw Ali recalled that elderly Mr. Morrisette often jumped up from his seat on the front row to wave his white handkerchief and shout his favorite words of encouragement to the congregation—"Come on up!"—over and over. Soon thereafter, Ali's Aunt Louisiana began to moan softly and chant her soft prayers for the dead, usually repeating these invocations throughout the service. The living usually could not make out exactly what Aunt Louisiana said, but she was not speaking to them. In a car outside the church, Aunt Annie Bett, who was both crippled and blind, also began to shout. Placed in the car by her brothers next to the church's open windows, Aunt Bett participated in the sermon even though she did not come inside, and after a while her familiar cries and vigorous clapping resounded even above the noise of the rest of the congregation.[50]

Black congregations sang loudly, shouted, and made a joyous racket that carried long distances, especially during the week-long revivals of August that some churches called "Big Sundays." As in the case of pastoral services, nearby communities often alternated weeks for their summer revivals so that neighboring congregations might attend. The hot month of August coincided with the yearly agricultural downtime, coming after crops were "laid by" and before the cotton harvest began. During these revivals (which also served as family and community reunions), churches sought to celebrate the faith of true believers, to restore backsliders ("turnbacks") to the fold, and to lure a few lost sinners (people with no "church home") from the road to hell.[51]

As several people attested, if word got around that one or more hardened sinners sought salvation and planned to attend a particular revival, this news greatly improved attendance. Ministers, often working in teams, gradually escalated their sermons during the week of Big Sunday, while everyone's attention focused on the troubled souls at the mourners' bench up front. People prayed for these people, stared at them, and sometimes touched them with their hands, in hopes that by the end of the week these souls "heavy with sin" would become "light as a feather" with Christian redemption. Salvation did not come easy, but by their teenage years individuals came under great social pressure to experience conversions at the summer revivals.

Powerful preachers sought these conversions with all their energies. At Mount Zion Baptist Church in Lewis's Bend, Refugio County, Reverend Isiah Weathers roared at his congregation in a "voice like a lion," and the singing became so loud that even Sunday-morning gamblers sometimes came up to stick their heads in the windows of the church to see what was happening. Mount Zion participants sang "Where You Running, Sinner?" to the people on the mourners' bench and laid their hands on them in encouragement. One Lewis's Bend woman explained: "Reverend Weathers was old-timey and made us get up and testify. The old-timers would get up and strut the floor, singin' 'Ride On, King Jesus.' . . . When I was comin' up, you had to pray and pray and pray until you saw something or felt a change. You had to be convinced you were saved. You had to have dreams and visions to prove you were saved."[52]

Big Sunday revival week came to fruition when people came forward to be baptized at the end in a momentous event that Reverend C. C. White first observed as a child. The place was a traditional site of baptism on Bell Creek in Shelby County, not far from White's home community of Possum Trot. As White and his mother walked cross-country to the site, they saw scores of other people doing the same. Reverend Jerry Mays addressed the crowd of hundreds about heaven and hell in a loud voice until "he got the people to humming and moaning and it made my stomach feel shivery." Then Mays walked out into the water

County Line Missionary Baptist Church at County Line,
Nacogdoches County. (Richard Orton)

singing "Oh, Mourner" and begging the people to come on in and be baptized. Folks began to scream and shout, and some of them was crying. They'd make their way through the water to where the preacher was standing. He'd say, "I baptize you in the name of the Father, and of the Son, and of the Holy Ghost," and he'd lower them backwards into the water till they went clear under. Then he'd raise them up. They'd come out shouting and singing.[53]

Although preachers at Big Sundays focused on saving souls, at County Line, Sand Hill, Vistula, and many other freedmen's settlements secular amusements tended to grow up on the sidelines during revival weeks as part of the constant tension between sacred and secular in community social life. Many of the secular amusements were grudgingly church-approved, since the midsummer revivals served as festive community reunions as well as religious observances, but such matters often aroused debate in the communities. County Line's revivals featured drink and food stands. Vistula's "Big August Meeting" ended with an epic Monday-afternoon fish fry, the fish having been seined that morning from overflow pools along the nearby Trinity River.[54] At Sand Hill in Nacogdoches County on Big Sunday afternoons, people with fine surreys and Model T Fords offered cheap joyrides to the public, while some young men slipped over to the playing field for a quick game of baseball. Sand Hill baptized in a nearby spring pond, but the place of baptism also invited secular activities. Boys at church offered to walk girls to the spring in order to get in a little courting, and local beer makers liked to cool their beverages there. At intervals, someone complained to the deacons about beer in the spring, and they launched a search to find it and pour it out. At fourteen, Helena Brown Patton tried her first spring-pond home brew with cousins, got sick, vomited on her fine church dress, and received a whipping.[55]

Parents tried to keep such things from happening, especially to their girls, and in strict families at conservative communities, secular social life shrank to the irreducible minimums. As at Sand Hill, some discreet courting went on in and around church activities. Girls seated at the back of the choir passed notes. With or without permission, boys managed to absent themselves for a game of baseball or a swim in the creek on Sunday afternoons, although they might have to return home in time for evening service. Families rather commonly visited around the community on Sunday afternoons, and even Vivian Lovelady's preacher father sometimes allowed her to travel to a nearby aunt's house where Hall's Bluff youths gathered to play.

The leash remained short, however, especially for girls. Lovelady recalled that her social life, "such as it was," centered around affairs at church and school. By World War I times, black church communities all across the eastern half of Texas had hardened their attitudes toward "Saturday night suppers," "country balls," and other parties in private homes featuring live music and dancing, and such affairs had become less common. Many parents were like Jessie May Amie's father at Lake Creek, Houston County, who allowed his children to attend no "suppers" except the supervised ones at church and school.[56]

At Sand Hill and other places, the traditional season of weekend parties lasted from hog-killing time in November to New Year's Eve, with a peak just before Christmas.[57] Some parents chaperoned dance-free parties for young people—"candy pulls," "play parties," and other affairs. Dancing in all but name sometimes went on at play parties, where couples stepped to the sound of a human voice. At Cologne, pairs holding hands marched to a small community brass band, but church people did not consider this to be dancing.[58]

Stricter families would have none of this. Larutha Odom Clay grew up in a landowner family at Shankleville, Newton County, and she remembered that her brothers got to roam around more: "The girls were well protected. I guess that our recreation was singing at convention and box suppers related

A prosperous landowner family of Carver, Harrison County, plays bingo in its front parlor, 1947. (Courtesy of Texas Agricultural Extension)

to the church. Everything was related to the church." Even at the church box suppers, she did not have any beaux to purchase her box "because everybody was kin."[59] Boys in looser circumstances often had Clay's problem. At their communities, too, "everybody was kin." On Saturday nights, Chester Denman and other teenage males of the Pine Springs community, Houston County, often got together to walk trails through the woods in a big circuit among several black settlements in search of girls unrelated to them. The boys trudged miles and miles without lanterns in this largely fruitless quest for female companionship, and some nights "you couldn't see your hand in front of your face."[60]

Freedmen's settlements varied in the frequency and intensity of their secular social life, and even in strict communities certain individuals always gambled, drank, seduced, and otherwise tested the limits of community toleration. After she married, Houston County resident Vivian Lovelady found that the Hopewell community she moved to with her husband allowed the Saturday-night dances strongly discouraged at her home settlement of Hall's Bluff. A brother-in-law of Wesley Taylor Fobbs, bored with the restrictions of the church community of Wheeler Springs, just north of Hall's Bluff, sometimes went cross-country to a certain place on the Trinity River, shouted at the west bank, then greeted Leon County moonshiners arriving in paddle boats.[61]

Gambling seemed even more a proclivity than drinking or dancing at remote country settlements, black or white. Men slipped out into the woods to play cards or shoot dice, at night illuminating their games with coal-oil lamps, jury-rigged from beer or pop bottles, or with light from burning stumps. With wary eyes on the teacher, boys at the Fodice community school shot craps for pennies at recess, not unaware that some claimed their Houston County community had named itself for the gambler's cry "Come on, fo' dice!"[62] Especially among the men (and as Leota Upshaw well knew), even innocent games and harmless competitions often led to betting—for example, Ed Stimpson's father and brothers shot at tin cans with .22 rifles during a family visit. At Sand Hill innocent community rodeos and baseball games had a "secret side," as Chester Gregory revealed, with men often wagering on the outcomes. At Ed Lathan's Mount Fall community in Washington County, black whiskey makers often showed up with pockets full of cash to gamble on local baseball contests.[63]

Sporting-life adherents at freedmen's settlements commonly slipped around (or went to town) for games of cards or dice, but other diversions also attracted their interest. "Chicken fights" were popular as well as the use of fast hounds for the coursing of rabbits. Roosters fought naturally after a little encouragement, and men bet on the outcome of fights involving their cocks or those of other men. "Greyhound races" were a black gambling specialty, although—like the black baseball games and the earlier rural horse races—these occasions were sometimes frequented by whites as well. Groups of men went out with their greyhounds until someone spotted a cottontail or a jackrabbit sitting motionless in the open some distance away. Owners then moved their leashed dogs into position while they and everyone else bet on whose dog would catch the rabbit. Finally, someone jumped the rabbit, handlers loosed their dogs, and the race began.[64]

Church communities disapproved of dog races and cockfights, and few of them tolerated the full-blown "Saturday night suppers" featuring live music, dancing, alcohol, and gambling, but residents of freedmen's settlements usually knew where to go to attend these. Just west of Vistula and southwest of Dixon-Hopewell and Hall's Bluff, the big Murray sharecropper farm along the Trinity River sometimes held such events on Saturday nights. Houston County remained dry, even after Prohibition ended, but the county sheriff rarely bothered this major landowner and even asked permission to go on his place to look for someone suspected of a crime. Blues-man "Lightning" Hopkins, originally from Houston County, often played balls at the Murray farm before he moved to Houston, Texas, and became famous. At the cropper farm's wild Saturday nights, musicians played in-side, courting youths danced, married women sat around and watched the dancers, men gambled outside or in a nearby "gambler's shack," and boot-leggers lurked in cars on the highway.[65]

Fights, "cuttings," and other violence often erupted at such wild affairs — one reason that Leota Upshaw and other church people vehemently opposed them. Black-on-black violence was indifferently punished in local courts during the Jim Crow era. Many racist lawmen tended to neglect these con-flicts among African American nonvoters and assumed a "blacks-will-be-blacks" attitude toward thefts, cuttings, shootings, and even "killings," so long as African Americans perpetrated these things only upon each other. When such matters did come to court, intervention by a single important white landowner might serve to get his sharecropper or hired hand off the legal hook. As a Grimes County landowner supposedly told his black em-ployees, "Stay out of the graveyard, and I'll keep you out of the pen."[66]

Because of such attitudes, cautious residents of freedmen's settlements took care which social affairs they attended. At Washington County, Ed Lathan of Mount Fall sometimes visited big cropper farm dances in Grimes County just across the Brazos River, often when his friend Mance Lip-scomb provided the music. Lipscomb always set up at a cool window at such affairs and played all night for the dancers, a strong right thumb boom-ing out a rhythmic base for his dance tunes on the acoustic guitar. But, as Lathan told an interviewer, he took care which affairs he attended and whether his friend played there or not: "Them protracted suppers, it was several classes: some was gambling, some was bootlegging liquor, some was courting, some was dancing with the girls, and some was so drunk they couldn't dance, and some was hunting something to steal. They's all type of people that visit them suppers, I'm telling you what I know. And lot of em, if I knowed a lot of bad people was coming here, I wouldn't go. They'd kill folks and shoot folks and cut folks, all that kind of stuff. That didn't happen ever time, but I pretty well picked my places to go."[67]

By 1940 in rural Texas, people held Saturday-night suppers with decreas-ing frequency. Although Saturday-night dances persisted at some big share-cropper farms, electricity had arrived in the countryside and with it loud music on jukeboxes. Around 1950 Mance Lipscomb put his acoustic gui-tar in the closet and took up an electric instrument to try to compete.[68] As at Sand Hill in Nacogdoches County, minor "juke joints" sprang up in and around freedmen's settlements, and Sand Hill's "joint" offered well-supervised entertainments at the community's Mason Hall. Every Saturday evening, Chester Gregory, who was renting the hall, prepared cold soda water and "Jack Macker" sandwiches for the public, opened all the doors and windows, and turned his jukebox on at maximum volume to alert Sand Hill that he was open for business.[69] Sand Hill's joint provided mild Saturday-night entertainments, however, compared with other alternatives. As previously with Saturday-night suppers, wilder juke joints operated in rural precincts outside the church communities, near big sharecropper farms, and in red-light districts in town.

In their essence, freedmen's settlements were usually church communities, "fortresses without walls," religious refuges from the Saturday-night side of things, but some of their residents always heard siren songs from the wilder side of life.[70] Ed Stimpson offered a wonderful description of Collin County juke joints where wayward folks from freedmen's settlements might or might not show up. Bootleggers circulated among the crowds in these places, identifiable because "they all ways wore ducking over alls and a coat too big" in which to carry their wares. Local police normally had been paid off by joint proprietors but operated in an unpredictable way. Sometimes they raided the joint and arrested bootleggers and patrons carrying weapons; sometimes they came in, sat down, drank free booze, and joked with the ladies. Searches for weapons invariably confiscated a good many guns, knives, and straight razors. "A lot of women carried straight razor and could slip it out of ther bosum as fast as a snake could strike and cut you so fast, make you look like shredded cheese." Professional gamblers at the juke joint fascinated Stimpson; they were cold, calculating, sober men with hard eyes, who almost always won. Desperate amateurs might cry to their dice, "I need this point bad as a dead man need a coffin!" but when they played the real gamblers, the dice (or the cards) seldom fell their way. Stimpson thought the reason was clear: "Crooked dice slip in a game or card dealer dealing from the bottom, or card put up ther coat sleeve." Again and again, at the end of the game, whatever the game was, "the money would all way wind up in two or three men hand." Outcomes like this easily provoked violence. Stimpson said, "I been in places when I was a kid whin a fight brake out, a gun shooting, a knife cutting, getting tromp on trying to get out of there."[71]

For reasons that can only be speculated about, African American red-light districts persisted in Texas market towns and county seats long after their white counterparts had been shut down. Many lawmen in police and sheriffs' departments often felt they had better things to do with their time than fight black vice, they allowed black "operators" to operate to serve as "snitches" about doings in the black community, and they sometimes pocketed modest protection money to supplement meager salaries.[72] Beyond that, certain significant white citizens in every community, although stalwarts about preserving segregated schools, had integrationist attitudes toward the sporting life.

As a religious country boy from the freedmen's settlement of Possum Trot, young C. C. White was shocked by what he found in Center around 1900 after he took a construction job with the railroad. A nearby vice district, complete with whore houses, serviced the black railroad men. White went there occasionally, although only to drink a little whiskey, look at the women, and go home with the rest of the bottle. The half-naked whores fascinated White, but he slept in a barracks with men "nearly eat up" by venereal disease. It seemed more prudent to walk out into the countryside to court country girls, and that is what he did. As a man transformed and a minister in the Holiness Church, White would carry the Gospel into the heart of Jacksonville's red-light district in 1928.[73]

Around World War II, a black vice district still operated in Longview, Texas, where Albert Race Sample lived with his mother into his early teenage years, helping her work as prostitute, bootlegger, and professional gambler. "Big Emma," as she was known, represented the opposite end of the continuum of black society from Leota Upshaw. "Sporting life" well described Big Emma, who whored, gambled, and bootlegged but did not usually steal or resort to violence. Emma's career demonstrated that at this sporting-life level of society integration already had taken place. A very pretty woman in her early years, she at first specialized in relationships with white men, who, after all, had the most money. Race Sample was Emma's son by a prominent Longview cotton broker. As the years passed, Big Emma continued to "turn tricks" with white men and black men, and at her weekend crap games both whites and blacks packed into her shotgun shack by the railroad to take part in the action. Emma probably had more trouble with blacks than with whites about her policies of integration (everybody's money being as good as anybody else's). Some blacks did not like the whites at the crap games, and some probably did not like Emma's white-looking son, Albert Race Sample, especially when he bested them at so-called games of chance.

He almost always did. If a rural black man from a freedmen's settlement came to Longview in search of the sporting life, he might end up sitting on the floor of Emma's shack shooting craps, and if so, he surely would lose his money. Emma, her son, and Emma's longtime gambling companion "Blue"

Sample had all practiced with dice until they could roll them to come out any way they wished. They "set" the dice in certain positions in their hand, depending on how they wanted them to end up, gave false rattles to suggest they shook them into random order, then made carefully controlled throws based on long practice.[74]

Out in the countryside, the greatest incursion of secular social events, with sporting-life overtones, came on Juneteenth, and ardent Christians in church communities remained suspicious of June 19, "Freedom Day," for this reason. Even normally innocent pastimes, such as baseball games, tended to get a little wild on Juneteenth. Interviewed in the late 1930s, ex-slave Preely Coleman of Cherokee County explained why he stayed home on Juneteenth: "I just never did like the celebration and picnics. Always too much trouble, too much red-eye, cause too many fights, cutting and slashing. I just don't like it. So I say to the folks this morning, 'Now you go on, and I'll keep the house today.'"[75]

Adults in families who felt as Coleman did often celebrated Juneteenths at home, with big dinners and special treats of soda water and ice cream made possible by ice brought out from town. Conservative land-owning families with several daughters especially tended to do things this way, despite their children's resentful knowledge that bigger doings were afoot elsewhere. In a good many instances, special white friends came out to attend these sober family Juneteenths.[76]

At most freedmen's settlements, Juneteenth was celebrated as a communitywide event but remained closely supervised by the church. At Peyton Colony in Blanco County the Baptists held a special service, then children marched in a circle from church to school to graveyard and back again in a symbolic reuniting of the living and the dead. Here, as at many other places, Juneteenth had begun a day or so before with a readying of the community barbecue pit, a massive butchering of goats and yearlings, and a long barbecuing of meat.[77] Barbecuing everywhere served as a male bonding ritual, with a crowd of men hanging out all night around the barbecue pit "lying and burning up meat," as one practitioner described.[78]

The actual day of Juneteenth was first and foremost a great feast and picnic, prefaced by certain ceremonies and speeches and usually followed by games and competitions.[79] Parades were common if there was some place to parade to. Clarksville near Austin, for example, featured a procession of decorated horsemen accompanying a "Juneteenth Queen" dressed as the Statue of Liberty.[80] Big baseball games followed the noon meal at many Juneteenths, but Peyton Colony favored horseback competitions. In "needle races" men raced their horses to women partners standing in wagons, handed them a needle to thread, then raced back to the starting place. "Cigar races" were similar, but required no partners; the men had to jump up on the wagons and light cigars before racing back. Another equestrian competition was called "tournament," with horsemen trying to spear four hanging rings while riding by at high speed.[81]

In areas with several freedmen's settlements, by mutual agreement Juneteenths might be rotated among communities, with each one taking its turn.[82] At places with fewer independent black communities, the Juneteenth celebration of the freedmen's settlements often developed into regional events, drawing black people from rent farms, small market towns, and the county seats as well as from other landowner communities. Freedmen's settlements in such places already served as unique tourist destinations—black communities run by and for black people, with whites seldom seen—so it was natural for their events to become regional in scope.

Proud Pelham in Navarro County had a long history of major Juneteenths. Every year on June 19, pigs and goats roasted over open pits or old bedsprings, while fish deep-fried in lard in big washpots hung from trees. "The day was full of programs, games, and enough food for a large army," someone recalled.[83] Friendship community in Delta County also staged major Juneteenths, usually on the property of the land-owning Blanton family. People traveled long distances to attend the celebration and camped out for several days. To accommodate tourists, local men strung lights between trees, built a board platform, and brought in a piano by wagon to share the stage with guitar players and fiddlers. Nighttime dances followed daytime feasts. Goats, the traditional Juneteenth barbecue animal, died in droves for the Friendship community's epic events of June 19.[84]

Perhaps no rural Juneteenth became as large and famous as that at Comanche Crossing on the Navasota River in Limestone County, a county with over forty-five freedmen's settlements. Henry Freeman attended Comanche Crossing Juneteenths from around 1870, and already by the late nineteenth century the event lasted several days. People came long distances for the free barbecues, dances, and speeches where "the politicians would come and tell us how to vote." This was before the white man's primary effectively excluded blacks from voting, and the white politicians addressing the festive crowd often offered more than speeches. The ones paying the most money got the most votes, Freeman claimed.[85]

In her book *Juneteenth at Comanche Crossing*, Doris Hollis Pemberton offered historical details of the celebration and an eyewitness account of the epic Bicentennial Juneteenth of 1976. The Limestone County Nineteenth of June Organization had begun in 1889, after scattered celebrations coalesced at Comanche Crossing, a convenient location by the river with a good spring for drinking water. Two large buildings had been erected in 1925, following a half century of Juneteenths held in the open. Baseball games remained a big event at Comanche Crossing, and opposing teams played hard, sometimes knocking each other's teeth out. Comanche Crossing Juneteenths could be wild and dangerous, Pemberton admitted. A few days after a Juneteenth held during the 1920s, or so she had heard, dead bodies left over from the big event floated to the surface of the nearby Navasota River.[86]

On the night of June 17–18, 1976, Juneteenth celebrations began with the chaotic arrival of thousands of people. Pemberton saw a Central Lines chartered bus roll in, bringing Jehovah's Witnesses from Waco, committed souls prepared to fight the devil on his own ground. A large black motorcycle gang also roared up at about the same time. Bands played in the pavilion all night long, and people danced and milled around, unwilling to go to bed. At first light on June 18, Pemberton observed various crap games in progress.

By three o'clock, six unarmed white Bexar County deputy sheriffs had arrived, hired to keep order by the Juneteenth Committee. Attorney General John Hill was scheduled to be the guest speaker on the 19th, and authorities felt a little nervous. As dark fell, the wild night of June 18–19 began. Pemberton described the crowd just before midnight—an exciting scene but closely approximating Preely Coleman's judgment of "too much trouble, too much red-eye." At Comanche Crossing on Juneteenth, the sporting life ran in high gear.

On the park grounds an estimated crowd of 18,000 of celebrants were enjoying themselves buying T-shirts, novelties, taking pictures or patronizing Henry, a night club photographer, in his stand, and partaking of food and drink. There were others who bought whiskey from bootleggers, and dope from dope peddlers. People of culture and people of sub-culture always respect each other's individual spaces on the 19th of June celebration in Booker T. Washington Park at Comanche Crossing. Violence, if any, was on the fringes of the main crowd.[87]

Day dawned on a more sober and solemn occasion, although Pemberton observed a sunrise Bingo game with "piles of greenbacks in front of every person—they were playing a serious game of chance, they were not playing Bingo."[88] This was but a holdover from the wild night before. Sunrise prayer service began at seven o'clock, conducted by several ministers, and, as Pemberton explained, "You could feel a reverence creeping across the park for this Sunday morning to solemnize the memory of the emancipation of slaves in Texas. The open-air tabernacle was enveloped in a layer of dignity."[89]

Whatever its flaws, this strange and traditional mix of sacred and profane, Saturday night and Sunday morning, must continue, Pemberton believed. "Come hell or high water, the Limestone County Nineteenth of June Organization will never give up the ghost. There will always be the JUNETEENTH AT COMANCHE CROSSING!"[90]

CHAPTER FIVE

School Days

Basic literacy, the ability to read and write and calculate simple arithmetic, had been a forbidden fruit for African Americans in the days before Freedom, and to a degree it remained so during Reconstruction. Both ante-bellum state law and social custom strongly discouraged the education of bondsmen, and the rare owners who for their own reasons chose to teach their slaves risked trouble. Attitudes could be extreme. During the 1850s, Sterling Boykin of Boykin settlement found that certain white neighbors so strongly resented his home education of mixed-race white, black, and Indian sons and daughters that on one occasion someone broke into Boykin's house and burned their books.[1]

Black schooling remained a precarious business for a decade after Emancipation, as freedman Joe Oliver noted of the school he attended at an unnamed Hill County settlement.

> After the Civil War was over they started a school for the white children and one for the nigger slaves' children. This is the first school that I went to. I was a good big boy then. We did not go to school but bout three months at a time. This was in the winter when we did not work in the fields. We had a little log schoolhouse with the benches made from a plank of lumber hewed from a big log. The boys had to take they turns at what they would call guard duty now, for the Indians and the stray niggers was passing all the time. Times was in the Reconstruction days, and no one could tell what might happen. Nobody felt safe.[2]

Perhaps Oliver told his white interviewer in the 1930s the whole truth about these educational anxieties, but probably he did not. Resentful whites were the main danger for black schoolboys during Reconstruction. Whites burned schools established by the Freedmen's Bureau in the late 1860s, harassed teachers and students on their way to class, and sometimes made it impossible for white teachers from the north to find lodging in communities.[3] Nor were Southerners of Boykin's persuasion immune from persecution. In Anderson County local people assaulted a one-armed Confederate veteran because he established a freedmen's school. In Travis County "Old Man Tilden" for a time held a school for black children on Williamson Creek about five miles south of Austin, but "Kluxers" visited the school, frightened the children, and threatened Tilden's life if he did not stop.[4]

Some whites had emotional reactions to former bondsmen attending school, just as they resented their new freedoms to travel the roads, keep firearms, leave their former owners, and farm their own land. But white resistance was not just a matter of the irrational aggressions of shell-shocked Confederate veterans or KKK hooligans who came by night. White hostility to black education often had rational economic motives, as historians Randolph B. Campbell and Kenneth M. Hamilton documented for Harrison County. Impoverished by the war and desperate to get their cotton plantations back into production, Harrison County landowners successfully strove to regain control of freedmen with labor contracts and sharecropper agreements. Black education was not on their agenda, and Freedmen's Bureau schools in the county were often harassed and broken up. White landowners could see no good at all coming from black schools, which took child workers from the fields and reduced overall control of the labor force. In 1870 and for decades thereafter, white farmers preferred to deal with black farm workers who could not read legal agreements or calculate profits at settling-up time.[5]

Freedmen, on the other hand, often wished to learn to read the Bible almost as much as they wanted to establish their own churches or farm their own land. African Americans flocked to Freedmen's Bureau schools during the 1860s despite constant overcrowding and occasional white attacks. With the demise of the bureau, some schools continued under Republican governor Edmund Davis's ill-fated free-school system, although white resentment and harassment perhaps became even worse. Democrats resumed control in 1873, and the Constitution of 1876 abolished the Davis free-school system for blacks and whites by adopting the "community system," returning all power to establish and maintain schools to local authorities. Hence, there were no local school districts and no taxes to support public education. Community parents could, if they chose, take up money, employ a teacher, and establish a one-year "subscription school," with the state of Texas defraying some of the operating expenses. Freedmen had little money to accomplish this, and state and local authorities often discouraged them, but so zealous were African Americans for education that—against all odds—678 black schools were operating in Texas by 1877.[6]

At Lincolnville, Coryell County, Ophelia Mae Mayberry Hall's grandfather ran one of these subscription schools as the county's first black schoolteacher. James Lothlen charged parents $1.50 a month for older students and $0.75 a month for younger ones.[7]

The 1877 count of 678 schools probably underestimated the true extent of black education in Texas. Much black literacy instruction went on informally within religious congregations, which by the 1870s were beginning to leave private homes and brush arbors to establish log churches. Reading, writing, and arithmetic education then often moved to the community church—a pattern that long continued at many settlements. At Lewis's Bend in Refugio County, for example, as one former resident reported: "The schoolhouse was the church house and the church house was the schoolhouse. We went to school in the daytime and church on Sunday."[8] His community's Mount Zion Baptist Church served multiple purposes.

Blacks for a time remained cautious about coming out into the open with their institutions and quest for literacy, and the church functioned as a shield. Ned Peterson, a community leader at the freedmen's settlement of Wellborn in Brazos County, had taught others to read and write and often interpreted complicated documents for his neighbors, but he continued to list himself as "illiterate" with the white census taker.[9] African American education long remained in black churches, partly for defensive reasons; this was the one community institution that black people truly could call their own. As late as 1920, over one-third of the black schools in Shelby County still operated in churches.[10]

In the Texas slave narratives recorded in the 1930s, freedmen sometimes commented on the strong fear of whites inculcated under slavery and how this still haunted them. Sending children to school for a once-forbidden education must have troubled such people. Vennie Brunson's "old folks" perhaps had such fears when she began to attend her first "free school" during the 1870s, although the cautions they raised about education (or the ones she reported to her white interviewer) were different: schooling might make Brunson and her siblings feel they were too good to work or might distract them from watching out for dangerous snakes, wolves, bears, and similar things in the natural environment.[11]

Despite occasional black apprehensions and white distaste for paying local taxes to support black schools, by 1880 most Texans believed they needed a return to some system of public education. The School Law of 1884 was the result, and it revived many of the bureaucratic supports for schooling begun by the Davis administration. Once again a State Superintendent of Public Instruction operated at the state capitol. Once again counties established permanent common school districts, which then elected three-person boards of trustees to run them. A county school superintendent and county board of education in the courthouse town loosely regulated the county's common school districts, which largely coincided with the geographic boundaries of dispersed rural settlements. "Independent school districts"—entities independent of the county system—were provided for in the 1884 statute but long remained restricted to the city limits of major market towns. All districts, common and independent, now had the right to supplement state funding by levying taxes to support local schools.[12]

School reformers had hoped for fewer school districts than under the subscription school system, but they got the opposite. Charters for common school districts now were granted on a permanent basis, and, as before, new districts regularly formed by means of the political pressure parents exerted upon county school boards. Instead of stabilizing the number of school districts as reformers had hoped, the School Law of 1884 increased the number of communities seeking to establish local schools and to draw from the state school fund. Each Texas county swiftly developed into a geographical maze of local school districts, with each district running its own white and black schools. By 1905 the state superintendent reported that no less than 10,169 rural common school districts operated in the state, as compared with 868 independent districts. In 1910 those numbers reached the all-time high of 11,682 common school districts and 1,001 independent school districts.[13]

Nor did the educational complexities diminish much over time. In 1934, for example, Bell County still had 120 rural districts and 9 town districts, Fayette County had 82 and 3, and Nacogdoches County had 84 and 7.[14]

Several hundred Texas freedmen's settlement schools were lost somewhere in this maze of more than 10,000 common school districts. Until 1899, districts operating both black and white schools usually elected separate three-man boards of black and white trustees to govern their respective schools of the district. Whites normally retained overall authority, and sometimes the black school boards were termed "sub-trustees." Districts usually took their names from the white communities. After statutory changes of 1899, one of the discriminatory Jim Crow political "reforms" of the post-Populist era, rural districts elected only three trustees.[15] This effectively excluded black trustees except at very remote rural districts, such as the freedmen's settlement of St. John Colony in Caldwell County, where only blacks lived. Blacks at St. John continued to elect trustees and run their own common school district until the consolidations of the 1960s abolished the last rural districts, and so did a score of other places, but across the decades most freedmen's settlement schools passed under the formal authority of the nearest white districts.

Independent black communities like St. John Colony perhaps lobbied more effectively for scarce resources with their county school superintendents and school boards than did black settlements with all-white trustees, but Jim Crow discrimination was the order of the day. Black community schools often remained primitive affairs in first-generation log huts and in churches long after nearby white communities had moved into specially constructed frame schools, with at least some instructional equipment. All across the eastern half of Texas, high teacher-student ratios, overcrowding, small one- and two-room schools, poorly trained teachers, low teacher salaries, inadequate facilities, worn-out school books handed down from the white school, and abbreviated school terms characterized black rural schools.

Whites' racist beliefs about blacks' inability to learn explained some of this neglect, but contemporary African Americans thought they detected other motives. Illiterate or ill-educated people were easier to keep "down" and in their economic place, which was first and foremost in white men's cotton fields and kitchens. "A nigger is a nigger," whites sometimes said, and a good education did not seem appropriate. Even grassroots liberals, who championed black education, often considered black people to be intellectually inferior, and local conservatives thought that black education— sometimes *any* education—spoiled black labor. (For one thing, they might want to read their cotton receipts.) Whites claimed that blacks could not learn but often acted as though they feared they could, with consequences that might cost them money.[16]

In Shelby County in 1940, Prairie View A&M graduate student Leo B. Chumley found impoverished schools, poorly supported by white authorities. Local whites, in Chumley's opinion, seemed to have little interest in black education, though some told him they wished to see in the curriculum more emphasis on teaching better manners toward whites. One-third of Shelby County's black schools still operated in churches, and eighteen schools were of the one-room, one-teacher variety long disparaged by educational reformers. Chumley found that the cost of instruction per student per year was $42.30 for whites, $16.42 for blacks, and that black schools operated about one month less, on the average, than white schools. The average value of black schools and school equipment was much less than that of white schools. Most black schools still used log benches, though there were a few real desks, donated by whites decades earlier after spotting the "Made in Michigan" labels on them. Whites had rejected these "Yankee" products for political reasons.[17]

Quantitative researcher William J. Brophy reported statewide statistics about black education to show that Shelby County was no exception. For one thing, the more blacks in a county, the lower the proportion of school revenues gained through local taxation. Brophy concluded that white voters seemed reluctant to support black education, even if their own children suffered.[18] Black teacher salaries averaged only 58 percent of white salaries in 1940. Black rural schools were smaller than white rural schools—for example, in 1935, only 3.2 percent of white students still attended one-room schools, but 18.1 percent of blacks did so. Black rural schools had "grossly inferior physical plants." In fact, the furniture in white schools was worth more than the total value of all black schools!

Lack of adequate funding also shortened the black school year—28 percent of black schools operated for fewer than 140 days in 1935. Furthermore, the disparity in public funding went right to the top. Prairie View A&M functioned as the only state-supported black university until 1947. From 1911 to 1939, the Texas Legislature had appropriated $163 million for higher education, but Prairie View A&M's share during that third of a century came to only $4 million.[19]

Town schools for blacks were also neglected during the era of Jim Crow, especially before World War II, and students going into town from freedmen's settlements sometimes reported bitter disappointment with the quality of instruction. One former student of the eight-grade County Line school reached the opinion that her high school teachers at the county seat of Nacogdoches "were as dumb as goats" and recalled that some even came to her for help with their lesson plans.[20] During the 1920s in Hunt County, at the same time that Saint Paul's School in the freedmen's settlement of Neylandville developed into an excellent rural secondary school, Greenville's black high school became a shabby disgrace. An interracial group of local leaders took a hard look at this school one day in midwinter, and, although they were residents of the county and used to Jim Crow realities, all were shocked by what they saw. Greenville's black high school had many knocked-out windows, doors that would not close, and inadequate fuel to heat the building on this cold winter day. The school grounds were poorly drained and very muddy, and the school itself had "a lake of water under the floor." There were no sidewalks, and paths to the school had become muddy quagmires. Toilets were dirty, unsanitary, smelly, too close to the building, and offered little privacy. Students crowded the classrooms, even on this day of cold weather and poor attendance, and some classes had few if any textbooks. In fact, "some of the grades were not furnished books throughout the year."[21]

Despite these discriminatory patterns, black teachers and students took the resources they had to work with, made of them what they could, and sometimes their educational efforts prospered. Even excellent rural secondary schools like Saint Paul's of Hunt County and Wellborn of Brazos County were issued old textbooks, but it all depended on what you did with them. Alandrous Peterson of Brazos County recalled that the Wellborn school he attended had books rejected by a local white school. "I remember seeing names of white families that I recognized in those old, very very used, books. But we took those old, marked-up, frayed books and learned everything we could from them to prepare us for some kind of a future in this country."[22]

On the same winter's day that Greenville's interracial committee visited the black high school, thousands of black students walked muddy county roads and trekked cross-county paths to hundreds of rural schools. Some lucky students lived close to their schools, but most walked or rode from some distance away, often several miles. Roads usually took roundabout routes, so students shortened their walks by traveling cross-country through private land, climbing over barbed wire fences, and crossing creeks across trees felled as footbridges. After a while, the passing of children's feet created a spider web of school trails radiating across the countryside to every rural school. Grover Williams remembered winter returns from his distant school through dark woods, feeling for the familiar trail with his feet.[23] In good weather the trip to school might be a lark, with students playing along the way and schoolmates joining the merry band, but cold or wet days were different. Children's footwear and clothing were often inadequate, they got wet and cold, and footbridges over rising creeks became slippery and dangerous.

Some parents kept their children home on such days, but others chose these times to send them to school. Rural schools taught basic literacy very well, but only if students could attend them often enough. Harsh economic realities and the relentless cycle of cotton agriculture strongly impacted rural school attendance all across Texas. As a consequence, Georgia Lee Wade of the Mount Fall settlement in Washington County learned to read and write, and Ed Lathan did not. Wade explained, recounting the experience of many others:

We would go enroll and get them books, and then we couldn't go back to school no more till that cotton is picked. When you finish picking cotton, long about maybe the middle of November, then we would go to school every day until about March. And when March come, well, you started to planting corn and cotton, and we'd be in and out of school. We would have to go to the field and plant that cotton and corn, and then go back to school until it got time to be chopped.[24]

Ed Lathan's family followed the same cycle of cotton agriculture in the same community, but Lathan's father had attitudes that were different from Wade's, or the family was more strapped for cash, or Lathan himself was more indispensable as a field hand. He told another common story: "Dry days, I didn't have a chance to go to school, I had to be in the field working with my folks. It rain, [they'd say] 'Get ready for school, boys, we can't work in the field.' I went in the school, but right in the main pinch of time, I might have to stay out of school two, three days every week."[25]

Smaller schools at freedmen's settlements often remained largely unchanged across half a century. The crude one-room log school that Joe Oliver attended in Reconstruction days in Hill County closely resembled others still used in 1920. Mrs. Corener Dean, for example, attended "a little log cabin, the only windows in it was logs sawed in two, and that made a light—one on the south and one in the north." Students in her school sat on crude, hewn-log benches and held their slates in the laps.[26] C. C. White's log school at the Possum Trot community of Shelby County had one window, one door, and a stick-and-daub fireplace at one end. School equipment was a blackboard, a barrel of different-sized switches, used for discipline, and students' slates. "We didn't have no desks, we set on anything we could get," White remembered. "The girls set on one side of the room and the boys on the other. We put our dinner buckets down in corner. There was an old wooden water bucket there, with a couple of gourds that we drank out of. The teacher wrote the ABC's on the board and made us say them over after him. Then we had to write them on our slates."[27]

Replacement of log schools with board-and-batten ones often changed little. Rebecca F. Grigsby taught for nineteen years during the 1930s and 1940s in the one-room Loco school of Eden Common School District in Nacogdoches County that she herself had attended. She described the school this way: "My school was just a plain wooden building of undressed lumber, just rough lumber. The windows were on either side, and in the end one door. We had homemade benches, we had no desks for students to write on. And of course there was no well, so we had to go up to the neighbor's house to get water." As she had done as a student, Grigsby kept a constant eye on the weather. Sudden rains might swell nearby Loco Creek and cut her students off from home.[28]

By 1915, most schools in freedmen's settlements were small frame one- or two-room structures like Grigsby's and very similar to the one-room Lincolnville school in Coryell County attended by Ophelia Mae Mayberry Hall and Rowena Weatherly Keatts. Keatts's father had donated land for the school in his pasture, and in earlier times it had served as the Lincoln-ville church. The Lincolnville school operated only six months of the year at a time when nearby Gatesville schools operated for nine months. The prob-lem was money, which was always short in the black rural schools. Teach-ers at Lincolnville rarely lasted more than a year or two before leaving for some place that paid better. About twenty-five students attended, on the average, virtually all of them blood relatives of Keatts and Hall, who de-scribed her school as "just a kinfolk outfit." The Lincolnville school had no desks, just "wash benches" that students sat on, holding their books in their laps. The textbooks themselves were ratty, discarded, hand-me-downs from white schools, as customary. Nevertheless, teachers were serious about instruction and discipline was strictly enforced. They would "put the brush on you" or "stand you in the corner on one leg, one foot." Teachers taught by subjects and grades, with each grade being "up front" reciting and taking instruction in turn. Ophelia enjoyed learning, and she diligently did her school assignments every evening. She and her two younger brothers lay on their stomachs on the floor around a kerosene lamp, studying their school books and crowding each other for more light to see.[29]

Rowena Weatherly Keatts passed through the same Lincolnville school, attended secondary school at Gatesville, a few miles away, then returned to Lincolnville to teach. By this time her family lived in Gatesville, so Rowena had a four-mile hike to and from her school every day. She went down the hill to the railroad track, walked the railroad, crossed the railroad trestle over the Leon River, crossed a man's pasture, walked across her family's pasture, and then went "right on down the trail to the school."

Absolutely nothing had changed. "It hadn't changed anything—it was just that same old building and most of those same old books." The benches were still there, along with several "old-fashioned desks." In the winter the desks stayed pushed against the walls to distance students from the big iron stove occupying the middle of the little room. Teacher and students periodically went outside to gather wood for the stove, usually to "get the wood in my daddy's pasture." Lincolnville school had a morning recess and an afternoon recess, when students played baseball, went into the nearby woods to pick black haws, or played in the nearby creek. On really cold days they remained in the building and played games devised by Rowena. Natural light illuminated the school, although lanterns might be used at the school's closing ceremony, the main social affair culminating the yearly round. Rowena's uncles, the fathers of several of her students, built a platform out in front of the school for these affairs, and the people attending "stood up and sat out in the old chairs and old benches in the yard" for a lantern-lit program of speeches, dialogues, solos, duets, and the like.[30] Many people came out from town to attend these "closing-out programs" and the picnics and baseball games that often preceded them.[31]

Despite their obvious lack of resources, small rural schools like the one at Lincolnville could be deceptively effective. If students could attend often enough (a very big "if"), such schools often successfully taught reading, writing, and arithmetic—the basics. Dora Session Griffith attended the school at the freedmen's settlement of Woodville in Cherokee County, the black secondary school at Rusk, and Butler College. After receiving her teaching certificate, Griffith taught for many years in various country schools, including Weeping Mary. Griffith had learned well and fast at the Woodville school, and she found that many of her students did the same. In her opinion, small schools could be effective because of good discipline, patient teachers, more time to learn, individualized instruction that let students go at their own speed, and the peer-to-peer instructions of older children. In Griffith's experience, older siblings were especially important in helping younger ones to increase reading skills. Children at a small country school got a "better foundation," had more direct participation in school activities, and received more attention from the teacher. School and community links were very close, and "a whipping at school meant a whipping at home," all across rural Texas.[32]

Whatever the occasional effectiveness of their instruction, many small rural schools remained shabby, poorly funded, makeshift affairs of "wash bench" seats, crowded classrooms, and underpaid and underqualified teachers right to the end, but by around 1920 other very similar schools were transforming themselves into excellent rural high schools. Almost without exception, these elite black rural secondary schools developed from humble origins at freedmen's settlements.

Transformation began early and reached remarkable dimensions at some places, as at Center Point, Camp County, a freedmen's settlement established in the late 1860s. Black settlers had lived on their wooded lands as squatters until about the time of the founding of the Center Point Bap-

*Terrance Dennis, great-grandson of community founder Guss Upshaw,
stands by the abandoned Upshaw Common School of County Line,
Nacogdoches County. (Richard Orton)*

tist Church in 1873, when community pioneers began to formalize their
land holdings. In the fateful year of 1889, community leaders organized an
"Industrial Union" to help local families buy land and make home improvements, successfully negotiated with white landowners for right-of-way to
build a new road to the county seat of Pittsburgh, and began a school. By
1897, the one-room log school had enrolled thirty-one pupils. The county
superintendent reported it in bad condition, worth only fifty dollars.[33]

For almost twenty years this little school, akin to so many others, sufficed,
but in 1908 a two-room frame school replaced it, and by 1916 an intense
"better schools campaign" and a bond issue resulted in a fine new five-room
school, which included secondary grades. Philanthropic assistance from the
Rosenwald Fund and (probably) the Slater Fund and General Education
Fund helped pay for this after 1921, as did the State Board of Education, but
Center Point citizens dug deeply into their own pockets to finance the new
school. By 1939 Center Point School had evolved into a excellent rural institution with ten classrooms, chemistry lab, home economics cottage, agricultural and industrial arts building, teacherage, school cafeteria, library of
6,000 volumes, and girl's dormitory. Center Point School was one of the
best in Camp County, with a campus valued at $14,000. Nine of the school's

ten teachers had at least bachelor degrees, and their average salary was the highest at any public institution in Camp County, black or white.[34]

Beginning in 1912, Center Point School also hosted the annual Northeast Texas Negro Fair, which drew participants and sightseers even from beyond Texas. In this, as in so many other things, Center Point School resembled what was undoubtedly its inspiration—Tuskegee Institute of Alabama. Like Tuskegee, Center Point had student work-study programs to defray tuition costs, a student-operated farm to supply its cafeteria, a canning center (preserving 6,000 cans a summer), and rich and varied extracurricular activities that included Interscholastic League academic competitions, football, basketball, baseball, rhythm band, chorus, weekly Bible study, community assistance programs, and more.[35]

Although closely associated after 1891 with Texas's black land-grant college, Prairie View A&M, the reform impetus to create schools like Center Point actually came from afar—from ideas and programs devised by Booker T. Washington and the concrete example of Tuskegee Institute, Alabama. By 1921 the Colored County Agents of the Texas Agricultural Extension Service and several philanthropic national funds, designed to improve rural education, had joined forces under Washington's influence to reform and revitalize freedmen's settlements.

The enigmatic Booker T. Washington, the "wizard of Tuskegee," profoundly influenced most of the community-improvement initiatives reaching Texas freedmen's settlements after 1915. Not every community became a Center Point, but most benefited to some degree from Washington's programs and from those of his disciples. Born a slave in Virginia in 1856, Washington educated himself and attended Hampton Institute in Virginia from 1872 to 1875. In 1881 he assumed the leadership of a new school for African Americans in Macon County, Alabama. Starting with a couple of run-down old farm buildings and a small amount of money from the state of Alabama, Washington built Tuskegee Normal and Industrial Institute into a showcase of African American enterprise and the best-known black school in the nation. Students received secondary-school academic training, but the focus of Tuskegee's curriculum was "industrial education," the learning of skills and trades that prepared students for jobs. As at Center Point, Texas, a third of a century later, students built various school buildings themselves, learning skills and crafts in the process. Many of the graduates then became teachers, spreading industrial arts training all across the South.[36]

Washington first gained national attention in 1893 when he spoke in the national capital as a member of Atlanta's delegation to request federal support for its Exposition. He addressed the congressional committee last and briefly, telling them that "he had urged the Negro to acquire property, own his own land, drive his own mule hitched to his own wagon, milk his own cow, raise his crop and keep out of debt, and that when he acquired a home he became fit for a conservative citizen." [37] Everyone liked this precursor statement to Washington's later "Atlanta compromise" speech, delivered before the Cotton States and International Exposition in Atlanta, Georgia, on September 18, 1895. At Atlanta, Washington reaffirmed the message given at the nation's capital two years before. He told black Southerners to work hard, acquire land, help themselves to advance, and remain in the South, accommodating to Jim Crow racial rules and customs. "Cast down your buckets where you are," Washington advised southern blacks. The races could be separate in social matters but work together for mutual economic progress.

Although Washington downplayed political struggles for black advancement and instead advocated gradual advancement by way of hard work and acquisition of property, these goals were but means to an end, and the end had to do with racial equality. In a less guarded speech in 1896 in Brooklyn, New York, he bluntly remarked: "We have spent time and money making political stump speeches and in attending political conventions that could better have been spent starting a dairy farm, or a truck garden, and thus have laid a material foundation on which we could have stood and demanded our rights." [38] Although Washington as political leader and racial spokesman never publicly departed from the principles expressed in Atlanta in 1895, he did expect that a more prosperous black race at some point would stand up and demand their rights. Furthermore, in addition to Washington's public pronouncements and Tuskegee example, he worked behind the scenes to advance more immediate improvements in civil rights. He privately fought the South's segregation laws, often keeping his involvement in court cases secret. He financially supported African American newspapers across the county, and he built up the "Tuskegee machine," a network of friends, supporters, and disciples that constantly fed him information.

As part of his political machine, Washington in 1900 founded the National Negro Business League to create a constituency of loyal political supporters. Prominent among this group was Robert L. Smith of Colorado County, Texas, founder of the Farmers' Home Improvement Society and (after 1915) first director of Texas's Colored County Agents program. Washington soon helped place Smith on the board of directors for the Anna T. Jeanes Fund, one of the several initiatives to improve black rural education with which he was closely associated. [39]

In Texas and elsewhere, as historian Edward Ayers aptly noted, "thousands of blacks had adopted Washington's strategy before they ever heard of him," and nowhere was this so true as at freedmen's settlements.[40] In these places black people already had acquired land, drove their own mules hitched to their own wagons, milked their own cows, and did their best to stay out of debt. From Texas to Alabama, Robert Smith and Booker Washington thus did not preach unattainable goals to African American rent farmers, who almost always knew of a few freedmen's settlements in their vicinities.

Such communities already practiced mutual support and self-help in their lodges and fraternal orders, as at the Colored Benevolent Association of Houston County, organized at Germany in the late 1880s. Members pledged to help each other if needed, paid monthly dues of ten cents, and met in a two-story lodge hall behind Germany's church.[41] Deceptively similar in its origins was the Colored Farmers' National Alliance of Houston County, organized at about the same time, with most members from the freedmen's settlement of Vistula. Fifteen black men and one white man formed this fraternal and home improvement society one evening in 1886, inspired by the all-white National Farmer's Alliance. Led by mulatto landowner John Jacob Shuffler of Vistula and white minister Richard Manning, this humble lodge-hall fraternity soon expanded far beyond its Vistula origins, absorbing other similar organizations along the way and becoming the Colored Farmers' Alliance, which claimed a national membership of 1,200,000 by 1891.[42]

Although the Colored Farmers' Alliance took strong public political stands, such as its support of the cotton pickers' strike of 1891, the rest of its agenda emphasized the virtues of self-reliance embodied in the freedmen's settlements of Houston County and the admonitions of Booker T. Washington. To educate its members on how to become better farmers, it established a weekly newspaper, the *National Alliance*, published in Houston. The alliance raised funds to pay for longer school terms for black schools and in some places founded private secondary schools, or academies. As appropriate for a fraternal organization, the Colored Farmers' Alliance solicited funds to help sick and disabled members. Its spokesmen preached a social message very similar to Booker T. Washington's. They advised promoting racial advancement and fighting Jim Crow with a familiar long-term strategy of landownership, self-reliance, education, debt avoidance, hard work, and personal sacrifice.[43]

Robert L. Smith of the Oakland community, Colorado County, did the same, but the organization Smith founded in 1890 to promote these policies steered clear of the direct challenges to segregation that destroyed the

Colored Farmers' Alliance after 1891. Smith's Farmers' Home Improvement Society and the Colored County Agent program that Smith later ran strongly affected Texas freedmen's settlements until World War II.

Robert Lloyd Smith had been born to free black parents in Charleston, South Carolina, in 1861. He attended Avery Institute and the University of South Carolina and graduated from Atlanta University. In 1885 Smith served as principal teacher at Oakland Normal School, a small teacher-training institution in Colorado County, Texas. By this time he was a follower of Booker T. Washington and an ardent advocate of self-help and racial solidarity as a route to economic growth for black Americans. In keeping with these ideas, Smith organized the Farmers' Home Improvement Society, which mirrored Washington's ideas and the examples of the Tuskegee Conference. Smith's organization encouraged African Americans to seek economic independence by home and farm ownership, cooperative buying, cash purchase, and by raising most of their own food. To promote this self-sufficient lifestyle, the FIS sponsored regional agricultural fairs, established cooperatives, paid sickness and death benefits, and founded a bank in Waco and an agricultural college at Wolfe City.[44]

Robert L. Smith's organization involved women through its Women's Barnyard Auxiliary, which specialized in gardens, canning, home crafts, and improved barnyard fowl and had members in twenty counties. Generalizing about his strategies, historian Debra Ann Reid noted that Smith and his agents tried to involve women and children as well as men, focused their efforts on black landowner communities, met mostly in rural schools, and ran meetings like religious services. Reid argued that farmers' societies like Smith's became increasingly important after 1900 as African Americans lost their political rights due to the rise of the white primary and Jim Crow.[45]

Smith preached the Washingtonian gospel against "King Credit," while his wife and other leaders of the Barnyard Auxiliary "organized local and state exhibitions of their canned goods, garden produce, livestock, and other items of handwork, such as quilts and clothes. The FIS used youth education to teach the value of rural life and farming as a profession." Smith encouraged education, including the reading of *Farm and Ranch* and pamphlets from the Texas Department of Agriculture and the USDA, but "he believed that the FIS provided a service that the government could not, the fraternal and social functions that helped keep community-based programs alive."[46]

The FIS peaked in 1912 at about 12,000 members, most of them within Texas, but Robert Smith soon reached a larger audience. One evening in September of 1915, Smith and home economic specialist Mary Evelyn

Hunter held the first community session of the new "colored" division of the Texas Agricultural Extension Service, created as a separate program to serve black farmers after passage of the Smith-Lever Act in 1914. To the casual observer, this affair must have looked like an FIS meeting. The place was the freedmen's settlement of Blackjack in Smith County, and the subject of the meeting was improved methods of canning food.[47]

From first to last, Robert L. Smith's African American version of the Texas Agricultural Extension Service (TAEX) remained focused on black landowner communities and upon strategies for improving the subsistence side of the farm. By 1920, twenty-five TAEX county agents served black Texans. By 1930, fifty-five agents worked in the field, and by 1940, eighty-seven agents, of which forty-six were in farm work and thirty-six in home demonstration work. Fifty-one counties had some sort of agent, thirty-one had both sorts.[48] Men served as agricultural demonstration agents, women as home demonstration agents, and during 1940 they enrolled 38,633 people in their clubs and in one way or another reached 504,708 rural black Texans with their programs.[49]

When both agricultural demonstration and home demonstration agents were present, as in the case of J. C. Bradford and Mrs. L. W. Ragdale in Cherokee County in 1928, they closely coordinated their efforts. Cherokee County men, women, boys, and girls met in their respective clubs at twelve strategically located sites across the county, usually the school buildings of freedmen's settlements. Agents found their natural audiences in these landowner communities, where people already had committed to a self-reliant, independent way of life. The agents in a sense preached to the choir at such places, but they offered valuable new information about better ways to do things. Agents worked rarely, if at all, at the black communities of major sharecropper farms, where they found themselves generally unwelcome. White landowners did not wish them there interfering with the labor, and the labor often had renter attitudes. Why practice home improvement on the landlord's sharecropper shack? Gardens, fodder crops, chickens, hogs, and other subsistence farming standbys usually were not even an option for black sharecroppers.

County extension programs for blacks usually paralleled extension programs for whites, but Colored County Agents placed greater emphasis on self-reliance and subsistence farming through various "live at home" campaigns rather than on cash crops and commercial farming (the emphasis of the white extension program, especially as time went on). Black agents concentrated on improving diet, health, and general living conditions. They promoted better and more sanitary toilets, the use of door and window

Cass County's Colored County Agent and a farmer examine the latter's farm records, 1946. (Courtesy of Texas Agricultural Extension)

A Colored County Agent and other men judge a "best hog" competition. (Courtesy of Texas Agricultural Extension)

screening, development of safe water supplies, and year-round gardens to help families escape high food prices at country stores.[50] Agents often sponsored the setting of concrete goals by families—enough fowls raised to provide chicken on the menu twice a week, enough garden vegetables canned to provide the family a can a day during the eight months of the year when the garden did not produce, and "a pig in every home."[51]

Agents worked hard, and they strategized in terms of the Booker T. Washington ideal, trying to make black farmers more effective, independent, and prosperous. As retired agent B. J. Pryor of Smith County told an interviewer, their goal had been to keep black people on the farm. Pryor and his predecessor, a man named Crouch, repeated the same admonitions for decades to the county's black farmers at thousands of meetings and demonstrations.[52] They told them to plant more feed crops for livestock, grow enough subsistence crops and gardens for self-sufficiency, and, as for cash crops, "diversify, diversify, diversify." Agents repeatedly advised farmers not to depend so completely on fickle cotton for their cash crop, but this admonition usually fell on deaf ears, at least until the Great Depression. Agents often freely offered more general advice, as did C. W. Rice at Greenville in 1921. Do not sell your farm if you are fortunate enough to own one, Rice told his audience. Reduce cotton acreage and plant more food and fodder crops. Do not be careless, gossip, loaf, gamble, abuse your farming tools, or buy autos and silk shirts when you make big crops. Instead, improve your farms and homes, cultivate better gardens, and raise more chickens.[53]

Agents followed similar organizational strategies in most counties, probably based on those worked out decades earlier by the Farmers' Home Improvement Society. They held demonstrations and made presentations at clubs organized around the county, often at twelve communities conveniently situated so that people from other communities could reach them. The clubs met in freedmen's settlement schools for the most part—neutral sites in communities divided along congregational lines. Club meetings began with prayers and songs and featured various types of audience participation familiar from church life. Men, boys, women, and girls had their own clubs, at least in counties where both male and female agents worked. Young people and women were less lashed to the economic wheel of public work or cash-crop agriculture than were the men, so they had time to participate more fully. Women's clubs were always larger and better attended than men's clubs. The TAEX promoted women as the natural reformers of the subsistence side of the farm in its so-called "balanced woman" program. Each club met once a month for a program directed by the club president, with the county agent attending in rotation. Periodically several adjacent

*"Best hog" and his happy
owner. (Courtesy of Texas
Agricultural Extension)*

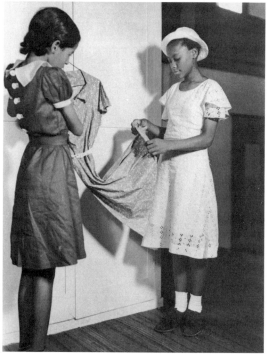

*County sewing winners
show their dresses at the
state competition, Prairie
View A&M, 1938.
(Courtesy of Texas
Agricultural Extension)*

A prize-winning seamstress displays a closet full of clothes she made herself, Harris County, 1947. (Courtesy of Texas Agricultural Extension)

The Colored County Home Demonstration Agent of Grimes County, Mrs. P. R. Brown, stands with contestants at the "egg table" of an agricultural fair. (Courtesy of Texas Agricultural Extension)

clubs met for a joint meeting and various skills and crafts competitions, and once a year all county clubs competed in a county meet, with winners going on to the statewide event at Prairie View A&M.[54]

An amazing amount of energy went into these countywide competitions and fairs. For example, in 1928, Cherokee County held a successful two-day community fair at the freedmen's settlement of New Hope. According to the county agent, "Four large rooms of the city school building were filled with canned goods, needle work, and farm crops." Several pure-blood poultry and hog breeds were exhibited. The fair at New Hope raised five hundred dollars, about half of it from whites. During the two days of the fair, an estimated 5,000 people attended.[55] At some point in the event, agents recognized Carrie Fuller of the freedmen's settlement of Pine Hill as "outstanding girl" of the county's girls' clubs for her projects during the year. Fuller had worked for money to buy seeds, planted her own large garden, and in the end sold a hundred crates of tomatoes at fifty cents a crate. Then she canned three hundred cans of tomatoes after the price fell, some of which she also sold. In addition, Fuller also canned okra, beans, peas, pickles, preserves, jelly, and jam, and did all the cooking and sewing for a family of six. She had won the dressmaking contest at Prairie View in 1928, making a nice dress in the short time given. She also kept a flock of Rhode Island Reds and sold eggs and fryers.[56]

County home demonstration agent Mrs. L. W. Ragdale had been at least as busy as Carrie Fuller during 1928, presiding over twelve girls' clubs and twelve women's clubs, with 689 and 739 members, respectively. Ragdale had supervised the canning of 8,750 quarts of pickles and the curing of 17,015 pounds of meat. Women and girls in her clubs had made 3,806 dresses and coats. Exactly 1,159 women and girls had been involved in club-related home gardening projects. A zeal for improved poultry had swept the county, although somewhat dampened by the "big rat plague" of the spring. Nonetheless, the value of all work in poultry raising in 1928 amounted to $16,075. Ragdale reported: "In Spring time when the hens are cackling and rooster crowing you can see the club women and girls going around gathering up the eggs getting ready for market on Saturday, sometimes now that they have cars they don't wait til Sat., they can go and sell the eggs and butter at noon and then get back to do the work they had planned." During 1928, Ragdale visited 403 homes on extension work. She spent 59 days in her office, 257 in the field, and wrote 282 letters.[57] Her male counterpart, agent J. C. Bradford, had equaled Ragdale's efforts. Bradford worked 56 days in his office, 248 in the field, wrote 196 letters, and conducted a staggering 546 "method and result demonstrations meetings."[58]

Brazos County women with prize-winning canned goods.
(Courtesy of Texas Agricultural Extension)

In Cherokee County, as elsewhere, many home and club demonstrations encouraged the canning of foodstuffs. Canning had been a big focus of the Farmers' Improvement Society and the topic of the TAEX's very first community session at Blackjack in 1915, and the emphasis continued. In the two decades after the Blackjack meeting, several hundred rural black communities, most of them freedmen's settlements, established canning centers. Smith and his agents believed a canning center served as ideal project, since it involved all members of the community. TAEX historian Debra Reid explained: "Personal and public networks combined as women and girls raised the funds, organized activities, and did most of the canning while men and boys helped construct, fuel, and operate the centers. Canning addressed many economic problems and provided a focus for community organization that had not existed previously."[59] Canning thus had a larger social meaning to the agents and participants: "Agents knew that canning offered a means to improve the nutritional value and variety of foodstuffs. Agents believed that a healthier black population had the potential to earn more and participate in society to a greater degree than those debilitated by pellagra and other diseases associated with the rural poor."[60] Special hard times launched agents into crash canning campaigns: "Farmers used canning as a means of defense. Some chose to can their beeves instead of selling cattle at low prices in times of drought [Washington County, 1925] or when counties passed stock laws that required farmers to fence their cattle in compliance with legislation passed to reduce fever [Houston County, 1924]."[61]

Canning grew so popular that even black communities in counties without a colored agent also established canneries. A TAEX bulletin, "Community Canning Plants," provided plans for a simple board-and-batten building with a shed roof measuring twenty by forty-eight feet, and local carpenters could handle this. Most communities purchased steam canner outfits consisting of a hotel-size retort that cost twenty-seven dollars, a sealer for tin cans that cost sixteen dollars, and tin cans that cost a few cents each. Communities used home-rigged open-kettle methods until they had raised enough money for the manufactured steam pressure canners. Some improvised with two washtubs, the smaller one modified with punched holes. Others used an oblong washer or laundry boiler with pieces of wire laid in the bottom to protect the jars from the heat source. The poorest operators made do with lard cans.[62]

In Leon County in 1933, two agents from outside the county visited the freedmen's settlement of Flynn to show that no lack of cash could stop a community canning program. Agents gave a canning demonstration at the local creek, which served as the community's water source. They dug a trench three feet long and three feet deep in the top of the creek bank, laid a piece of galvanized iron sheeting over the hole to hold the retorts and cookers, built a fire in the makeshift furnace, and processed three hundred cans of beef in an afternoon.[63]

For the individual family, canning was an important activity in the group of strategies promoting increased cash flow, independence, and landownership. Canning helped families improve their diet and stay out of debt to the mercantile store. Canning centers also helped agents accomplish their goal of strengthening rural communities. They increased community solidarity by requiring cooperation and planning. They lessened feuding and bickering in communities beset by conflicts between multiple churches by offering a beneficial communitywide project. The canneries also served as new social centers, apart from any particular church.[64]

Results were remarkable. In 1929 black families in TAEX programs canned more than one million containers of food, an average of 115 cans or jars per family. At least 368 community steam pressure canners operated

during the canning season, a large number of them at freedmen's settlements. People paid for using the facility—a set fee usually taken as a proportion of the canned food to pay the operating costs of the plant.[65]

Sixty-four additional community centers began during the Depression
1930s, this time with direct government support, and the government also
promoted the establishment of community mattress-making centers that
used free surplus government cotton. Agents taught short courses in mattress making all across Texas, and at the height of the program an average
of twelve mattress centers existed in each county with a black demonstration agent. During 1940, the centers produced 32,810 mattresses, utilizing
an astonishing 3,281 bales of government cotton.[66]

Wheeler Springs settlement in Houston County demonstrated how government programs could come together at an individual community, head-
quartered here—as was so often the case—at the school. Teacher Lula
Denby Dailey took the lead at Wheeler Springs. Born in 1878, educated at
Prairie View A&M, Dailey taught as principal teacher in the community's
two-room school for fifty-two years. During the 1920s she closely allied herself with the county's black home demonstration agent. At Dailey's urging,
community men built in succession a clubhouse for local TAEX club meetings, a combined canning plant and butchery, and in 1932 a log house where
women held meetings, quilted, made comforters, and stuffed mattresses.
Nearby, Dailey raised a school garden to provide vegetables for hot lunches
prepared for her school pupils.[67]

As Booker T. Washington and Robert L. Smith both realized, many
campaigns for African American advancement began in the rural schools
of black landowner communities like Wheeler Springs. From around 1905,
Washington successfully attracted philanthropic support from white businessmen and industrialists for programs to improve black education. At
the philanthropists' behest, Washington designed the Jeanes Fund, General
Education Fund, Rosenwald Fund, and Slater Fund programs, tested them
out for a few years in Macon County, Alabama, and adjacent counties, re-
fined their operational strategies, then set them in motion across the South.
Washington's Texas friend and follower Robert L. Smith, who served on
the board of the Jeanes Fund, once described himself as a "practical sociologist," but surely that term applies to Booker T. Washington with even
greater force.[68]

Washington worked within the system to get everything he could for
black Southerners. Programs promoting improved education for African
Americans in the South had a basic problem during the era of Jim Crow:

Professionally attired women of Pirtle stand in front of their canning center, a few miles from Kilgore. Community men built the canning center themselves at a cost of $317.50. (Courtesy of Texas Agricultural Extension)

Rug-making demonstration led by the Colored Home Demonstration Agent near Riesel, Texas. (Courtesy of Texas Agricultural Extension)

many whites thought that such reforms operated at cross-purposes to their self-interests. After his 1930s field study of Sunflower County, Mississippi, John Dollard observed: "It is really the fervor of Negro belief in education as a means of advancement that has been responsible for much of the development. After all, from the standpoint of the white caste, why spend money for Negro education if it tends, as most suspect, to unfit them for their caste and class roles?"[69] In Dollard's opinion, Booker T. Washington had advanced the cause of black education in a clever and effective way by "meeting the white-caste stipulations." By social necessity, Washington emphasized industrial and agricultural training for blacks, useful trades that had been emphasized on the slave plantation as well. Southerners found it harder to disapprove of this sort of black education, despite the fact that industrial and agricultural training might ultimately lead to black economic advancement and (at least potentially) to greater assertion of rights.[70]

Washington's correspondence often revealed his pragmatic, clever social engineering within the domain of Jim Crow, as in a letter to Wallace Buttrick from Tuskegee Institute on October 11, 1911. Clearly, Washington calculated how best to use northern money to apply the Tuskegee model far and wide.

I told you sometime ago that I would make you a written report about the use of the Jeanes Fund which I control in this county. As I stated to you verbally, I acknowledge that on the face of matters it seems as if we have spent a great deal of money, but it has not been without a definite plan in view.

First of all, we thought it worth while to thoroughly equip one county in school buildings, in teachers, etc., to see to what extent the people and county authorities would continue the work after we have given it up and moved to another county.

Second, we wanted to see after the schools had gotten to the point where they did really first class work in their local communities, whether this would not win the support of the white people residing near those schools.

Third, we have tried to make an object lesson in the way of showing how rural schools might be partly supported through the use of school farms especially in communities where cotton is the main product.

In all this work we have cooperated with the Demonstration Agents, and the result is that there is a general improvement in agriculture throughout the county among both white and colored people.

The results so far seem to demonstrate the wisdom of our course.[71]

Jeanes Industrial Teachers, sponsored in part by the Anna T. Jeanes Fund, begin working in Texas just after World War I. Jeanes Fund teachers, all of them black women trained in home economics, visited rural schools to assist teachers by giving lessons on personal hygiene, sanitation, home economics, home and community improvement, and practical skills such as sewing. Also called "Jeanes Supervisors," such teachers worked directly under the county school superintendents and were paid partly by the counties, partly by the Jeanes Fund. They normally spent one or two days at one rural school before moving on to another. Twenty-two counties employed Jeanes teachers in 1930, about the maximum number.[72]

In practice, Jeanes teachers often assisted at rural schools also benefiting from Rosenwald Fund and Slater Fund programs, many of them at freedmen's settlements. Such schools also served as community centers for county extension demonstrations, PTA meetings, dances, Juneteenth celebrations, plays, fund-raisers, church services, and political meetings. Jeanes supervisors thus played a role in enhancing the community-center functions of black rural schools.[73]

These organizational activities perhaps made white county school board members a little suspicious. Only twenty-two counties had Jeanes supervisors in 1930, while nearly four times that many had Rosenwald schools. Walker County appointed its first Jeanes supervisor in 1927 at the request of the county superintendent. The school board abolished the position in 1929 but reinstated it in 1932. In 1942 Jeanes Supervisor Estelle Jordan, with a bachelor of science degree from Wiley College, met with teachers, organized community PTAs, and tried to put some industrial arts training (sewing and woodwork) even into one-teacher schools. Her special program of the 1941–1942 school year had been "a pig in every school." Students fed the pig with scraps from their lunches throughout the year, then at the end of the school term the teacher awarded the valuable school pig to his or her choice for the outstanding student. This had not worked out very well, perhaps for the obvious reason: for only one student and family did the school year not end on a sour note. Nonetheless, Miss Jordan's official motto remained, "Work and keep on working."[74]

In part because of people like Jordan, industrial arts programs often developed at even the smallest rural schools. At one Caldwell County school, instruction ceased during a certain part of the school day while the male teacher and his students made brooms. At the freedmen's settlement of Doak Springs in Lee County, teacher Ed Kerr strongly promoted the making of items of immediate use to students' families, with raw materials gathered from the nearby woods. Smaller boys made children's chairs from apple boxes and hat racks from rattan vines. Older boys made tables, chairs, cabinets, wagon wheels, shoes, and other useful things.[75]

None of the Washington-inspired programs impacted so many black rural schools in Texas as the Rosenwald Fund, which helped construct 527 educational structures, including 424 schools. The Rosenwald Fund had been established in 1917 by Chicago philanthropist and president of Sears, Roebuck and Company, Julius R. Rosenwald, with a gift of 20,000 shares of Sears stock worth about $20,000,000. Rosenwald worked with Booker T. Washington and Tuskegee Institute from 1913, running test programs and refining the plan. The Tuskegee strategy utilized the carrot of Rosenwald money to galvanize local self-help, since Washington insisted that significant matching funds be required from both local people and the respective states. This worked very well. For the 527 buildings erected in Texas between 1920 and 1935, $419,375 came from the Rosenwald Fund, $397,851 from local blacks, $60,494 from local whites, and $1,623,800 from the state.[76]

Across the South as a whole, the Rosenwald Fund helped build over 5,000 schools, each intended to be an excellent example of rural school construction. Besides the new schools, the fund offered grants for extensions on existing Rosenwald school buildings and for new industrial arts buildings, teacherages, and privies.

To be eligible for Rosenwald money, a school had to meet for more than five months, the site and buildings had to be deeded to authorities, and considerable matching funds had to be raised. As at Germany in Houston County, many a freedmen's settlement school now left its community church for the first time. In 1922 Germany constructed a fine new two-room school. At the opening ceremony, citizens met first at their old church/school for a prayer service, then marched together to the new institution.[77]

Not every Rosenwald school was located in a freedmen's settlement, but a very large percentage of such communities built Rosenwald schools, with the relative contributions made by the fund, the state, and local people varying with circumstances. For example, Jakes Colony in Guadalupe County built a four-teacher school in 1920 that cost $4,475, and local blacks paid $3,275, whites paid nothing, the state paid nothing, and the Rosenwald Fund paid $1,200. At Mill Creek a one-room Rosenwald school worth $1,425 replaced a log cabin and adjacent brush arbor in 1921, and black parents paid $125, whites paid nothing, the state paid $800, and the Rosenwald Fund paid $500.[78]

More resources and funds came together at Sweet Home in Guadalupe County, as was often the case with secondary schools based in freedmen's settlements. After construction, this rural high school had four classrooms, a teacherage, a kitchen, and other facilities, and also served a three-county area as "county training school" for vocational and agricultural education. Hence, it was also a John F. Slater Fund school, one of fifteen such schools at the time of its 1924 construction. A local German businessman donated land for the new school. The school cost $5,500 to build, blacks paid $1,600 of this, whites (i.e., the German benefactor) paid $500, the state paid $2,300, and the Rosenwald Fund contributed $1,100.

Sweet Home subsequently had five classrooms as well as a teacherage, a home economics building where girls learned sewing and cooking, and an industrial arts shop where boys were taught blacksmithing, carpentry, mattress making, and auto mechanics. Sweet Home Colored School was finally consolidated into the Seguin Independent School District at the late date of 1962.[79]

Although historians of education in the South have spared them hardly a glance, county training schools like Sweet Home brought a remarkable renaissance to the communities and hinterlands lucky enough to have them. Thirty-two county training schools operated in Texas by 1932, the maximum number. Although the counties with training schools are recorded, no complete list of community locations has been found. However, in every instance where community affiliation is known, that community was a freedmen's settlement.[80]

In 1932 Cornell University graduate student Lawrence A. Potts offered an excellent portrait from life of Texas county training schools. The Slater Fund supported such schools, "which in reality are high schools located for the most part in the center of the Negro population." Each developed county training school resembled nothing so much as Booker T. Washington's famous black institution at Macon County, Alabama—Tuskegee Institute. Potts wrote:

> The cooperation of the county board of education and Superintendent, a minimum term of eight months, a minimum salary of $1,000 for the principal and not less than $500 for assistants, and a good school building are the essential requirements for the establishment of one of these schools which local people often refer to as "county colleges."
>
> Farm, shop, home economics, and agriculture are emphasized in the course of study offered at these schools. Boarding departments are available for students who live in distant parts of the county. These training schools are the social centers for the county. Rural organizations such as the interscholastic league, the progressive farmers of Texas, mother's

clubs, and basket-ball contests that are organized on a county basis usually have their meeting at the training schools. The boarding departments, dormitories, and able teaching staff at county training schools have attracted visitors and meetings to the extent that they are not only community but county social centers.[81]

Texas's thirty-two county training schools seem to have developed on the explicit model of Tuskegee Institute, and like that institution, they sought, as one of their purposes, to prepare industrial arts teachers for positions in other black schools. Additional black rural high schools soon formed on the county-college pattern, which was the Tuskegee model—for example, Fodice School in Houston County.[82] County demonstration agent Pryor in Smith County often held meetings at three black rural high schools during his tenure as county agent, only one of which could have been a county training school. Partly because of these new rural high schools, black secondary education greatly improved during the 1920s. Some 6,200 blacks attended high schools in 1920, but 19,136 did so by 1929.[83]

Slater Fund schools or not, the new rural high schools had many things in common: they almost all grew from typical one- and two-room schools in freedmen's settlements, they emphasized industrial arts training, their students helped to build some or most of the schools' infrastructure, they often developed busing and boarding programs for students from well beyond the local area, and they came to serve as social gathering places for black people from all around.

Pelham High School in Navarro County was such a school—an institution of great pride to its community. Built in 1921 with Rosenwald Fund assistance, the high school followed two earlier institutions, the first established in 1878 at a Methodist church. Pelham developed a rich community life, all focused on the school. Active organizations included the Farmer's Improvement Society and the Juvenile Society (begun in 1912); Young Men's Association (1915); Canning Club (1925); Home Demonstration Club and 4-H Club (1928); Juneteenth Organization (1930); and Boy Scouts of America (1940).[84] Theresa Carroll Wright Davis recalled attending Pelham School during the late 1920s. Her father was the famous principal teacher and superintendent, Zeno Wendell Carroll; her mother was a teacher and the dean of women. Zeno Carroll was a college graduate, fluent in Spanish and two other foreign languages, and a highly motivated teacher-administrator. Pelham School under Carroll enforced high standards. Boys wore ties and kept their shirttails in at all times; teachers in-

*Abandoned rock school at the remote Fodice community of Houston County.
(Richard Orton)*

spected students every morning for proper hair, shoes, and "hygiene"; and nobody could say or even think, "I can't do that." Pelham School allowed no such negative thinking. Buses transported many out-of-district students daily into Pelham to attend school, and the school put the vehicles to other good use. Pelham students attended the Interscholastic League state meet at Prairie View A&M and the Paul Quinn College Annual Basketball Tournament for High Schools; they visited Baylor University to see the Harlem Globetrotters as well as the county seat of Corsicana to view the movie "The Ten Commandments."[85]

As schools like Pelham developed, other smaller black schools consolidated with them. Some rural high schools were built up entirely of such consolidations. In Houston County, Smith Grove joined with Center Hill to become Center Grove School; then, over a decade or two, White Rock, Thankful, Bluton Farm, Vistula, Post Oak, and others merged with Center Grove. Some parents fought such consolidations in keeping with the rural belief that the death of the school meant death of the community. A native of Smith Grove, teacher W. C. Williams rose to become principal of proud Center Grove High School, a Tuskegee-like institution with glass cases full of Interscholastic League trophies. Upon occasion, Smith went to other communities to negotiate consolidations, and local patriots sometimes remarked that Williams had "come to tear up our school." But in public meetings he responded with Matthew 5:17: "I am come not to destroy but to fulfill."[86]

CHAPTER SIX

Working
for the Man

Hours before daylight one morning in 1923, thirteen-year-old Henry Earl of the Smith Chapel community of Panola County rose from his bed, dressed, ate a quick breakfast, lit a pine-splinter torch prepared the night before, and set out on a several-mile walk down cross-country trails to his first day of work at a Timpson sawmill. Assessing his situation in a poor family with many mouths to feed and inadequate farmland, Henry had made an early decision to turn to "public work"—nonagricultural wage labor for whites outside the freedmen's settlement. "Working for the man" did not mean the end to Henry Earl's relationship with Smith Chapel, however. Dead tired at the end of his first long work day at the sawmill, Henry set off for home after the mill's final whistle, as he would for many years thereafter.[1]

By 1920, many younger sons and daughters at Texas freedmen's settlements had been forced to turn to part-time or full-time employment outside the community. The larger farms of the freedmen's generation fragmented at their deaths into the hands of their children, and most of the land accumulators had large families. Born seventeenth in a family of eighteen, W. C. Williams of Smith Grove in Houston County inherited very little from his father and soon became a schoolteacher.[2]

Nor was land division among large families the only factor forcing residents of freedmen's settlements into work outside the community. By the 1920s, many crops of cotton and corn had come and gone on family fields, diminishing soil fertility, and after 1905 the boll weevil also reduced cotton yields. In addition, commissioner's precinct after commissioner's precinct opted for stock laws, gradually closing rich men's woods to the ranging of poor men's hogs and cattle and to their ancillary moneymaking activities of tie chopping, stave making, fur trapping, and others, all of which had brought in a little cash.

Every black family at a freedmen's settlement told stories of land lost and land regained. Some miles to the north of the Williamses of Smith Grove, Vivian Gardiner Lovelady grew up at Hall's Bluff on a eighty-six-acre sandyland farm painfully acquired by her father. Mr. Gardiner's freedman father had once owned much better land on the edge of the Trinity bottoms—or so he had thought. The elder Gardiner made payments for many years on property supposedly purchased from a white man after signing papers that the illiterate ex-slave could not read. Finally, having by his calculation more than paid off the note, Gardiner asked the white man about this, only to discover that he had been tricked. As the papers confirmed, all these long, laborious years he had been only a renter.

Shattered by this betrayal, Gardiner died young, leaving wife and children in the hands of his oldest son, Vivian Lovelady's father. The younger Gardiner rent-farmed, did day labor, and not only took care of his widowed mother and younger siblings but gradually accumulated enough cash to purchase a farm. He and his wife had ten children, while Gardiner struggled to keep up payments on the land and hand it down to his offspring. He succeeded in this, but most of the younger Gardiners had to find their way elsewhere. One-tenth of eighty-six acres did not make a farm, and the family's land was poor. The freedman Gardiner's lost acres of rich bottomland, cheated from him by the white man, lay within sight, close to where Hurricane Bayou passed into the Trinity River valley, but his son's family owned property in the infertile hills above. As Vivian Gardiner Lovelady recalled, "A lot of that land he was not able to work—it was up on a sand hill, and it was sloping."[3]

Vivian Gardiner grew up on the sand-hill farm, attended Mary Allen College in Crockett, then married a man named Lovelady from a more fortunate landowning family in the freedmen's settlement of Hopewell, south of Crockett on the Pennington road. Thereafter, in their mixing and merging of farming with outside employment, the couple's life during the 1930s and 1940s resembled that of most landowner families at freedmen's settlements. The Loveladys had been one of the pioneer families of this community, and Vivian Gardiner's new husband inherited fifty-eight acres from the family farm, but this was not enough to support a growing family. For a quarter of a century, Vivian and her husband and children used their land as homeplace, garden site, and small subsistence and cash-crop farm while they rented additional cotton acreage nearby. From a cash-crop perspective, most of the family's income came from the rental places. Mr. Lovelady also often did wage work outside the community for extra money in the winter downtime, and the entire family, adults and children, sometimes trekked south to the Rio Grande Valley to pick early-maturing cotton in July after their own Houston County cotton fields needed no further cultivation and were laid by.[4]

In 1920 many landless black farmers hungered for forty acres and a mule just as much as a half century before, but these things had become harder to obtain. At most places, land prices had gone up much more than cotton profits or agricultural day wages, and squatting on unclaimed lands was no longer possible. Some diligent or lucky farmers, however, still worked and saved their way to forty acres and occasionally much more than that. At the Doak Springs settlement of Lee County, John and Willie Welborn began married life on a few acres of inherited land in 1909. They worked very hard and gradually, over the years, accumulated 204 acres, ten children, and an eight-room farmhouse. Willie Welborn raised chickens and sold fifty dozen eggs each week for ten cents a dozen. John Welborn grew cotton, corn, and sugar cane, operated a syrup mill, and served as the community black-smith, shoe repairman, casket maker, and jack-of-all-trades.[5] Most new landowners had a harder time of it and were less successful than the Wel-borns. At the freedmen's settlement of Woodville in Cherokee County, dur-ing the 1920s and 1930s, Leader May Session's father accumulated money for land purchase by clearing "new ground" at fifty cents a day and by walk-ing twenty miles back and forth into Rusk for wage work, while his wife and children ran the rent farm back home. Session succeeded in purchasing land for his family, but—after several disastrous boll-weevil years in succession—he saved his farm from repossession by the bank only by the subterfuge of selling it to a schoolteacher daughter.[6]

As perhaps at Woodville, the geographical areas of freedmen's settle-ments often expanded very little after 1910. Land prices had risen beyond what most poor black farmers were able to pay, and whites on the periph-ery of the communities often proved unwilling to sell any additional land to blacks. Certainly this was the case at Promiseland, South Carolina, intensively studied by sociologist Elizabeth Bethel. Promiseland remained bounded within the several square miles of land purchased by the original freedmen landowners.[7]

Something similar probably was the case at many Texas freedmen's settlements, and for the same reasons. Within the original boundaries of each community, family lands were divided and subdivided across the gen-erations, and each pioneer's original farm became something of a family compound, with informal leadership residing with the oldest and most im-portant landowners of each family. Because of this, by 1920 or so, freed-men's settlements no longer so closely resembled white farming settlements.

Freedmen's communities had become defensive black islands in a rising tide of Jim Crow.

With the passing of time, landholdings in freedmen's settlements became smaller, family solidarity and cooperation more intense, and the role played by landowner-leaders more important. At every community, major landowners like the Taylors of Wheeler Springs or the Givenses of Givens's Hill served as community patrons, employers, landlords, protectors, and negotiators with outside whites.[8] Virtually every scholar of black landowner communities has commented on this. In the black settlements of Sunflower County, Mississippi, during the 1930s, Hortense Powdermaker noted that the landowner class had "an influence all out of proportion to its numbers. Its role is not without an element of consecration. It is the privileged class; but it is also the class that works in behalf of the others."[9] After careful study of the deed, probate, tax, and census records for several unnamed Gregg County freedmen's settlements, dissertation researcher Deborah J. Hoskins believed that she had discerned something very different about the black communities. She characterized the typical Texas settlement as follows:

A few families had accumulated a reasonable amount of land. They used it to benefit an extended family and to preserve and enlarge a racially-identified community.

They managed this by a wide variety of means. The largest black landowners could borrow money or buy land on credit from white landowners, and did. They alone, apparently, felt secure enough to coopt a white system to black-devised purposes. . . . They also bought and sold land among themselves, and often, perhaps in response to the shifting needs of their families. They usually took the trouble to register their transactions at the county courthouse immediately, including not only transactions with whites but also sales among themselves, perhaps as a means of protecting the black community as a whole.

But then the largest landowners in these communities turned this property around to other blacks. Brothers and sisters, together with their spouses, sometimes purchased land collectively and also inherited land collectively from their parents.

Some families had accumulated sufficient landholdings that they were able to hire tenants. Usually, they hired their own children, who eventually inherited the property, both sons and daughters, when the elder retired from active farming, although not always without strings. Other elders gave small plots to stake their children to an independent living upon marriage. Some of the largest black landowners also lent money to non-kin blacks, starting new farms and keeping old ones solvent. Some sold off small plots of their own property to other members of the community who were not directly related . . .

This African East Texan rural economy functioned very differently from its white counterparts. This economy served a community, a collective, rather than existing to enrich any one individual or segment of the society. Family networks grounded the collective nature of this culture. Family members tended to live close to each other whether they owned land or not, and the extended family seemed to have vital functions, both socially and economically.[10]

By around 1920, these extended families at Texas freedmen's settlements had evolved complicated strategies for economic survival that almost always involved some dealings with whites. Agricultural day labor outside the community probably was most common. Those with enough land for both subsistence and cash crops raised them to maximum advantage; then, more often than not during the winter downtime, the agricultural pause after the summer laid-by time, or during cotton-picking season, many of these families did cash farm work for others.

Census takers classified farmers into owners, tenants (renters who brought their own work stock and equipment to other people's farms), and sharecroppers (renters who brought nothing but their labor), but families like that of Vivian Gardiner Lovelady so commonly "made a day" on the nearby white cotton plantations that they virtually represented a fourth agricultural status: small landowners/day laborers. The big Murray farm in the Trinity River valley just to the west of Hall's Bluff often needed every man, woman, and child it could get to chop or pick and thus offered a dependable source of supplemental income for the Gardiners, who viewed the Murrays not as agribusiness exploiters but as part of the yearly round of making do and getting by on a sandyland farm.[11] Picking cotton for cash had a special satisfaction for black people like the Gardiner family. Usually Jim Crow economic disparities did not operate in the cotton field, and a pound of cotton picked was a pound of cotton paid for. If a thirteen-year-old black girl picked more than a white head of household, she got more of the landowner's money.

Rather often, white farmers like the Murrays did not wait for hands to show up looking for work but went to nearby freedmen's settlements to recruit labor. They might notify a major community landowner or preacher that they wanted so many choppers or pickers or fence builders or hay hands at such-and-such a day and time, or, more impatient, they might pull up outside people's houses and shout or honk their car horns for them to come out. Whether people wanted work or needed to make excuses about why they could not work, they came outside.

According to strict Jim Crow decorum, to mount a black man's porch and knock politely on his front door implied an unacceptable degree of social equality. Instead, whites so frequently sat in their cars and honked for blacks to come to them that they acquired the secret derogatory nickname "honkies." Conversely, an occasional white man might choose to walk up on the porch, knock on the door, and perhaps even address the black woman as "Mrs."—another and much more grievous breach of racial etiquette. Jim Crow rules remained more variable in the remote countryside, where whites enforced them or dispensed with them as they wished.

Many families combined work on their own farms with periodic skilled or semiskilled labor for others. Such services were often bartered for other goods and services within the black community and performed for cash outside, often for whites. Farmers with special skills periodically laid aside their plows and hoes to build chimneys, break work stock, butcher beeves, do carpentry, fix farm machinery, build log houses, dig wells, and a variety of other things. Race usually had remarkably small effect on such transactions.

For example, a white farmer in need of a new well cared little if a black man dug it, and black well diggers usually charged flat rates for their hard, careful, dangerous work. Arthur Cotton of the Sulphur Springs settlement of Sabine County learned well digging with his father, then did it on his own after crops were laid by and in the winter downtime. Cotton charged whites or blacks between two and three dollars per vertical foot—at a time when other people cleared new ground or chopped cotton for under a dollar a day, sunup to sundown. He dug his wells precisely vertical and exactly 33 inches wide with a posthole digger, and he was so comfortable on the bottom that he often had his dinner sent down to him for the noon break. Cotton simply avoided looking up at the ever-diminishing circle of daylight. Only a block-and-tackle and an assistant at the top protected Cotton from a well job gone wrong—from "bad air" or impending cave-in. He periodically lit a match to test for the former, and if the match did not light, beware. Although Cotton never had the earth actually collapse on him and only got sick from bad air a few times in his career, well digging was dangerous. Many a white farmer sharpened his own posthole digger, considered saving money, then decided to pay Arthur Cotton three dollars a vertical foot.[12] Some rural whites classified well digging as "nigger work," exceptionally hard and dangerous, but the racist designation carried an undertone of respect. Many blacks from freedmen's settlements also did seasonal work in the logging crews of major lumber companies, the most dangerous industrial labor in the United States, riskier even than coal mining. Blacks also often broke horses and mules, sometimes breaking their own bones in the process. Harrison Barrett of Barrett settlement broke horses for whites at five dollars a head, and so did Mary Moore's father in Lee County.[13] As she recalled, "The horses would pitch and shake him so hard he could smell his own blood."[14] At Peyton Colony in Blanco County, Neiman Johnson worked as a horse breaker from his teenage years, breaking over three hundred horses in his career and ending up with a bad back. Johnson also did dangerous cowboy work as a "mustanger," cutting wild mustangs off from the brush, crashing into them and knocking them down with his big saddle horse, then getting a rope on their necks before they could stand up.[15]

Horse and mule trading was another risky trade performed by blacks in agricultural downtimes, but the dangers were of a different order. "A deal is a deal," people said, and an uneasy equality prevailed among traders of different races, but a black man had better be well down the road before a white farmer discovered something wrong with the mule he had just swapped for or purchased. Grover Williams of Flat Prairie, Washington County, reported that Burton mule traders often took advantage of his illiterate black grandfather, but the shoe could be on the other foot. "Let the buyer beware" was the basic rule in stock trading. During the 1920s and 1930s, Nelson Jones of Caldwell County bridled at the Jim Crow restrictions he lived under and took a secret revenge by becoming a "road trader." Jones often paid one hundred dollars a head for a pair of mules or horses, then set off across the countryside to find a white man (or a black man) who would double his money. The process sometimes took a couple of days, but Jones usually found his buyer. As Jones noted, whites were incredibly touchy in Jim Crow times, and blacks had to treat them "as if they were covered with feathers and the wind was high," but people like him had become skilled at smoothing ruffled feathers, which made them well suited for stock trading.[16] As John Dollard noted of 1930s Mississippi, "A Negro informant said that Negroes learn to get along with white people by outwitting them, by studying them closely, and by marking the points at which they are susceptible to influence."[17] A legendary stock trader at Pelham in Navarro County played this game to perfection. Dolph Martin could not read or write, though he subscribed to several newspapers and had others read them to him. An acquaintance described Martin this way: "That man could trade. He'd leave in the morning on his horse going to Hubbard. He'd trade that horse and get some boot and keep on going making other trades.

By the time he got home, he would be on his original horse but have $150 in his pocket."[18]

Many black families at freedmen's settlements farmed their own limited lands, then used agricultural downtimes to produce something else to sell outside their communities. At Richardson Chapel, Nacogdoches County, small landowner C. C. White often peddled excess garden produce, butchered yearlings, and barbecue in nearby Nacogdoches. To be within peddling distance—under ten miles, depending on the roads—of an important white market town opened many possibilities. In the wood-stove era, the wagonloads of stovewood prepared every week by the other sons of "Big Charlie" White found a ready market. Town whites also purchased kindling wood of "lighter pine," resinous heartwood from long dead trees gathered from the forest floor. At Wheeler Springs in Houston County, one family occasionally took a week off from field work to fish the Trinity River, accumulated the catch in rived-board live boxes, then took fresh catfish and other river fish into Crockett to sell to regular customers. If whites in the courthouse town wanted fresh fish to eat in the 1920s, they either caught them themselves or bought them from this family.[19] Many other countryside commodities were sometimes peddled in town. Garden products were probably the most common, but blacks also made the rounds with such things as hickory nuts, chinquapins, mayhaws, blackberries, black haws, and others.

Certain bulk products could be processed from family lands or nearby open woods, required little more than hard labor to produce, might be prepared at one's own speed and convenience, and often found ready markets closer to the freedmen's settlement. Steam gins dotted the countryside, and every one of these consumed hundreds of cords of stovewood every ginning season. Each such gin was a major customer for firewood. Timber crews of lumber companies bought many wagonloads of lighter pine, which they used to fuel the company locomotives, loaders, and skidders. That the "fat pine" might have been gathered from their own forests did not matter. Charcoal, prepared from cordwood by slow burning in conical mounds under piles of earth, was sold to blacksmith shops and to more affluent households.

Rived cypress shingles and white oak barrel staves found a steady sale at the nearest railroad stop, but these trades paled to insignificance beside the market for railroad crossties. Railroads (including the tramway systems of lumber companies) bought a prodigious number of hand-hewn ties—several thousand for every mile of track laid. Ties sold for ten to twenty cents each, depending on the length and whether they were hewn on all four sides or only on two. Tie making was hot, hard work and best pursued in the depth of winter, most part-time tie hackers thought. Two-person teams of family tie makers took ax, broadax, and crosscut saw into their woods or somebody else's woods (it often mattered little), felled a hardwood tree of the right diameter, "bucked" the trunk into correct lengths with the cross-cut saw, then began to make ties from each length. First, one person "score hacked" a side of the round log, then the other hewed it down flat with the heavy broadax. Repeated three times more, the process produced a rectan-gular crosstie worth an average of ten cents. A team of veteran tie hackers from a freedmen's settlement, perhaps a father and his oldest son, might produce thirty common ties in one day. Then they marked the ties with their name, stacked them at a designated place along the railroad, and waited for the check in the mail. Although railroads forced black people to ride in des-ignated cars on their passenger trains, they did not discriminate among tie makers; to the railroad, a tie was a tie.[20]

Whiskey was also whiskey, and that produced by blacks in freedmen's settlements could also pass to buyers sight unseen. According to Sheriff Frank Brunt of Rusk County, the Dogtown settlement along the Nacog-doches County line specialized in moonshine whiskey. A buyer knew to drive to a certain bridge over a creek, honk his horn, leave money in a cer-tain hollow stump some distance from the road, wait awhile at his car, then walk back to pick up his whiskey. Thus did the black whiskey maker cut out the middle-man bootlegger and protect himself at the same time.[21]

During national Prohibition and long thereafter, moonshine whiskey re-mained the poor man's preference, and, although freedmen's settlements tended to be straitlaced church communities, it was fairly common for some community members to make whiskey. Local markets determined this to a great extent. After the Mexia oil boom of 1921, many people at the numerous Freestone County freedmen's settlements ventured into whiskey making. The raw materials were cheap, the manufacturing process was easy to mas-ter, and the nearby oil-field roustabouts provided a ready market. There re-mained only the sheriff to worry about, and most minor whiskey men must have hoped to stay lost in the crowd. Many people made whiskey in Free-stone County during the 1920s.[22]

Whenever major cotton farms with their resident communities of black sharecroppers lay close to freedmen's settlements, someone in the settle-ments often made whiskey to supply the company quarters. This was the situation between Vistula and the Murray farm quarters in Houston County and at the Washington County "Bluffs." For Mount Fall and other com-munities along the Bluffs, the huge cropper farms in Grimes County on the other side of the river provided a thirsty market for part-time whiskey

*Cotton pickers weigh cotton before dumping it into the wagon, Ellis County, 1937.
(Courtesy of Texas Agricultural Extension)*

cooks. What is more, as Ed Lathan suggested, some "big white people" probably were involved, perhaps even the fearsome Moore family. "Everybody round the country made liquor," Lathan told an interviewer, "cooking whisky, homemade whisky—they had more barrels and distilleries on branches and little thickets. People round here made whisky for big white people, and they bootlegged it like the black folks, and lot of 'em drank it." For two decades, the law did not intrude, and it seemed that nearly every little thicket along the Bluffs had a whiskey still. Moonshine sold in Navasota, Washington-on-the-Brazos, and Brenham for three or four dollars a gallon, and, as Lathan concluded, "You get four dollars for a gallon of whisky, you got some money, you can buy yourself some groceries in them days, and that's the way lots of people survived and fed the kids."[23]

A cautious man, Ed Lathan steered clear of moonshining and also avoided relationships with the huge Grimes County sharecropper plantations across the Brazos River. Washington County blacks could hear the bells of these operations pealing out the daily round. Well before daylight, a bell to get up and eat your breakfast, then a bell to be at the mule lot to catch your work stock for the day, then a bell to be on station in the field, waiting for enough daylight to begin to plow. A bell at noon signaled lunchtime, but no bell sounded an end to the day on the Terrell family's Allenfarm or the farms of the Moore brothers, and no bell was needed. Farm work on these big agribusiness plantations ceased only when it grew too dark to see.[24]

At Mount Fall in Washington County, Vistula in Houston County, and other freedmen's settlements, younger sons sometimes signed on as share-croppers at nearby cropper farms for a season or two, but most soon moved their families elsewhere. At their worst, such places seemed strange and terrible, unlike any previous experience for young blacks used to a high de-gree of personal freedom. From places where Jim Crow realities hardly in-truded on daily life, they had arrived at Jim Crow "boot camps." Raised in Washington County freedmen's settlements, Annie Mae Hunt moved to a Grimes County sharecropper farm with her parents in 1922 and found that, while "Washington County was a free country," her new life was "like slavery times." Within a year, she found out how bad things could get. A careless comment by her stepfather to a white overseer triggered a disci-plinary raid on the family that left Hunt with a shattered arm, her sister with a broken nose, and her mother beaten so badly she did not work for three months. The real target of the night visit by two cars of white men had been the stepfather, but he escaped, swimming the Brazos to the "free country" of Washington County.[25]

Ed Lathan's friend Mance Lipscomb had grown to manhood in the harsh environment of the bottomland sharecropper farms, and he tended to take these places rather for granted. Some were much worse than others, but most of the big farms required gang labor enforced by armed white "pushers" on horseback that created cotton-field scenes indistinguishable from 1850. Each family's housing was a one-room shack, their "furnish" was the standard salt pork, meal, and molasses, drawn from the farm commis-sary at usurious rates of interest, and their home "cropper plot" was mostly fictive. On the big farms, work gangs labored on the "through and through" system, without respect to family rental plots, and families had nothing to do with the sale of cotton off their plots at the end of the season. Landlords hauled it away by wagon to the gin, then told each family how it had "come out" for that year. News often was not good, but no one dared to dispute the white man's word. One memorable year, Mance Lipscomb's family made thirty-one bales of cotton on the wonderful Brazos Valley alluvial soil, but the plantation overseer informed them that they had exactly broken even.[26]

At Mount Fall, Vistula, Hall's Bluff, Wheeler Springs, and other freed-men's settlements, small landowners like Ed Lathan heard the bells ringing at the bottomland cropper farms but stayed away, tilling their own ground.

Most valued this ground beyond all else that they had, and Lathan and many others feared social and economic entanglements with whites that might cause them to lose their land. Black landowners had more to lose than share-croppers or wage hands, and many had followed the dictum of "cash and carry or starve to death" long before Robert Smith and Booker Washington began to preach the evils of buying on credit. Like many others, Ed Lathan ran a subsistence farm on his small acreage at Mount Fall while renting better land from a local white man on which to grow cotton and corn. This thirds-and-fourths rental avoided the necessity of borrowing money from the bank to make a cash crop on his own land, and Lathan also carefully avoided any debts to the white landlord. The white man—something of a friend—urged Lathan to buy a tractor, but he refused to do this and re-mained a mule farmer to the end. Tractors required a credit purchase from whites, and unforeseen circumstances and missed payments on credit pur-chases might cost you your farm. Lathan explained: "I never got that big, and I always spent wise, renting the other fellow's land. I's born a free man, you understand what I mean? I ain't never been under slavery, no white man riding up and down the middle behind me telling me what to do in my crop, like a lot of them people. That's what I mean, free."[27]

Many landowners at freedmen's settlements followed similar cautious strategies. In Nacogdoches County Leota Freeman Upshaw's parents both had inherited land at County Line, but they preferred to reside as the only sharecropper family on the small farm of a white landowner named Roark just beyond the perimeter of the black community. The Freemans' relations with the Roarks were cordial. The renter family had the use of an adequate house, work stock, farming equipment, and a free two-acre garden plot, and they stayed out of debt to everyone but Roark, whom they trusted. Nor did the white man lurk behind them in the field and try to tell them how to farm. Roark stayed out of the way and allowed the Freemans to manage their own crops in a sharecropper relationship little resembling circumstances on the large bottomland farms.[28]

For the Freemans, two inheritances of land still had not added up to a viable farm, and other families were in the same situation. More and more people, especially the younger sons, found themselves hiking to public work like young Henry Earl of Panola County. As family farms shrank in size, supplemental income was needed. Women walked into town for domestic service as the maids and cooks of white families, and men took seasonal jobs at sawmills, logging fronts, and cattle ranches and in railroad gangs, construction projects, and turpentine camps.

Sometimes the burden fell most heavily on the women. Deola Mayberry

Adams's father still made three to five bales of cotton a year on limited family land at Lincolnville in Coryell County, but this was not enough. To help make ends meet, Deola's mother walked several miles into Gatesville three times a week to wash and iron for white families, often staying overnight. On those days, Deola's grandparents at Lincolnville took care of Deola, her brothers and sisters, and many of their other grandchildren. "Grandma Lou" and "Grandpa Bill" Mayberry sometimes looked after no less than nineteen children at their unpainted "old-make house," which had five rooms and a "boxed-in" front porch used as a bedroom for the boys. After Deola's mother walked home with her small wages and occasional handouts of food and clothing, she assumed the usual heavy burdens of a farm wife. She sewed "britches quilts," often several a week, for sale in town. She managed the household, including cooking, gardening, and food preservation, and she labored beside her husband in the field, as needed. Deola's father was a kind man but only a little less of a taskmaster than the Brazos bottom pushers. The Mayberry family often worked the fields from first light to dark, "from can see to can't."[29]

The availability of seasonal employment varied from place to place and depended on local circumstances. At Lewis's Bend and other communities along the San Antonio River, men left the wooded bottoms to take jobs as cowboys, cooks, fence builders, and hay hands on nearby cattle ranches. At Barrett in the East Texas pines, they floated log rafts down the Neches and Sabine rivers, worked in the woods crews of lumbering operations, and labored on county road crews.[30]

Rather often, some sort of public work ultimately arrived close by the remote freedmen's settlement, and in these cases many more residents participated. Turpentine camps, logging crews, and a quarry cutting stone for the Galveston seawall operated around 1905 near remote Boykin in Angelina County, and local people took jobs with all of them. Pioneer Jim Runnels became a "powder monkey" at the rock quarry, handling dangerous dynamite. Helen Darden's mother married in succession two black outsiders brought in by the quarry and a turpentine camp.[31] Shankleville in Newton County was equally remote, but after 1918 the last great bonanza lumber company established its company town of Wiergate only three miles away. Wier Longleaf Lumber Company employed any Shankleville man and boy who wanted to work in its sawmill, woods crew, and turpentine camp, and most of them did. As at other places, the small cash crop and subsistence farms at Shankleville continued to operate while the older males took part in public work. As Larutha Odom Clay explained, "Those people [the men] could walk and ride horses to the mill and work and come on back home,

and the women and the children did the farming—that was how we lived."
Wiergate also provided a place to peddle local farm products: "Ladies would
go there to sell their eggs and butter and whatever gardening things that
they had."[32]

Shankleville families could have relocated to the Wiergate quarter, where
facilities included homes with electricity and running water, baseball fields,
and even a company swimming pool for African Americans, but most of
them did not. By and large, the forced move into public work remained seasonal or part time for people at freedmen's settlements. For a long time, few
residents chose to give up their land or their community residence, even if
they only made it home on weekends. Most people clung with determination to their homes and communities.

For example, at Cedar Branch in Houston County, economic circumstances after 1930 often forced Larry Leonard to leave his wife and children to run the family farm while he commuted long distances to public
work, but in his mind Leonard never left home. After the railroad construction job he followed moved south to northern Harris County, Leonard still
continued the trek from Cedar Branch, now beginning his drive to work
just after midnight. "If I had of could've made a living, I wouldn't of left,"
Leonard told an interviewer. "Here is where I want to be. Well, I didn't
leave! When I laid my crop by, I went and got the other fellow's job and
then tend to mine."[33]

Over eighty years of age at the time of his 2001 interview, freedmen's
settlement resident Larry Leonard had lived half his life in the era of Jim
Crow. Leonard said little of the bad old days of segregation and discrimination to a white stranger, only telling of his decades-long failure to get
county commissioners to pave the road to the Cedar Branch church and
his enduring bitterness over loss of the community's Rosenwald school to
Lovelady Independent School District.

Many other things remained unsaid, but for every person of Leonard's
generation, the racist past still haunted the present. At the end of an interview several years earlier with the same white man, Ed Lathan of Washington County refused to sign the form giving permission to place his oral
history tape in an archive. Lathan understood and agreed with the purpose of the interview; the document was the problem. Lathan had not been
able to attend the Mount Fall school often enough to learn to read, and
white strangers with unknown legal papers to sign triggered bitter memories and present alarms. Many black landowners of Lathan's generation had
been robbed with a fountain pen. Moreover, nightmare ghosts of Jim Crow
haunted some places with special force, including Lathan's landscape along

the Brazos. People there still passed down oral traditions about black men murdered on the old iron bridge crossing the river, the pogromlike attack on African American families at Old Washington, and other violent events. Lathan's close friend Mance Lipscomb had seen a hoe hand shot down in the field by a pusher and had endured the race murder of a cousin and the lynching of a close acquaintance. Such things could not be forgotten this side of the grave.[34] No wonder Ed Lathan refused to sign the paper.

During the 1920s, black people like Lathan and Leonard looked out from their freedmen's settlement refuges at complicated social landscapes dominated by Jim Crow. All directions, lines of travel, neighboring settlements, crossroads market towns, and county seats were not the same. In those days, as an elderly white Washington County farmer explained, "Fifteen miles down the road was like another land," but these differences were even greater, and infinitely more important, for blacks. Jim Crow customs varied across the landscape with great complexity, and a black person had to know the lay of the land. Some crossroads stores in the countryside welcomed black customers, others forbade them to enter their doors or even to pause on the public road outside. A good many white communities had rules forbidding black presence after sundown, and some communities enforced whites-only customs at all times. Oscar Allen of Angelina County once observed a black family from the freedmen's settlement of Nigton, in adjacent Trinity County, grinding through the white Hudson community on a shredded tire, having suffered a flat where no black motorist could afford to stop.[35]

At the periphery of every freedman's settlement, black lands verged on white lands, and more often than not the relationships with these immediate neighbors and neighboring settlements were good. Blacks and whites had usually known each other from childhood and had often established close personal relationships—even friendships—that to a degree transcended Jim Crow.[36] As in all other such things, however, whites made the call. Teenager Marion Upshaw occasionally did day labor for different white neighbors at County Line, and he recalled that some of them ate noon meals with him in their homes and some of them followed Jim Crow customs and ate first and separately.[37] Sitting down at a dinner table with a black person implied social equality and represented a huge violation of racial norms, but rural whites might do it. At their own farmhouse in the deep countryside, who was to know?[38]

Factors other than personal acquaintance contributed to good relations with nearby white settlements. Close involvement between communities sometimes went back to slavery times, as in the case of black Sand Field and white Reilly Springs in Hopkins Country. Many whites and blacks at these places had the same last names, testifying to the old relationship. As in Hopkins County, whites also regarded adjacent black communities as convenient and customary recruiting sites for day laborers like Marion Upshaw. For blacks, this was both a blessing and a curse. Rather often you might be happy for a day's work chopping or picking for a familiar white man, but if you had something else planned for the day, it was difficult to say no.

Blacks at freedmen's settlements said no to whites more often than at other African American communities, however, one reason that neighboring whites respected them and to a degree protected them from strangers who did not know their independent ways. An incident at Cologne in Goliad County was rather typical. A young white farmer recently arrived in the county rode up to black landowner Jim Walls working in his field and brusquely ordered him to send his daughters over to pick cotton on the white man's farm. Walls refused, saying that his daughters did not work for others but that he was sure his sons would be happy to come over after their own labors were completed. Astonished, then humiliated and angry at this insult to Jim Crow norms, the white outsider raced his horse into nearby Fannin to start trouble for the black man, but local whites proved totally unsympathetic and told him to forget it. The black farmer was well known and respected, and, besides, everybody knew Cologne blacks behaved differently. They would not only say no but fight back. After news of this incident got around, the young white farmer found no blacks willing to pick his cotton, his crop failed, and he soon returned to Jackson County, "where niggers do what they are told to do." [39]

In the Jim Crow countryside, a freedmen's settlement was fortunate if it had a friendly white neighbor of property and social importance to intervene in time of trouble or to assist local people in their dealings with outside whites. Stockman and farmer Baxter Moss played the role of patron and protector for Sand Hill in Nacogdoches County. He maintained a friendly relationship with the community and allowed black residents to take up as many of his wandering range cattle for temporary milk cows as they wished, insisting only that the accompanying calves receive his mark, an entirely cropped ear.[40] White landowner P. O. Green played a somewhat similar role at Wheeler Springs in Houston County. Green often employed local blacks on his place, and he drove others back and forth into Crockett to public work for small fees at a time when no Wheeler Springs resident had an automobile. Green also served as labor organizer for local blacks; after a while, if a big white farmer needed day hands, he had to go through P. O. Green.[41]

Major black landowners like French Taylor often played something of this role as community protector and negotiator with town whites. Taylor's master and father taught him to read and write, recognized him as his son, brought him to Texas, and helped establish him as a farmer at Hall's Bluff. After the man's death, Taylor retained friendly relationships with his white half-brothers and sisters and their families, and he had major white friends in both Crockett and Lovelady. White relatives sometimes sent an automobile to pick up French Taylor to eat Christmas dinner with them at their home, and there were similar social contacts.[42]

Even blacks inclined to avoid whites had to go to town sometimes and needed working relationships with such minimal market facilities as mercantile stores, cotton gins, gristmills, and post offices. Howard Matthies recalled a family of blacks from Flat Prairie in Washington County rolling into nearby Burton in a dilapidated wagon pulled by the only work stock they had, an emaciated old mule and a milk cow.[43] Blacks at Germany in Houston County found their services at the small white town of Belott on Highway 21, and every freedmen's settlement needed such a minimal point of white contact.[44] People from Friendship in Delta County customarily traveled to the white community of Klondike to gin their cotton and to shop at Hollon's Store, a business that gave credit to black farmers at reasonable interest rates. Hollon's also "ran a chicken peddler" into black Friendship as a much-appreciated public service. Mr. Hollon was friendly, but paternalistic and somewhat bossy. No family could have over five hundred dollars in credit between cotton seasons, when all debts came due, and Hollon felt free to inquire about how you planned to use the money. "You don't need that much just to do that," he might say.[45] Green's Mercantile Store in Giddings played a similar role for blacks from the numerous freedmen's settlements of Lee County. Mr. Green also offered credit—"story accounts," George Francis observed, tongue in cheek, in a play on words on "store accounts." To get cash, you went in to Mr. Green and told your story.[46]

In Washington County, Burton stores also offered credit to Flat Prairie and Post Oak blacks—in fact, they insisted on it. As Grover Williams observed, even small purchases like snuff and chewing tobacco automatically "went on the book," the primary subterfuge for charging black people more money, Williams thought. No receipts were ever given, and when bills came due, blacks, as usual, could not question the white man's word. Another Burton store not only forced most blacks into credit purchases but also played tricks like "accidentally" adding the day's date into the bill or including a stray broom that happened to be on the counter with the legitimate purchases.[47]

No wonder that freedmen's settlement families preferred to deal with black businessmen whenever they could, which was not often. Very occasionally, families found their necessary stores, gins, gristmills, and post offices at a small black market town, as at Nunnsville in Lee County, Easton in Gregg County, Cuney in Cherokee County, and a few other places. By the early 1920s, Cuney, in particular, had become a considerable town. It remained unincorporated, with no formal city officials or municipal water or sewer systems, but had multiple gins, stores, various small black-owned businesses, several churches and lodge halls, a hotel, a black high school, a telephone exchange, and even a semipro black baseball team.[48]

At least once or twice a year, sometimes much more often, a family traveled longer distances to a larger white market town, usually the county seat. Freedmen's settlements had often established themselves along county lines, seemingly as far away from such citadels of Jim Crow power and authority as they could get, and residents faced trips to town with both anticipation and apprehension. Birdie Wade of Nacogdoches County recalled that trips to her county seat often began with stern admonitions about appropriate behavior from her parents the night before. Adults tried to shield children from the rebuffs of Jim Crow, but they also worried about them doing or saying things that might get the family into trouble. Children lacked impulse control, and those from freedmen's settlements were less accustomed to being around whites. Birdie Wade's parents emphatically ordered Birdie and her siblings to keep quiet and stay in the wagon. Nacogdoches was not particularly friendly to black visitors. It had no black hotel or black cafe, though a store close to the wagon yard sold cheese, crackers, and other snacks. While at Nacogdoches, black children had to stay close to their wagons. Parents could walk downtown to shop but could not drive there in their wagons, and everybody had to be out of town by sundown.[49] Nonetheless, the inhospitable courthouse town remained something of a tourist destination for rural African Americans starved for urban novelties. Nacogdoches, for example, had electric lights, brick streets, and bananas. Mrs. Velio King lived with her new husband half a day's journey away, but she recalled that they often went to town during their first married years. "We would go to Nacogdoches every Saturday in a wagon. We'd go down to the hitch-yard, just set and look, and buy a banana and come home. Lawrence would buy bananas because he liked them."[50]

For children from a remote black settlement, a trip to the courthouse town served as a crash course in the rules of Jim Crow. Some customs were nearly universal and came into play on the trip in—for example, blacks in wagons or automobiles gave the right-of-way to whites and refrained from passing whites on dusty roads. Andrew Eleby recalled riding with his grandfather when the prosperous Vistula landowner pulled his car entirely off the road and braked to a stop to let a white man drive by.[51] As they did on city sidewalks, blacks avoided the eyes of the whites that they passed on the road, since even a hard stare could get you into trouble.

Black travelers also dressed appropriately for their visits to town, and at many places—especially on weekdays—that meant dressing like field hands in overalls, straw hats, sunbonnets, and other items that looked like work clothing. Courthouse communities varied a good deal in how rigorously they enforced these sumptuary customs, but silk shirts, Stetson hats, and dress pants could arouse white disapproval, especially during the work week, when blacks were supposed to be in the field. The county seat of Rusk enforced such rules, and on one occasion Sheriff Bill Brunt made a black man in dress pants stand while he cut them off above the knees with his pocket knife—thus literally "cutting his britches off," as the old saying described this sumptuary castration.[52] At Houston County, Texana Randolph's husband took a job working for a rich white man known as "Telephone" Cook soon after their marriage, and only then could he go into Crockett at midweek wearing his good suit. Now, as she laughingly told an interviewer, Mr. Randolph had become "Telephone Cook's nigger" and could wear anything he pleased.[53]

Navasota, the county seat of Grimes County, either had an unusually severe dress code for black visitors or Mance Lipscomb and Glen Alyn's other African American friends simply told him more of the common Jim Crow reality. As Bubba Bowser and others affirmed, blacks walking Navasota streets carrying cotton samples and trying to sell their own cotton often got into big trouble, as did blacks with inappropriately good buggies, fine horses or mules, and luxury motorcars.[54] All strange blacks, not of the town, attracted white attention, and they had to dress like field hands or else. Willie Lipscomb explained: "Any Negro that went there with a silk shirt on, they'd tear it off and spit on it—tear that shirt off you! You couldn't wear a silk shirt to Navasota, and you couldn't wear nothing during the week but blue duckings or khakis and a straw hat. You go out with a white Stetson on and you'd come back with it all flopped down round your head!"[55] From an African American perspective, some Jim Crow courthouse towns were much worse than others. Musician and sharecropper Mance Lipscomb had worked on Grimes County cotton farms all his life, and the usually mild-mannered Lipscomb turned vitriolic on the subject of Navasota. "A dog call that a dirty hole," he told Glen Alyn, "that's what I call it. That's the dirtiest place in the world, Navasota. More niggers killed there'n any place in the world. Yeah, man! They killed niggers for the fun of it. Specially if a man tried to hold up for his rights, they gonna kill him, get rid of him."[56] Mance's friend, John Cameron, had been riddled with bullets by a white mob in a Navasota jail cell, then hung from a telephone pole.

Besides observing appropriate dress and demeanor, black travelers approaching the county seat made sure they kept their wheels turning through certain whites-only communities (like Hudson) on the way in, even if they had a broken spoke (or a flat). Upon reaching town, they parked their wagon in one of the hitch lots and began to take care of business—shopping, visiting relatives, paying taxes, and other necessary things.

Adult African Americans, especially the men, now had to concentrate on controlling every aspect of their public behavior. This was not the "small friendly place full of harmless relatives," as Beatrice Upshaw Ali described her home of County Line. Every county seat had its unique set of Jim Crow rules governing the movement of blacks in time and space, and these had to be learned anew for every place. A black educator noted, "Every town had its own mores, its own unwritten restrictions. The trick was to find out from local [black] people what the rules were."[57]

Town blacks lived in neighborhoods or quarters, often with derogatory nicknames such as Lockhart's "Cocklebur," Kountz's "Fly Blow," and Lufkin's more common "Niggertown." These black neighborhoods often included black business districts on the edge of town, which also sometimes had their own names—for example, "The Flats" at Greenville. Traditional lines of black travel passed downtown from the quarters and black business districts, often coinciding at the courthouse. Long periods might pass on other streets and sections of the white business district without anyone seeing a black face. African Americans usually could stand around and socialize on one side of the courthouse square, though some towns insisted they move a block away to do this. In such places they moved briskly into the square to shop or conduct public business, then moved away again. No black stores in black business districts dared to exclude whites, but many white stores excluded blacks. To prevent embarrassment, African American shoppers had to know when the sign in the window, "We reserve the right to refuse service to anyone," simply meant, "No blacks allowed." Blacks freely entered many stores and were welcome, though they might have to access them by special doors. Many restaurants excluded blacks entirely; others allowed them to go around to the back. A restaurant at Greenville followed this policy, and one man recalled that black customers had enjoyed certain advantages along with the customary humiliation of entering the back door. They got the same food for about half what the whites up front paid, and the black cooks gave seconds. African Americans were well aware of the white-owned stores that treated blacks courteously and fairly, and they gave them their business. At the county seat of Wharton in Wharton County, the men's clothing store of Horton Foote Sr. had such a reputation. Blacks often brought Foote legal documents to read and interpret for them, which he did free of charge.[58]

At any given time, certain parts of the town were forbidden areas for blacks. Texas laws requiring segregation in public transportation (1889, 1891), prohibiting racial intermarriage (1881), and prohibiting cross-race adoption of children (1907) were but the tip of the iceberg of Jim Crow rules, most of which remained informal and unwritten, though often vehemently enforced. A law of 1907 allowed amusement facilities, roller rinks, movie theaters, and even public parks and libraries to segregate blacks or to completely exclude them, as they wished, and rather often they chose the latter option. Greenville's public library excluded blacks, although a friendly white librarian sometimes provided black readers with requested books wrapped in brown paper at the back door—this to prevent whites from seeing which library books were being "polluted" by black use.[59] In the white courthouse town at midday, there were many places where black people simply could not be, and after sundown the forbidden areas expanded. At dark, varying with each town and its local customs, blacks had to be in their quarters or on their side of the railroad tracks.

Time and space customs varied from place to place, but certain Jim Crow rules operated everywhere, varying only in the intensity of their enforcement. At Greenville, as one black man recalled, it was permissible for a black man well acquainted with a white man to call him by his first name, but not so at Palestine.[60] Blacks everywhere in the South got out of the way of whites on sidewalks, spoke only if spoken to, removed their hats during interactions, and invariably addressed whites with the respectful "Mr.," "Mrs.," and "Miss." Blacks never were so addressed by whites, only by their first names, by "boy" or "girl" or (if they were elderly and well known) by "uncle" or "auntie." African Americans recalled that whites patrolled the Jim Crow rule of "no salutations" with special diligence. Blacks dared not refer to other black people as "Mr." or "Mrs." in white company, telephone operators sometimes broke in to rebuke blacks who did this on the telephone, and postmen occasionally delivered letters to black homes with the "Mr." or "Mrs." penciled out. Jim Crow was a stickler for this rule and for its converse. A story circulated that racial decorum required black customers at certain Brazos Valley mercantile stores to say, "Can I please have a can of Mister Prince Albert Tobacco?"

Black visitors to the courthouse town might pass white people on the street whom they had known all their lives, with the whites refusing to recognize them, and of course blacks could not initiate the interaction. James Wade remembered that "they would ride by you and turn their head, fore they'd speak to you."[61] Sometimes this was for the best, because if whites did speak to you, blacks immediately had to assume their best "white folks manner"—deferential, friendly, agreeable, and nonthreatening. Field worker John Dollard followed Mississippi whites and blacks around for months during the 1930s observing these interactions, and he became fascinated by them. To his northern eyes and ears, the black performances of deference often appeared overblown and phony, but his white companions seemed to take them at face value. Blacks were lavishly subservient and respectful, giving "a continual flow of agreement" to the white person to which they were talking, such as " 'Yes, boss,' 'Sho nuff,' 'Well, I declare,' and the like." Dollard generalized: "The Negro must maintain a position of continuous affirmation of the white man's wishes and ideas, showing thereby his lack of contrary intent, independence, aggressiveness, and individuality. A 'good nigger' from the white man's point of view is one who has mastered this technique. It stuck me repeatedly that the deference of Negroes, in addition to being pleasant, has the function of allaying anxiety among white people."[62]

With some blacks, "rebelliousness shines through the white-folks manner," Dollard observed, though perhaps local whites did not notice this. As the black visitors from the countryside walked around the courthouse town, shopping in stores and interacting on the street with whites and blacks, they had to be very careful to maintain white-folks manner and to observe complex Jim Crow etiquette, or trivial violations might snowball into terrible consequences. In stores white customers always took precedence over black ones. If a black man had waited through three white customers to ask to purchase a certain hat and another white came in, he had to wait through that one, too. This was true everywhere, without question. Furthermore, after that customer left, the black customer had better know his hat size. Blacks could not try on clothing before purchase, since according to Jim Crow customs prohibiting racial contagion, no white could wear or use things that blacks had worn or used. (Black midwifes, wet nurses, and prostitutes excepted, of course; Jim Crow was not strong on logic.) From a black perspective, whites always seemed incredibly sensitive about these matters, as about everything else. Sidney Green of the Moab community of Lee County often went to the courthouse town of Giddings on Saturdays, and Green recalled, "We were divided along that [racial] line, you couldn't hardly touch nobody going down the street when it was crowded. Lots of them came to me, and, you know, I would actually hit them when the streets were crowded, and they'd follow me clear on down to the depot and want to jump on me. And I told 'em, I just don't remember running up against 'em."[63]

Everywhere in the South minor transgressions of Jim Crow customs sometimes led to drastic events, as for the black man who forgetfully entered a store at Apple Springs in Trinity County with his hat on and was shot dead by the owner.[64] In Alabama Nate Shaw worked with a white female clerk trying to fit his son with a pair of new shoes until an older white man became incensed by all this white female attention shown to a black boy. The man challenged Shaw, then found himself confronted with a formidable individual who did not back down or assume a white-folks manner. The outraged white set up an outcry and others rallied to the scene until authorities intervened to vouch for Nate Shaw.[65] Things could go bad for black people just that quickly, since whites acted as though violation of one small Jim Crow rule challenged the whole system of white dominance, black deference, and racial apartheid. God, or perhaps the devil, was in the details. A black man, defiant or suicidal, repeatedly entered the wrong door into Kreuz's Meat Market in Lockhart until whites finally beat him to death.[66]

Black men walking sidewalks in courthouse towns had to be especially aware of white women in order to maintain maximum avoidance. They took care not to brush against them in passing or even to look at them, and, as one Mississippi man bluntly summed things up, "If you smiled at a white woman, you'd be hung from a limb."[67] Every black man from a northeast Texas freedmen's settlement must have walked town streets in full knowledge of the horrible public torture death of Henry Smith at Greenville in 1906 and the burning of two brothers at Paris in 1920. "Any accident or minor mishap may appear to whites as a cover for latent aggression, thus provoking a counter response," John Dollard observed.[68] Black males always felt themselves to be tiptoeing around a lion's den, forever fearful about what might happen out of nowhere. A black man had to control his behavior, not just to protect himself but to protect his family and community. Dollard wrote: "The threat of lynching is likely to be in the mind of the Negro child from earliest days. Memories of such events came out frequently in the life histories of Negroes.[69] Every Negro in the South knows that he is under a kind of sentence of death; he does not know when his turn will come, it may never come, but it may also be at any time."[70]

Mance Lipscomb tried to explain this to an unbelieving young white friend in the 1970s. Blacks had been afraid of whites under Jim Crow, he affirmed, and with good reason. "The way I come up in the world, my parents was scared of 'em, and we had to be scared of 'em," Lipscomb said.

"You was born scared of 'em."[71] Black parents visiting the courthouse town left their children back at the hitch yard for more than one reason. They did not wish the children to see them humble themselves in interactions with whites, and they feared what children might say or do. Adults tried not to frighten children about whites, but these fears were communicated nonetheless. Young Osceola Mays grew up in the Waskom community out from Marshall, and she too was "born scared of 'em." As a child, Mays had little personal contact with whites, but adults frightened her by how they lowered their voices when they talked about whites and by how they acted around them. Mays grew up believing that if "anyone around Waskom got out of the rules and regulations of the white people, the mob would come and get them. They'd go and hide out down in the woods or go to visiting somebody else's house. They wouldn't stay home that night. White folks would take people and burn them and cut their feet off. Them kind of stories made me scared to sleep."[72]

Occasionally, Osceola Mays's nightmare of white mobs attacking black farmsteads was a reality. In times of racial trouble, black families at isolated communities often hid out in the woods around their homes as a precaution against the terrifying mob that came by night. Such reports survive from the violent days of Reconstruction, from the sporadic political violence of the late 1880s, when white Democrats drove the last black local officials from office, and from the time of troubles after World War I. Freedmen's settlements, however, usually gave would-be white aggressors cause for concern. Attacking a black family at an isolated farm was one thing; facing off against a unified black community on its home ground could be quite another. African Americans in such places had somewhat different attitudes, and at least nearby whites knew it.

During the first years after Emancipation, freedmen's settlements like the White Rock community of Grayson County sometimes regarded their white neighbors with misgivings. Residents of White Rock knew very well that some people did not like the idea of an independent black community in their midst. Until about 1880, White Rock people feared for their personal safety and that of the White Rock Baptist Church. The attack on White Rock never came, but at Tod Davis's unnamed landowner community in Nacogdoches County, "white cappers" often came around at night to harass the community. They kicked in doors and took people outside to whip them at gunpoint, so much so that families began to hide out in the woods. After a while this harassment increased until "they interfered with the working of the land," which perhaps was the whitecappers' intention.[73]

Deadlier attacks occurred in Bastrop and Matagorda counties. White

Democrats had reassumed political control of Texas by the middle 1870s, but blacks continued to vote, and in populous freedmen's settlements they sometimes elected their own local officials. During the late 1880s, whites no longer tolerated this. With the help of his former master, a freedman named Cal Thompson had purchased over five hundred acres of Bastrop County land and founded the Cedar Creek community, which elected a black justice of the peace and a black constable in May of 1888. A white attack on Cedar Creek ensued, leaving at least four men dead, two black and two white. Thereafter, whites swore revenge on all blacks involved, especially Cal Thompson, previously described by the Bastrop newspaper as "a Negro of much influence in the community." One by one, whites waylaid and murdered the black defenders of Cedar Creek or forced them from the county. Two white men shot Thompson as he left Bastrop one day. At least a hundred whites witnessed the murder, but all refused to reveal who did it. By now, the local newspaper's position on Thompson had changed, editorializing that the mulatto community founder had been "nothing but a troublemaker and both sides were glad he was killed."[74]

Similar events had happened the year before, when Vann of Matagorda County became the scene of a violent attack from white vigilantes from Matagorda, Wharton, Brazoria, and Fort Bend counties. Here, also, black local officials trying to do their jobs had served as a flash point for the conflict. In 1887 Matagorda County freedmen still had a black legislator in Austin, a black county commissioner, two black justices of the peace, and a black constable. Trouble began when two white men refused to work the roads with a group of blacks under the supervision of the black commissioner. A black justice of the peace ordered constable Jerry Matthews to summon the two whites before him, but Matthews died in the attempt. Black residents armed themselves and launched a posse to find the killers, and the word of this "uprising" got out. Some eighty-five armed men from Matagorda and surrounding counties, led by the Matagorda County sheriff, soon attacked fortified blacks at Vann on Live Oak Creek. A number of blacks died in the gun battle, though leader Oliver Sheppard managed to make his escape. The fight at Vann effectively ended black participation in local government in Matagorda County, and, as a white local historian noted: "For several years afterward, the Negroes were expected to take off their hats when they met a white man and keep them off until the white man had passed. The Negroes remained relatively subjugated until the Civil Rights Act of 1964."[75]

During the period from 1918 to 1925, however, many Texas whites did not perceive blacks as "relatively subjugated," and this time of troubles during and after World War I witnessed attacks on black communities, lynchings, and what John Dollard termed "lynch-like events." In times of racial violence, public lynchings were but the tip of the iceberg of violence against blacks. Black fugitives from local lawmen all too often ended up dead, and Dollard observed, "How many of these semiofficial shootings are actually disguised lynchings one cannot tell."[76]

Dollard and other observers argued that increased white fears triggered white violence, and by 1918 whites had authentic causes of worry. Blacks had begun to fight back against white aggression. One December evening in 1918, a preacher in the local AME church at Kildare, a mixed-race community on the railroad in Cass County, delivered a blistering lecture that was being repeated from other pulpits. Its title was "On the War and After the War." Blacks had learned to fight white men overseas; now they needed to go to war for democracy at home, the preacher thought. The government had "forced the Negro to go 3,000 miles away to fight for democracy when they should have been fighting for democracy at home." Now the time had come for blacks to demand their full rights as citizens, even if it meant opening "another war for democracy right here at home." Black veterans should lead this fight—men "not afraid to die" and "experienced in killing white men." Audience members should "arm themselves with Winchester rifles" and prepare to defend their families.[77]

Such lectures had their effects. Thirty-two chapters of the National Association for the Advancement of Colored Peoples formed in Texas between 1917 and 1919. Blacks did not riot and agitate, but they did become less passive before white violence. Historian Steven Reich generalized: "This call to arms stands out as neither an isolated incident nor the wishful fantasy of a deluded preacher. On the contrary, African Americans echoed these themes in churches, fraternal societies, union halls, and social settings across Texas and throughout the South from 1917 to 1919, the years during and immediately following American involvement in World War I. African Americans resisted [white] oppression, posing a formidable threat to the status quo."[78]

Southern whites certainly seemed to perceive the threat as significant, since they responded much as they had during the time of Reconstruction. Walter L. Buenger noted that "blacks' willingness to defend themselves, as well as efforts to organize resistance to discrimination, increased after World War I. This newfound black assertiveness often demanded a response, joining the KKK."[79] Klan members, local and state officials, and the newly formed Federal Bureau of Investigation soon joined forces in harassing the new chapters of the NAACP.[80]

The lynching of brothers Herman and Ervin Arthur in Paris, Lamar

County, on July 6, 1920, typified the new circumstances and sent shock waves all across eastern Texas. Herman Arthur was a World War I veteran, and when his landlord tried to use armed force to keep Herman and his brother from moving off their farm, Herman responded in kind, although more successfully. Herman Arthur shot and killed both the white landlord and his son. Two days later, on July 6, a white lynch mob came for the Arthur brothers at the Paris jail, and lawmen handed over the blacks to be burned at the stake. A near race riot then ensued at Paris. Lynchings often ended in generalized attacks against the local black communities, but black war veterans had been urging African Americans in Paris to arm and fight back since 1919, and officials feared actual combat. Perhaps in recognition of this, the Paris mob threatened but failed to drive home its attack.[81]

Although members of economic elites in the South had sought black recruits for the World War I war effort, many southern whites had opposed this. Blacks in U.S. uniforms, consorting with French women, and armed with rifles set off many Jim Crow alarms and anger, and ultimately these blacks (like Henry Arthur) would end up back home. From 1919 on, groups of whites, often KKK members, sometimes appeared at southern railroad stations to strip uniforms from returning black soldiers and to otherwise reacquaint them with the power of Jim Crow.[82]

Apprehensions remained, however. Alarmed by the nearby Paris lynchings, an interracial committee formed at Greenville in 1920 to survey white concerns about blacks, and the fears it recorded in its interviews typified those all across the South. Whites distrusted local black people's "white-folks manner," for they were "suspicious that the negro does not reveal the state of his mind to the white man with whom he talks, but that he thinks one thing and says another." More specific fears focused on whites' beliefs about the presumed effects of the war: "They are suspicious of the number of guns and the amount of ammunition that the negroes are constantly buying. They are suspicious of the negro secret societies. They are fearful of the result of army life and especially of the French attitude toward the negro soldiers. They rebuke the dangerous arrogance and the self-assertiveness of the young negro."[83] In keeping with such attitudes, many Hunt County whites had joined the Klan in an attempt at keep the "new Negro" down and in his place. Over six hundred Klansmen marched through the county seat of Greenville in December of 1921, ending at the 24-foot-long electrified sign erected earlier that year. The sign read, "Welcome to Greenville: The Blackest Land, the Whitest People."[84]

Freedmen's settlements had existed largely unnoticed for half a century in the rural nooks and crannies of southern counties, but in the wave of paranoia after World War I they began to attract white attention. The popular mind conjured up rumors about bands of blacks marching about the countryside and "entire black communities gathered in secret places to study the arts of war."[85] In 1923 a county sheriff and the state governor stood by and did nothing when KKK-led mobs attacked and burned the freedmen's settlement of Rosewood, Florida, climaxing a long period of north Florida lynchings and assaults on black communities that had begun in 1920. The official death toll at Rosewood was two whites and six blacks, but the unofficial black death toll ran much higher. Blacks at Rosewood were killed or run off and their property confiscated. The mob burned homes, a church, a Masonic hall, and a store. Despite the magnitude of this attack, a county grand jury found insufficient evidence to prosecute anyone.[86]

Whites launched other assaults on freedmen's settlements, that much is certain, but just how general was the "Rosewood phenomenon" is difficult to say. Authorities hushed up and denied the Rosewood incident for many years, just as they did the even more violent attack on blacks near Elaine, Arkansas, in 1919.[87] On some occasions, white attacks must have been repulsed by black communities willing to fight back, as was the case at St. John Colony in Caldwell County around 1920. The conflict between St. John Colony and the nearby white market town of Red Rock registered in no newspapers or other documents, but Reverend S. L. Davis offered a tersely worded account of events in an interview of 1976. Davis refused to elaborate further, but much may be read behind his brief comments. Was this simple harassment by white hooligans or a potential Rosewood repulsed by armed force? Of a certainty, local race relations were very bad. The events described had been preceded by several murders of blacks in the Red Rock area.

There was a bad little place, seven miles from Saint John, known as Red Rock. You could be on a train and look out the window and read on a big sign, "Nigger, don't let the sun go down on you." Yes, that was the signboard. Well, we regarded that, we just didn't let the sun go down on us. There was other places we can go, we don't have to go there. But they decided one time they were going to come up and break up our Nineteenth. We got the news early, before the Nineteenth, and every old musket, and every old rifle, and every old shotgun, they don't care whatever kind, and every old cap-and-ball pistol—we had a tent there, nothing else but weapons was in there. They came to do it, but they went back. They was glad to get back. Didn't come back.

There was another [incident] after another crop grew up. I guess they heard about what the others did. They came back a little worse that time.

They got some horses' ears knocked down, some buggies tore to pieces, and so forth. We let them know that was our territory. We're not going to invade yours and you're sure enough ain't going to invade this. It's known as Saint John, today, and we don't bother nobody. Nobody![88]

Northeast Texans lynched forty-six black people between 1883 and 1923 (which was the last), but lynchings and attacks on black communities disappeared rather abruptly at about the time that blacks began to fight back.[89] A lynching that did not happen ended in a rifle skirmish at the freedmen's settlement of Kellyville, a few miles southeast of Jefferson in Marion County on August 8, 1920, just a few months after the Arthur brothers burned at the stake in Paris. The affair began with a disagreement between young McKinley "Buck" Beal and a white girl over the purchase of a watermelon. He agreed to buy the watermelon for a dime, but she refused to give him his rightful change and thrust the dollar down the front of her dress. Beal's unwise attempt to recover his money triggered loud screams from the girl, then a shotgun blast from an elderly white woman, and at that point Buck ran for his life.

Back at the farm of Alf Beal in Kellyville, Buck told his story, and his family—knowing full well what was about to happen—prepared to defend themselves against the inevitable white mob. They placed a dummy to draw fire, and Alf Beal and his sons armed themselves with rifles and took up firing positions in, around, and under the house and outbuildings. Several cars of whites soon roared up. Their passengers jumped out, shot at the dummy, and began to take deadly fire from the Beals. Sheriff Will Terry arrived immediately thereafter, just in time to haul a carload of wounded vigilantes back to town. The mob asked to parley, Buck crawled out from under an outbuilding, and his brother Manse shot him dead. Presumably, Manse Beal did this to save the rest of his family from the mob and to save Buck from the horrible fate of burning alive. At this point the mob retreated. Besides Buck, one white man died the next day and another was crippled for life, but nothing ever was done about the matter, which was hushed up. Local law enforcement officials filed no charges. After a time, overcome with guilt about what had happened, the white girl admitted her role in the tragedy and soon went insane, spending the rest of her days in the Austin State Hospital.[90]

Two years later a violent chain of events at Freestone County also ended in an attack on a freedmen's settlement. Teen-aged Eula Ausley turned up missing in May of 1922, and searchers found her body. She had been viciously murdered—stripped, violated with a stick, and stomped and beaten to death. Soon a posse led by first-term sheriff Horace Mayo scoured the countryside. At about the time that the sheriff began to suspect John Hill, a former white neighbor of Eula Ausley's grandfather, of murdering the girl, his out-of-control posse predictably turned on local blacks. Over the sheriff's weak protests, whites seized three men, cut off their genitals, ears, and noses, tied them to a iron-wheeled riding plow at the town of Kirvin, and burned them alive.[91]

Klansmen and other racial avengers had rushed in from surrounding counties, but many failed to arrive in time for the lynching. Now, having tasted blood, the mob of locals and outsiders began a month-long reign of terror among Freestone County's black community. They murdered black men caught abroad in the countryside and shot into people's homes at night; an unknown number of local African Americans died in this pogromlike aftermath to the Kirvin lynching. With little or no protection from the law, black people remained in their homes, avoided all travel, and stayed away from windows and from lamps at night. Some families left their houses after dark to sleep in the woods. Doubtless others moved closer to trusted white employers, friends, and protectors. Meanwhile, local newspaper accounts of the lynching and its continuing aftermath were full of lies and omissions, as editors tried to prevent further violence, defend the community against outside criticism, and protect important local whites from the consequences of their actions.

Nearly a month after the triple lynching, a twenty-two-year-old black man named Leroy Gibson believed things had calmed down enough to allow him to visit his girlfriend at Kirvin. Gibson came from one of the black families on John King's farm, and he must have believed this affiliation with a powerful white landowner would protect him. He soon found out otherwise, escaping Kirvin on the run with a bullet wound in his leg. Then Gibson went for sanctuary to the only place he knew to go—the freedmen's settlement of Simsboro, nine miles from Kirvin, where his grandparents and other relatives lived.

Early on the morning of June 2, 1922, Leroy Gibson's relatives heard him singing the Twenty-third Psalm from a field across from their house. Perhaps he feared that whites might already be in Simsboro and chose to test the waters in this way? In any case the psalm proved appropriate. Gibson's relatives helped him, but the white mob showed up on the afternoon of June 3, took the wounded Leroy from the house, and riddled him with bullets in a nearby field. Thirteen-year-old Lutisia Gibson, Leroy's niece, recalled that the mob seemed to depart, but when her brother, Allie Gibson, took a rifle and left to check on his mother, a white ambushed him and shot him down at the gate. At that point, Floyd Gibson, Allie's uncle and a World War I veteran, rushed out, grabbed Allie's gun, threw himself down in the prone rifle position, and began to fire on the mob. Lutisia Gibson explained, "Uncle Floyd said, 'Oh, they done shot Allie.' He went and picked up Allie's gun and just leveled it, and we don't know how many he killed. With that rifle he just laid down and just began to shoot. He'd been in the army, and they'd taught him to shoot laying down. He was an expert with the rifle. He only stopped because he ran out of shells."[92]

After that, the Simsboro families stayed home and prepared to defend their community; they had nowhere else to go. The white mob had fled, probably carrying a dead man, a dying man, and several wounded. (Though this would be entirely suppressed, and the Simsboro incident completely distorted in the local newspaper.) As Lutisia said, "Everybody was scared. We were scared to stay home and scared to leave."

Then, something very significant began to happen—armed blacks from outside the Simsboro community, perhaps relatives, arrived to help defend Simsboro. Foster Foreman, then a boy working on a nearby cotton farm, witnessed armed men rolling into the freedmen's settlement by the wagonload. "It didn't matter who they was," Foreman recalled, "if they was white, the people down here was gonna shoot them. They was barricaded in the bushes. They weren't out in the road. There would be a group here, and you'd go another half a mile and there'd be another group. If you got by this, that other'n was gonna get you."[93]

After word of the Simsboro confrontation got out, whites gathered at Kirvin and angrily paraded in the streets, but somehow the crowd never got around to going to Simsboro to get the rifle-carrying blacks out of the bushes. A day passed, then another, and the red haze of the racial pogrom began to dissipate in Freestone County. People came to their senses as from a bad dream. Important citizens spoke out against the violence, Sheriff Mayo made law-and-order speeches, and the KKK members and other recreational racists from outside the county began to drift home to wives and families.

After the Simsboro incident, World War I veteran Floyd Gibson immediately departed Texas to spend the rest of his life in Washington State, returning secretly only once. The attack on Simsboro and the triple burning and racial murders haunted Kirvin for decades—not that people talked about these things very much. When Lutisia Gibson told the story of the attack on Simsboro to researcher Monte Akers, her grown children had not heard it before.

Monte Akers believed that Floyd Gibson had served in the much-decorated 36th Colored Infantry, which fought in Europe under French officers and marched down Harlem streets through cheering crowds just before disbanding. In Gibson, the worst Jim Crow fears of the black rifleman home from France and accustomed to killing white men had come true.

CHAPTER SEVEN

Decline and
Remembrance

Whites received a good many surprises at freedmen's settlements over the years. Elelia Upshaw, wife of an older brother of N. E. Upshaw, walked her property one day in 1938 when two white man came by, one of them named Buck Bradshaw. They saw a calf that Luther and Elelia Upshaw owned and asked her what she wanted for it. It was not for sale, she told them, and this refusal of a white request immediately provoked the two men. Blacks in Jim Crow times were not supposed to say no to whites, even on their own land at a remote freedmen's settlement. Bradshaw offered five dollars for the calf, but Elelia again refused. At that point he told her she had only two options — sell it to them or they would take it. Once again, Elelia Upshaw declined to sell the calf, and when the men began to catch it they discovered she had a third option — firing both barrels of her shotgun.

The boom of the shotgun set in motion a chain of events leading to the establishment of County Line's California enclave. Elelia Upshaw shot hastily, so only a few pellets struck home, slightly wounding one of the white men in the mouth. After the whites fled the community, County Line residents got their guns and took up defensive positions to repel attackers, while Elelia Upshaw hid in the woods. But after a day or so it became obvious that the angry whites had made the same choice as the Kirvin mob. Nacogdoches County sheriff's deputies began to visit the community, inquiring about Elelia Upshaws's whereabouts, but Luther Upshaw said he did not know where his wife was. After a while, Luther got the help of a white friend in Lilbert, who contacted a white lawyer in Nacogdoches on the Upshaws' behalf. Elelia turned herself in, pled guilty, and received a two-year suspended sentence for her use of excessive force in repelling cattle rustlers. Elelia Upshaw had visited her probation officer only twice when the man told her she did not need to come back. At that point Elelia immediately moved to

Monel Upshaw, younger brother of Luther Upshaw. Unlike Luther, Monel remained at County Line for the rest of his life. (Richard Orton)

California, not to return to County Line for over thirty years. Doubtless the shotgunned whites nursed bitter grievances, and Elelia's continued presence in County Line perhaps endangered other Upshaws. Luther Upshaw soon followed his wife to "the Golden State," the first of many County Line residents to do so. Over the years, Luther and Elelia's home often served as first stop and temporary residence for people relocating to the West Coast.[1]

Already by World War I times, most freedmen's settlements had developed expatriate communities in larger Texas cities or in northern or West Coast cities. Freedmen's settlements often failed to expand beyond the original landholdings, and property fragmented across the generations until farms became too few or too small to support everyone. While some younger family members stayed behind, others moved to nearby county-seat towns or to major urban areas. Links to what one man called "the plant bed" remained, however—ties never to be broken so long as the freedmen's settlement persisted.[2] People returned home every year to community reunions and revivals, even from distant Oakland or Chicago. Sons and daughters born in the city made summer visits to country cousins, uncles, and aunts, and sometimes the country cousins made reciprocal visits. Letters and packages passed back and forth between city and countryside.[3]

After 1930, Texas freedmen's settlements became caught up in the general decline of black rural population that took place all across the South. Many factors contributed to this, including land fragmentation, soil exhaustion, boll weevil incursions, stock laws, and federal programs of the Depression years, which negatively impacted renters and small landowners. Most freedmen's settlements weathered the storm despite the loss of population, but for the Crown community of Atacosca County a boll weevil attack during the 1937 crop season proved the final straw.[4] The community disbanded. Other marginal communities died soon after the arrival of good roads, which finally replaced often impassible dirt tracks into nearby white market towns and facilitated people's moves first into public work, then into town.[5] Other settlements merged into the ever-expanding urban areas of Houston, Dallas, Austin, and other cities.[6]

The coming of stock laws closing the woods to poor people's cattle and hogs hit many communities especially hard, including Boykin in Angelina County. Residents had relied on the old free-range rights to help fill the economic gap left after the cultivation of sandyland cotton.[7] In poor crop years, hunting, fishing, foraging, tie making, and half-wild hogs and cattle roaming pine woods and bottoms allowed communities like Boykin to survive. Boykin pioneers Jim Boykin and Jim Runnels owned only a few hundred acres each, but they ranged stock across thousands of acres of unfenced woods. Helen Darden's mother was present when white friends visited Jim Runnels to advise him to buy all the additional land he could. A day soon approached when Runnels would not be able to even "break a riding switch" from another man's property, a visitor predicted. No longer would Runnels's hogs fatten themselves on other people's acorns or his sons cut railroad ties from other people's trees.[8]

During the 1940s, the white men's prediction came true, and barbed-wire perimeter fences and "No Trespassing" signs rose up all across southern Angelina County, but the war years had even more significant effects on Texas freedmen's settlements. Many rural people, black and white, now went into military service or war industry work, never to return to the countryside. Texas experienced little decline in black rural population until around 1930, but then the state's population declined more rapidly than almost anywhere else in the South. Between 1930 and 1940, 3.9 percent of black Southerners left the countryside, a figure that included 13.9 percent of black Texans. The war decade of 1940–1950 saw the biggest drop in black rural population—27.5 percent in the South as a whole, 47.3 percent in Texas. Sixty-four rural counties in eastern Texas lost black population during the decade, mostly to Texas cities, not to cities of the North.[9]

Black landowners resisted the move to town, and there had been a lot of them—12,513 heads of households in 1890. By 1910 no less than 31 percent of black Texas farmers owned land. The general percentage of African American landownership in the lower South during that year, including Texas, stood at 20 percent. Across the South as a whole, black farmers owned over 15 million acres in this peak year of 1910—a remarkable achievement, considering the obstacles to land ownership faced by freedmen and the sons and daughters of freedmen.[10]

In truth, southern blacks probably owned and had the use of more land than the official high-water mark of 15 million acres, since census takers often ignored purely subsistence farms, and lands in the possession of squatters were not enumerated. After the stock laws began to be strongly enforced during the 1940s, the squatter settlements of Lewis's Bend in Refugio County and Evergreen in Titus County (and doubtless other places) finally began to disperse, having barely registered on the official censuses or county tax rolls.[11]

Between 1910 and 1990, official black landholdings in the South fell from 15 million acres to 1.1 million acres, and many a painful family story resided behind those figures.[12] As noted above, various social and economic factors operated against survival of the small family farm, black or white, and sheer poverty often drove rural people to sell out and move to town. Blacks at freedmen's settlements, however, often valued the land above all else and hung on to it until the bitter end, which often came after whites also began to value their land. As Deborah Hoskins noted of the freedmen's settlements of Gregg County: "Black people had carved their autonomy from 'free spaces,' weak points in a white power structure that whites had not yet shored up, places where whites were not looking, sites that had not yet become important enough to the preservation of privilege that whites cared what blacks did there."[13] Gradually, however, with the passing of time, lands of freedmen's settlements became more valuable and less "free spaces," and by fair transaction, legal trickery, or coercion, most of them passed into white hands. This became emphatically true in Gregg County after 1928 and the arrival of the East Texas Oil Field, as Hoskins noted. Great oil wealth lay under the sandyland farms of these freedmen's settlements, and every black land deed came under predatory legal scrutiny.[14]

Some land was lost by black carelessness and inertia, though white land speculators lurked in every courthouse town, waiting to take advantage. A black landowner who offered his land as collateral for a loan from an unknown white took a huge chance. The creditor might bide his time, lie low while a few payments were missed, then foreclose on the valuable property. Some white "Snopeses" went around setting these traps for blacks almost as a business sideline, and many people were dispossessed by this entirely legal means. Wary of white lawyers and complicated documents, black landowners often died intestate, thus fragmenting their land among numerous children, a few of which might sell out at this point. After another generation had passed, with one or two other part owners also dying without wills and passing on their land claims to multiple heirs, properties became hopelessly entangled, with many part owners residing elsewhere. By this point the family land was very vulnerable. If any of the multiple owners failed to pay their taxes and other owners failed to fill the gap, the land might be taken by the county and sold, often to one of the white courthousewatchers. If any of the multiple owners—aged, sick, deranged, or financially needy—sold a speculator his claim to the land, the buyer could petition a judge for a legal procedure called a partition sale. Partition sales put the land on the market to the highest bidder, more often than not the land speculator who had begun the process. Such lands often sold well below market value, and a great many black acreages passed into the hands of whites by this route, also entirely legal.[15]

Legal trickery was much more common than illegal coercion in the taking of black property, though coercion certainly occurred. Black landowners at Hunt County in 1920 told interviewers that KKK members had visited them by night and ordered them to sell their land and move out of the area. They had done this in entirely legal transactions, but not of their own volition.[16] A black Mississippian complained in 1913, "If we own a good farm or horse, or cow, or bird-dog, or yoke of oxen, we are harassed until we are bound to sell, give away, or run away before we have any peace in our lives."[17] The attack on black landowners south of Slocum, on the Houston-Anderson county line, in 1910, and the KKK-led assault on Rosewood, Florida, in 1923 seem to have had their economic sides, since whites subsequently got the black properties.[18]

Legal trickery was the norm, however, and often the crudest kind sufficed at a time when blacks had no real recourse in local courts, and no white jury would take a black man's word over that of a white man. An illiterate Houston County man signed a purchase agreement for a plot of land and paid money on it for many years before finding out it was only a rental agreement. "When you can't read and write, then you is looking to be cheated," a Hopkins County man affirmed, telling of a Sand Field neighbor who went to the bank to make the final payment on his farm, only to have the banker inform him the interest had been miscalculated and he must pay on the property three more years.[19] In Sunflower County, Mississippi, a white land speculator got around blacks-only deed restrictions placed on forty-acre plots sold to freedmen by using a black stand-in. The man bought several plots from original freedmen purchasers, then resold to the specula-tor.[20] As in this case, black cheaters also stalked landowner's properties. In Jasper County, Nellie Forward worked with her siblings in the wash house and cotton field for years to accumulate money to buy a small farm around 1880. However, sometime later their deed burned in a house fire, and they did not know how to replace it. Soon thereafter, a young black man named McRay "come fooling around me and making love to me, and he find out we don't have no deed no more, and he claimed the farm and took it away from us, and leave me with a little baby boy that I named Joe Millie McRay."[21]

In Freestone County, freedman Anderson Willis's 3,000 acres was "too much land for a nigger," whites had said. According to Willis's descendants, he was defrauded out of his land in 1904. As a *Dallas Times Herald* reporter wrote, their 1984 lawsuit alleged "that promissory notes were forged, pledg-ing the land as collateral. The family claims that negotiable notes passed through several hands before banker John Riley foreclosed on the land and had it sold by the county sheriff at public auction." Several of Willis's signa-tures appeared on key documents about the land, though the ex-slave could not read and write, and no other signatures by him were known. The *Dallas Times Herald* reporter continued, "[Loraine] Watson said that her father and other Willis descendants years ago had tried several times to document the loss of the family land, but they weren't allowed to view land records in the county courthouse because of their race and because they couldn't find a local lawyer to handle their case."[22]

Apparently what happened to Anderson Willis's land was far from un-usual. In an eighteen-month investigation reported in 2001, Associated Press researchers documented "a pattern in which black Americans were cheated out of their land or driven from it through intimidation, violence, and even murder. In some cases, government officials approved the land takings; in others; they took part in them." The AP researchers interviewed over 1,000 people and examined thousands of public records in a study of "107 land takings in 13 Southern and border states." In these cases alone, 406 black landowners lost more than 24,000 acres of farm and timber lands, plus 85 smaller properties. Besides these, reporters found evidence of many more land seizures that could not be fully documented because of gaps in the pub-lic records. Fifty-seven of the land takings studied had involved violence.[23]

AP reporters generalized, "The true extent of land takings from black families will never be known because of gaps in public records, deed books with pages torn from them, and records that had been crudely altered." An extreme case of record tampering involved the rather common event of southern courthouse arson, as at Paulding, Mississippi, on September 10, 1932. KKK groups had been harassing black landowners from their lands for some time in the eastern half of Jasper County, then mostly settled by African Americans. Whites' burning of the courthouse and its black land deeds greatly facilitated the process, including the resale of thousands of acres of formerly African American land to a local timber company.[24]

In Jim Crow times, the more a black man owned, the more he had to worry about. No wonder some landowners avoided all debts to whites, or that Andrew Eleby's prosperous grandfather pulled entirely off the road to let white men pass, or that the richest black man in Sunflower County, Mississippi, declined to walk into Indianola shaded by an "uppity" umbrella. Little things meant a lot in the time of Jim Crow, and black landowners walked a fine line. Prosperous mulatto farmer Anthony Crawford of Abbeville, South Carolina, took a wagon of cotton into town one day in 1916, spoke a harsh word to a white mercantile store owner while haggling over the sale of cotton seed, and ended up lynched by sundown. Nor did Crawford's wife and children manage to keep his fine 427-acre cotton farm in the months thereafter. A bank seized the land for an unpaid debt and sold it to a white man for a fraction of its actual value. Anthony Crawford seems to have been one of those prosperous black farmers that commanded increased respect from whites, but once he made a Jim Crow mistake, poor whites and the economic elite swiftly joined forces to strip him of his life and inappropriate wealth.[25] According to Loren Schweninger, a University of North Carolina expert on black landownership, for many decades successful blacks "lived with a gnawing fear that white neighbors could at any time do something violent and take everything from them." Ray Winbush, director of Fisk University's Race Relations Institute went even further, telling the AP reporters, "If you're looking for stolen black land, just follow the lynching trail."[26]

Black landowners in freedmen's settlements had a greater measure of protection from direct white aggression. Such places were defensive communities, where black property owners had circled the wagons against outsiders—a "fortress without walls," one historian called the Georgia community he studied.[27] At every community, properties might from time to time be lost to whites because of failure to pay taxes or to keep up loan payments, but usually the whites sold the lands back to other African Americans. Freedmen's settlements were black enclaves that kept to themselves, and until the end of Jim Crow few whites wished—or dared—to live there.

During the 1940s and 1950s, and into the early 1960s, the rural black population of Texas ebbed away into urban areas, but most freedmen's

settlements maintained a diminished community life. A hard core of old-
timers clung to the land and resisted moves to town. "Integration" held no
charms for some people in the freedmen's settlements, who still felt the same
way as freedman Garrison Frazier in 1864, who informed U.S. Secretary of
War Stanton that "we would prefer to live by ourselves rather than scattered
among the whites."[28]

"When the school dies, the community dies," was the old country saying,
and during the 1950s and 1960s community patriots who felt like Garrison
Frazier joined forces with white segregationists to expand freedmen's settlement schools. In virtually every county in eastern Texas, certain freedmen's
settlement schools developed into proud rural high schools — in the beginning with money from the Rosenwald and Slater funds, then with money
from nearby white independent school districts, which viewed such schools
as great places to send their black students (and avoid integration).

In Houston County the relationship between Center Grove School and
Lovelady Independent School District was typical. Center Grove began
around 1926 as a consolidation of the two one-room freedmen's settlement
schools of Smith Grove and Center Hill, and over time Center Grove ab-
sorbed several other freedmen's settlement schools. Center Grove, now one
of the black schools of Lovelady ISD, continued to develop. Principal W. C.
Smith, a native of Smith Grove, persuaded the Lovelady school board to
sponsor a new gym in 1950, a football program in 1954, and a band in
1955. Around 1960, Lovelady closed its black school in town and began to
bus all black students in the district out to Center Grove — a move that
staved off full integration of schools at Lovelady until the late date of 1969.
W. C. Smith of Center Grove led local blacks through this inevitable integration, which not all of them preferred. Smith himself integrated Lovelady High School administration as its first black "vice-principal" (a special
title). Soon, at the request of parents of both races, the legendary coach
took charge of the new integrated girls' basketball team.[29]

This same pattern repeated itself at many other places across eastern
Texas, born of the same uneasy alliance between freedmen's settlement
patriots and white segregationists in town. In Nacogdoches County, Winter's Hill School began as a one-room school of rough lumber in the freedmen's settlement of that name. Then it became a two-room school, built
with Rosenwald Fund assistance, and, after consolidation with Douglass
ISD, it became the new five-room black school of Douglass, which now
shut down its own black school and bused all students out to the freedmen's
settlement. Around 1960 a scant few years before forced integration, Douglass ISD demonstrated its commitment to this arrangement by building a

new six-teacher brick school for Winter's Hill after the old wooden school burned.[30]

The freedmen's settlements that consolidated into Center Point, Winter's Hill, and similar large rural schools did so with mixed feelings. Vistula, Post Oak, Thankful, and Fodice lost their own schools when they consolidated with Center Point, but at least they still sent their children to an independent black community where blacks—more or less—ran their own show. Community vitality lost by the demise of home schools coalesced at other freedmen's settlements, which flourished with special vigor into the 1960s.

Such a place was Center Point in Camp County and Neylandville in Hunt County, the home of Saint Paul's School of Common School District No. 53.[31] Saint Paul's had begun as a simple freedmen's settlement school in the late nineteenth century, but it got money from the Rosenwald and Slater funds and developed into a rural high school and county training school. By 1943, although still operating in a common school district with all-black trustees, Saint Paul's had become the dominant black secondary school of Hunt County and beyond. Saint Paul's featured well-paid and well-educated teachers and the only "full high school department" of the area's black schools. In fact, most other Hunt County black schools had closed their doors and bused students to Saint Paul's. Eighty-seven students resided in the district, and 223 transferred in, for a total enrollment of 310. Some of Saint Paul's bus routes ran over one hundred miles, round trip, bringing students from adjoining counties. Primarily because of the growth and success of Saint Paul's, only three other black schools still operated in Hunt County in 1943, two small schools at the far edges of the county and one in Greenville, the county seat. Commerce, Wolf City, and other white market towns now chose to bus all or most of their black scholars to Saint Paul's.

This compromise between flourishing Saint Paul's School and economy-minded white segregationists in Hunt County's common school districts and town ISDs lasted into the 1960s, when Saint Paul's met the fate of other such schools. Whites liked having most county blacks lumped together over at Neylandville, but they did not want to pay more money to maintain this arrangement, and the Saint Paul's school district found it more and more difficult to collect local taxes. Perhaps times were hard, or perhaps many Neylandville taxpayers now disliked paying money to preserve this patriotic segregation. In any case, only about 20 percent of Neylandville's residents still paid their school taxes. With not enough money, Saint Paul's physical plant fell into disrepair, and the Texas Education Agency, having looked the other way at violations of state requirements for decades,

Abandoned classroom in Fodice's rock school building. For some years after consolidation, Fodice residents used the former school as a community center. (Richard Orton)

found that it could no longer do so. The TEA issued ultimatums, and Saint Paul's School consolidated into unhappy Commerce ISD in 1965.[32] Probably some black people at Neylandville approved of this belated integration, but others did not. Ellis Brigham, great-great-grandson of the community's founder, freedman Jim Brigham, told a *Dallas Morning News* reporter: "Integration hurt us. When you've got an all-black community and you pull the only school out, you break the backbone of the community." Blacks at Saint Paul's had been free to do things their own way. Lenel Lee, longtime Neylandville resident, said, "We didn't pledge allegiance to the flag, we would start the day singing the black national anthem, 'Lift Ev'ry Voice and Sing,'" the song written by James Weldon Johnson for Lincoln's birthday celebration in 1900.[33]

Even after the last school consolidations of the 1960s, a hard core of long-term residents held the line at many Texas freedmen's settlements. Death of the school did not bring about the immediate death of the community, despite the old saying. Family land yet remained, and for some the landhold lasted for life. Lenel Lee observed, "Land is like a birthright. Once you relinquish your land, you're at the mercy of other people. We were brought up to be independent. We never believed in renting."[34] Larry Leonard at Cedar Branch in Houston County felt the same way. Now elderly and retired, he stayed home, contributed money for a Texas Historical Commission marker for the Cedar Branch church (which still baptized people in Leonard's stock pond), and persisted in his efforts to get white county commissioners to pave the road.[35] At Wheeler Springs in Houston County, teacher Lula Denby Dailey continued her attempts to sustain and revitalize the community until she died in 1976. In 1960 Dailey worked with the Texas Extension Service to recycle the abandoned school, cannery, and log sewing hut as a Wheeler Springs community center, serving on the board of this community improvement project until her death. Then, in 1978, Dailey's former assistant, Wesley Taylor Fobbs, recycled the old buildings yet again, this time to assist senior citizens by preparing and delivering two hot meals a day and by accumulating used furniture and clothing for redistribution. Fobbs also organized the planting of a community garden for the elderly very near the site where Lula Denby Dailey had raised food for the schoolchildren of Wheeler Springs.[36]

As community populations declined, members of the old guard like Fobbs, Dailey, Leonard, and Lee played important roles in organizing the summer community reunions and revivals. At Woodville, Dora Session Griffith lived on twenty-six acres of family land, paid taxes for herself and all the rest of the numerous part owners, and organized two annual family reunions for the two sides of her family, as requested by her father just before his death. The family reunions also served as general community reunions for Woodville people.[37] Not far away in Houston County, only six families still lived in Germany in 1990, but some among them organized the Community Reunion in June, the Berryman Family Reunion in July, and the Church Homecoming in September, when many people returned to the community from distant cities.[38]

These reunions were a special time, when seemingly abandoned communities filled with people as "old friends and family members, separated by time and distance, were drawn together again in a spiritual collective which endured all human trials."[39] At its summer reunion, the area between Vistula's old graveyard and its now defunct church usually filled with cars and people, many of them with out-of-state license plates.[40] Communities like Pelham and St. John Colony in Caldwell County staged even more exuberant reunions—in St. John's case, incorporating an annual wagon-train reenactment of the founding families' move from Webberville on the Colorado River to St. John's post-oak wilderness.

Leota Upshaw, daughters, and other relatives leave Leota's home to attend the annual homecoming service of the County Line Missionary Baptist Church, 1991. (Richard Orton)

Leota Upshaw visits with a friend in front of her house during County Line's homecoming, 1991. (Richard Orton)

The demise of church congregations often signaled the real death of a community, or at least the beginning of that death. In 2001 Jessie Mae Amie reported that one church at her home settlement of Lake Creek in Houston County was defunct and the other one in precipitous decline and that she was one of the last black residents of the community. Amie recounted other ominous (and familiar) omens of the bitter end of community—cleared fields reverting to woods, whites buying black land, and packs of coyotes prowling closer at night. Even the weather had changed for the worse, she thought.[41] The squatter settlement of Lewis's Bend in Refugio County had begun a long decline from World War II, ending when people moved the community church out of the San Antonio River bottoms. A former resident noted:

When they moved the church in Lewis's Bend out on the prairie, the people didn't like it at all. It ruined the feelin' of goin' in those trees for church. Black people love shade trees and the river, and the spirit was lost when they moved out of the bottom.

Nowhere else was like the Bends. Any distance from there was another world.[42]

Jenks Branch community began with the arrival of three Miller brothers to Williamson County from Rock Hill, South Carolina, after the Civil War, and it ended when Manual Miller lost the last fifty-five acres of family land for nonpayment of Georgetown ISD school taxes in 1989. Miller eulogized the death of Jenks Branch in these words: "We turned out some great men—doctors, lawyers, a professor down at Austin, a preacher who had churches all over Oklahoma. Everybody helped each other with a living. If I were younger I'd be real sad about losing that place because I wouldn't know any better, [but] I'm too old to feel bitter. It didn't seem real fair, but I feel like I've been set free. I've got my mind on another direction of looking, east, west, and straight up to the Kingdom of the Lord where I'm going next."[43]

Other places had produced more than their share of "great men"—a treasurer of the United States (Azie Taylor Morton) from St. John Colony, a National Merit Scholar and the first black student to enter Rice University from Center Grove, among many others. Black folklorist John Mason Brewer had come from Cologne, a nearly defunct community by the time Frederick Young penned its 1970 epitaph. "Gone are those days, and the great singing, praying, and witnessing Christians are forever departed," Young wrote. "No children are being born. We are all old people. The young people have deserted the village for the great cities of the country and of the world. Cologne has become the 'deserted village' of our day."[44]

At Wilson Creek in Matagorda County, Courtney L. Grigsby's landhold had passed into the hands of others, church congregations had disbanded, and even the graveyards were grown up in brush. The story of the mixed-race community founded by red-haired Frenchman Antoine Deadrick and his mulatto wife Mary Washington had been almost forgotten. Grigsby wrote in his memoir, "Another Matagorda County History":

> What Wilson Creek land that does remain in the family is no longer being lived on by any of Antoine's descendants as of this writing. Wire is rusting where it is held in place on sagging fence posts, held loosely by staples hammered in decades past. Lilies bloom and wilt among weeds. Where once picnics were held, gates no longer open and shut. Cities host the hopes and dreams of Antoine's grandchildren. The graveyards lie unattended, the bones that they hold in their bosom are losing their names. Property paid for with toil and troubled brows has been sold or lost to taxes. Such is change, as constant as the winds, as relentless as aging.[45]

However, as some Texas freedmen's settlements passed entirely away during the 1980s and 1990s, other surviving settlements quickened ever so slightly with new life. A few young families drifted back to the ancestral communities, and faithful attendees of summer reunions returned to family land or bought back into communities at retirement. County Line, Weeping Mary, Pelham, St. John Colony, and other places reached their lowest ebb, then began a slow increase in population. New brick homes sprang up along the highway at St. John in Caldwell County and Post Oak in Lee County. The descendants of Anderson Willis lost their 1984 lawsuit to recover stolen family land, but by 1990 1,100 acres of the lost 3,000 already had been repurchased by family members.[46] At Woodville in Cherokee County, Alvin Carter finally completed his long quest to recover full title to his mother's 117 acres, previously scattered among 172 heirs. Carter had corresponded with relatives in California and New York and sought them out at community reunions for nine years to accomplish this.[47]

Helena Brown Patton, granddaughter of freedman community founder Ben Brown of Sand Hill in Nacogdoches County, retired to East Texas after a life spent at Michigan, California, Germany, and other places. She had been born in Sand Hill in 1922.[48] At County Line, Marion Upshaw, grandson of freedman Guss Upshaw, purchased seventy acres once part of great-

Community founder Jim Upshaw's house at County Line, 1998. (Richard Orton)

*Younger Upshaw relatives converse near barbecue rig during
County Line's 1997 homecoming. (Richard Orton)*

Leota Upshaw mows her yard at County Line in 1990. Although in poor health, Leota still resided in the community in 2003. (Richard Orton)

uncle Jim Upshaw's land. Upshaw bought this property for the clear spring that once served as County Line's drinking water, the foundation of Uncle Jim's steam mill, and the small log structure still showing the marks of Jim Upshaw's broad ax. Upshaw hoped that his children would bond with this land he felt so strongly about and where he felt the presence of his dead father and mother every time he visited.[49] At Weeping Mary in Cherokee County, deputy sheriff James Green had returned from his previous career as a Houston policemen. Old-timers like Bessie Mae Parker bemoaned the decline of community spirit at Weeping Mary, where "No one rings the church bell now," but Green noted signs of community vitality in the big summer reunions, church services held twice a month, and the largest youth group membership of any congregation in the area.[50]

A few communities actually came back from the dead. Antioch Colony in Hays County had disappeared from the map by 1955, with most of the property sold to whites or lost after taxes went unpaid by absentee owners. Antioch began around 1870, when a white man named Joseph F. Rosley bought 490 acres west of Onion Creek for exclusive sale to blacks. At its peak around 1920, Antioch had a church, school, syrup mill, and 150 to 200 residents. Antioch's family farms were small, but residents raised what cotton they could, practiced the usual subsistence austerities, and worked for

Monel and Leota Upshaw's daughters, joined by Cline Wade, sing gospel music during the County Line homecoming, 1991. (Richard Orton)

whites in nearby Buda. They ran their own small farms while they share-cropped, built fences, dug ditches, did stone masonry, and hoed and picked cotton. The community dwindled away after 1930 for the usual reasons until it became entirely deserted.[51]

Then an improbable rebirth began. The black landhold at Antioch Colony had shrunken to 10.5 acres, left behind when the Harper family moved to Arizona in 1955, but in 1978 Winnie Martha Harper Moyer returned to Antioch. As the years passed, her parents and twin sister, Minnie Mary Harper Nelson, joined her, followed by five other sisters, one brother, one great-granddaughter, and four grandnephews and grandnieces. Other former residents also began to return.

Emily Harper Hill, who was seventy-three in 2000, explained, "It's just nice and quiet and in the country, the way I was raised up." Despite spending all their adult lives elsewhere, those who returned said that they had always considered it home. "This is my roots, my history," said LeeDell Bunton, who had not lived in Antioch since he was nine years old, but who purchased 7.1 acres along Black Colony Road in 1996. Bunton was one of the leaders of the return. He organized the first Antioch reunion of the new era, attended in 2000 by 300 people, and he helped in reestablishing the Antioch church.[52]

Bunton's seven acres, purchased for $13,900, were part of the forty-five acres that his great-great-grandparents, Dave and Mary Bunton, bought from Joseph Rosley in the early 1870s. Bunton often visited the Antioch property from his home in Phoenix and planned to retire there. He liked to walk the land, observing the marks of the past still visible: the old overgrown wagon roads; the limestone springs where his ancestors' horses drank long ago; the rusted chain used for stringing up hogs at hog-killing time, now half embedded in the gnarled branch of a live oak; wild sage planted for medicinal tea; and the white day lilies that still bloomed at the house site of his great-grandmother, Kate Bunton, though every other visible trace of her house had disappeared.

"It would be a shame to erase this and never know it was here," LeeDell Bunton told an Austin reporter. "We're not saying it's right or wrong. We're just saying we should never forget. For those who own property now, they should try to hold onto it, so 100 years from now their great-grandchildren can tell their children, 'This is where our beginnings were after slavery.' I think that means something. It should mean something to everybody."[53]

Appendix

FREEDMEN'S SETTLEMENTS AND OTHER
RURAL AFRICAN AMERICAN LANDOWNER
COMMUNITIES, BY COUNTY

This is a "working" list and probably contains some communities that might be deleted after an exhaustive on-site study of local sources. Also, the list is doubtless incomplete.

Alternate community names (and alternate spellings) follow in parentheses. A single asterisk (*) indicates a description of that community in *The New Handbook of Texas* (as updated online, June 2003). A double asterisk (**) indicates a marker file for that community name (or the name given) in the marker research files of the Texas Historical Commission, Austin, Texas. Identification of a community by the respective county historical commission is indicated by a dagger (†).

ANDERSON

Bosman* (Bozman), Davenport*, Beulah, Flint Hill*, Sand Flat*, Tucker* (Green Bay), Union Hope Church*

ANGELINA

Boykin

ATASCOSA

Crown* (Lagunillas)

BASTROP

Alum Creek, Cedar Creek*, Center Union*, Colorado*, Crafts Prairie†, Flower Hill*, Hills Prairie†, Hopewell†, Lone Star*, Pleasant Grove*, St. Mary's Colony*, Saint Litton, Salem*

BELL

Sampson Hill*

BLANCO

Peyton* (Peyton Colony, Boardhouse)

BOSQUE

Bibles Hill†, Rock Springs* (The Colony), Wash Lock Hill (Westpoint)†

BOWIE

Beaver Dam*, Cedar Grove (Born), Garland's Colony

BRAZORIA

Anchor, Cedar Grove*, Chenango, Green Hill*, Jerusalem*, Lake Jackson*, Latonia*, Linnville*, Mims*, St. Paul

BRAZOS

Mudville* (Steele's Store), Wellborn

BURLESON

Teals Prairie, Tunis, Yellow Prairie

CALDWELL

St. John Colony*/** (Wynn's Colony)

CAMP

Center Point*, Harvard* (Harvard Switch), Living Green*, Miller Grove*, Myrtle Springs*, Rocky Mound*, West Chapel

CASS

Bethlehem, Nickleberry*, Shiloh

CHAMBERS

Black Branch (Babylon), Double Bayou

CHEROKEE

Blounts Chapel (Blunts Chapel), Bulah*, Church Hill (Churchill), Cuney*/** (Andy), Delmer†, Elm Grove, Holly Springs†, Lost Ball†, Macedonia, Mount Comfort*, Mount Haven, Mount Olive*, New Hope, Old Larissa, Pine Grove, Pine Hill, Pleasant Plains*, Pleasant View†, Shady Grove, St. Thomas Chapel*, Rock Hill*, Sweet Union* (Hog Jaw), Weeping Mary*, Woodville (Black Ankle)

CORYELL

Lincolnville*

DELTA

Cross Roads* (Union, Clem, Hog Wallow), Friendship*

DEWITT

Hopkinsville*/**, Lockart†, Pleasantville*, Westville*

FALLS

Big Creek, Highbank, Spring Hill

FAYETTE

Armstrong Colony, Cozy Corner†

FISHER

Center* (Center Point)

FORT BEND

Dewalt*, Kendleton*/**, Pointers*, Powell Point*

FREESTONE

Beulah†, Bethlehem†, Board Bottom†, Brown's Creek (Titus Farm)†, Carter's Place (Grove Island)†, Coutchman†, Davis Chapel†, Frazier†, Gibson Chapel*†, Grove Island*†, Hopewell, Jerusalem†, Jones Academy†, Keechi†, Lake Creek†, Landsville†, Lee*†, Lepan†, Lone Star†, Lookout†, Lynnville†, Mount Livingston†, Mount Pleasant†, Myrtle Grove†, Patterson Prairie†, Pine Top†, Plum Creek*, Post Oak* (Post-oak, Post Oak Grove), Prairie†, Rhode Island* (Rischer Town)†, Rocky Mound†, Salem*, Sand Hill*, Shiloh*, Simsboro, Spring Seat†, Tabernacle†, Tea Color (Tehaucana Grove)†, Tehaucana†, Thomasville†, Titus Farm†, Union Chapel*, Washington†, Woodson's Chapel†

GALVESTON

Highlands†

GOLIAD

Cologne* (The Colony, Perdido, Centerville, Ira), Manahuilla, St. Paul

GONZALES

Bascom (Brasco Lake)†, Dement*, Elm Slough†, Harris Chapel†, Hood's Point†, Lone Oak†, Mount Eden (Hickston)†, Nash Creek, Sand Hills, Terrysville (Terryville)*†, Walsh†

GRAYSON

Independence Springs†, White Rock†

GREGG

Camps, Easton*, Elderville, Fredonia, Greenville, Mason Spring, North Chapel,

Pleasant Green*, Red Oak, Ridge* (Freedman's Ridge), Rollins, Shiloh*, Stump Toe, White Oak

GUADALUPE

Brushy Creek, Hoover*, Jakes Colony*, Mill Creek, Sweet Home*, York Creek

HARDIN

Fresenius†

HARRIS

Barrett*/**, Borderville*, Hufsmith*, Kohrville* (Korville, Pilotville), Lily White*, McNair*, Riceville*

HARRISON

Hughes Spring, Leigh* (Antioch), Lott*, Nesbitt*, Piney* (Pine Ridge)

HAYS

Antioch Colony* (Black Colony)

HILL

Irene†

HOOD

Mount Zion (The Colony)†

HOPKINS

Birch Creek†, Cherry Grove*, East Caney†, Galilee*, Mount Sterling†, North Caney†, Pleasant Hill*, Prairie View†, St. Luke†, St. Mark†, Sand Field†

HOUSTON

Allen Chapel*/**, Cedar Branch*/**, Center Grove*/**, Center Hill, Dixon-Hopewell, Fodice*/**, Germany*/**, Givens's Hill*/**, Glover*/**, Hall's Bluff*/**, Hopewell*/**, Lake Creek, Mount Zion*, Pine Springs, Shady Grove, Smith Grove, Thankful, Vistula*/**, Wheeler Springs*/**

HUNT

Neylandville*

JASPER

Holly Springs, Magnolia Springs, Mount Union, Prairie View

JEFFERSON

Pear Orchard

KARNES

Flaccus* (Brieger)

KAUFMAN

Egypt*, Frog*, Pyle's Hill†, Rosser†

KINNEY

Seminole Camp*

LAVACA

Good Hope*

LEE

Antioch, Betts' Chapel, Doak Springs*, Dockery, Globe Hill*, Jones Colony*, Leo* (Field's Spur, Leo Switch), Moab†, Nunnsville*, Pin Oak†, Post Oak†, Sweet Home (Liberty Valley)†

LEON

Flynn

LIBERTY

Ames, Macedonia*

LIMESTONE

Cedar*, Bethlehem* (Woodland), Elm*, Mustang*, Nazro*, Rocky Crossing*, Sandy*†, Sardis*, Sims Colony*, Smith Chapel*, Webb Chapel*

MADISON

Antioch, Ottowa*

MARION

Bethlehem*, Belview*, Corinth*, Douglas Chapel*, Frazier*, Friendship*, Gethsemane*, Judea Church*, Lewis Chapel* (Louis Chapel), Logan* (Logan Chapel), Macedonia*, Mount Carmel*, New Zion*, Rock Springs*, Shady Grove Church*, Sunview* (Murrey League), Union*, Warlock* (Ero)

MATAGORDA

Bell Bottom*, Cedar Lake* (Dura, Duroc), Cedar Lane* (Sugar Land), Grove Hill*, Hudgins*, Liveoak* (Grapevine), Mount Pilgrim*, Podo*, Price, Vann* (King Vann African), Wilson Creek†

MCLENNAN

Harrison*†, Willow Grove*

MEDINA

Mission Valley*/**

MILAM

Six Mile*, Sneed Chapel*

NACOGDOCHES

Center Point, County Line (Upshaw*), Mount Gillion*, Oak Flat*, Pine Flat, Pleasant Hill (Loco), Redland, Richardson (Richardson Chapel), Sand Hill, Walnut Grove, Winter's Hill

NAVARRO

Babylon*, Brushy Prairie (On the Prairie)†, Elm Flat†, Goodlow* (Goodlow Park), Samaria* (Goodnight)†, Pelham*/** (Forks of the Creek), Philips* (Philip's Chapel), Rural Shade†, Timothy†, Union Hill†, Vann*

NEWTON

Biloxi, Cedar Grove, Galloway, Huff Creek, Indian Hill, Jamestown, Liberty, Pleasant Hill, St. John, Shankleville*/**

PANOLA

Corinth* (Longbranch)†, Eleven Hundred†, Evergreen†, Four Mile†, Harmony (Deberry)†, Holland's Quarters*, Paradise†, Pleasant Hill†, Walnut Grove*, Mims Chapel*, New Boggy†, Old Bethel†, Pope Quarters†, Saint Rest†, Shady Grove, Shiloh (Beckville)†, Smith Chapel, Social Point†, Walnut Grove*, Zion (New Zion)†

POLK

Barnes*, Darden*, Lily Island, Palestine

RED RIVER

Peters Prairie*

REFUGIO

Black Jacks, Lewis's Bend, Sprigg's Bend, Robinson Bend

ROBERTSON

Hammond*

RUSK

Chapel Hill, Dogtown, Mayflower, Springfield, Valley Grove, Water's Chapel

SABINE

Weeks Quarters

SAN AUGUSTINE

China Chapel†, Greertown (The Preemption), Pisgah†, Mount Dena†, Mount Horeb†, Pleasant Hill*, St. Luke†, Sunrise†, Union Grove†

SAN JACINTO

Camilla†, Darby Hill†, Drew's Landing†, Maynard*†, New Hope†, Palmetto†, Patrick's Ferry†, Rose Hill†, Spring Ridge†, Stephen Creek†, Stringtown†, Swartwout†, Urbana†

SHELBY

Africa* (Webb, St. John), Bell Chapel*, Coonville*, East Liberty*, Gates Chapel*, Hot*, Hughes Town*, Mount Gillion*, Nettleridge*, Possum Trot*, Sand Hill*, Todd Springs*

SMITH

Bethlehem*, Blackjack†, Clear Springs*, Cold Hill, Douglas*, Dunbar*, Fairview*, Galilee*, Jackson*†, Jamestown* (Berrien, Jimtown), Jones Valley, Lanes Chapel†, Liberty†, Mount Olive*, New Bethel*†, New Hope*, New Mountain, Old Hopewell, Omen, Pleasant Grove*, Shady Grove*, Spring Hill*, St. Louis†, Siloam*, St. Violet, Starrville, Thompson Hills* (Thompson), Union†, Universe*†, Wallace Grove†, Waters Bluff*

TARRANT

Mosier Valley*

TITUS

Evergreen*, Piney*, Whiteoak†

TRAVIS

Burdett's Prairie, Clarksville*, Kincheonville*, Littig*, Masontown*

TRINITY

Antioch*, Cedar Creek*, Nigton*, Lacy*, Pine Grove*, Red Branch*

UPSHUR

Elam Springs*, New Caney, Pleasant Grove* (Nubbin Ridge), Snow Hill*, Stracener*, Summerfield*, Union Grove*, Valley View*

VAN ZANDT

Blaine*, Red Land*, Wynn*

VICTORIA

The Commons†

WALKER

Galilee*, Grant's Colony* (Harmony Settlement), Wynnwood*

WALLER

Lawrence Key* (Lawrence-Key), Lewisville* (Louisville), Pointers* (Pointer), Silent Grove, Sunny Side*

WASHINGTON

Bluffs, Cross Hogs Branch†, Flat Prairie*, Graball*, Jerry's Quarters*, Lott*, Mill Creek*, Mount Fall, Post Oak, Pleasant Grove*, Sauney Stand*, Spain's Settlement*

WHARTON

Burr, Dinsmore* (Roberts), Elm Grove*, Hudging's Cut Off, Sandies*, Sand Ridge*, Sorrelle*, Mount Pilgrim*

WILLIAMSON

Bailey†, Damascus†, Miller Community (Jenks Branch, Liberty Chapel)†, Rocky Hollow*, Walker†, Youngstown†

WILSON

Crew's Colony†, Doisedo Colony (Dorcy Colony)†, Hay's Colony†, Montgomery Colony†, Nockenut Colony†, Steven's Colony†

WOOD

Center (Fouke)†, Green Grove*, Muddy Creek Church*

Notes

CHAPTER I

1. Schweninger, *Black Property Owners in the South,* 162.

2. Ibid., 164.

3. Litwack, *Trouble in Mind,* 135.

4. McMillan, *Dark Journey.*

5. Fisher, "Negro Farm Ownership in the South," 483–485; he was the only scholar we found to offer such a regional overview. Studies of freedmen's settlements outside Texas include Bethel, *Promiseland* (South Carolina); Montell, *The Saga of Coe Ridge* (Kentucky); Grindal, "The Religious Interpretation of Experience in a Rural Black Community" (Florida); Nathans, "Fortress without Walls" (Georgia).

6. Hamilton, "The Origins and Early Promotion of Nicodemus"; Taylor, "Black Towns"; Painter, "Exodusters"; Althearn, *In Search of Canaan.*

7. Scholars from other disciplines have sometimes expressed puzzlement over historians' neglect of settlements. See, for example, anthropologist Thomas H. Guderjan, "Forest Grove: A Dispersed Farming Community in East Texas." Anthropologist Oscar Lewis discussed settlements at length in his 1948 study of Bell County, Texas, *On the Edge of the Black Waxy,* noting that settlements' informal geographical boundaries closely paralleled those of common school districts. Cultural resource management historians and archeologists rather commonly write about settlements. See, for example, the survey of forty-one settlements on the 350 square miles of countryside that later became Fort Hood, Texas (Freeman, Dase, and Blake, "Agriculture and Rural Development on Fort Hood Lands," 183–206). Historian Frank Owsley discussed settlement formation and development in *Plain Folk of the Old South,* 63–64.

8. Hoskins, "Separate Streams of Discourse," 55.

9. For a study of Mound Bayou, which in its origins did resemble some Texas freedmen's settlements, see Hermann, *The Pursuit of a Dream.*

10. Traylor, "Harrison Barrett"; Mears, "African-American Settlement Patterns in Austin, Texas." Another useful master's thesis is Wright, "I Heard It Through the Grapevine," primarily focused on the Mims settlement of Brazoria County.

11. Hoskins, "Separate Streams of Discourse"; Reid, "Reaping a Greater Harvest."

12. White and Holland, *No Quittin' Sense.* See also Hunt and Winegarten, *"I Am Annie Mae";* Stimpson, *My Remembers;* Sample, *Racehoss.*

13. For an excellent example of such a study of a true freedmen's settlement, see Green, Peter, and Shepard, "Friendship."

14. Rawick, *Texas Narratives.*

15. Powdermaker, *After Freedom;* Dollard, *Caste and Class in a Southern Town.*

16. Dollard, *Caste and Class in a Southern Town,* viii.

17. Alyn's interview tapes are in the Lipscomb-Myers Collection of the Center for American History, University of Texas at Austin. Reverend White's edited oral autobiography was published as *No Quittin' Sense.* Sitton's interviews are in the archives of the Houston County Historical Commission, Crockett, Texas.

18. Wesley Taylor Fobbs interview, August 10, 2001.

19. Edward L. Ayers wrote, "We have focused so much on the limitations Southerners endured that we have lost sight of the rest of their lives." (Ayers, *The Promise of the New South,* ix.)

20. Bethel, *Promiseland,* 7.

21. Andrew Lee Eleby interview, August 31, 2001.

CHAPTER 2

1. Traylor, "Harrison Barrett," 20.

2. Tyler and Murphy, *The Slave Narratives of Texas,* 113.

3. Rawick, *Texas Narratives,* 3:611.

4. Ibid., 3:637.

5. Ibid., 2:135.

6. Ibid., 6:1937.

7. Ibid., 3:648.

8. Smallwood, *Time of Hope, Time of Despair,* 38.

9. Tyler and Murphy, *The Slave Narratives of Texas,* 121.

10. Rawick, *Texas Narratives,* 5:1581.

11. Calvert, "The Freedmen and Agricultural Prosperity," 461–471.

12. Crouch, *The Freedmen's Bureau and Black Texans,* 39.

13. Smallwood, *Time of Hope, Time of Despair,* 55; *New Handbook of Texas,* "Black Codes," 1:562.

14. Hamilton, "White Wealth and Black Repression in Harrison County, Texas," 346.

15. Ibid.

16. Ibid.

17. Smallwood, *Time of Hope, Time of Despair,* 55.

18. Rawick, *Texas Narratives,* 2:198; Tyler and Murphy, *The Slave Narratives of Texas,* 114.

19. Smallwood, "Through the Eyes of the Freedmen."

20. Crouch, *The Freedmen's Bureau and Black Texans,* 65.

21. Smallwood, *Time of Hope, Time of Despair,* 126.

22. Ibid., 137.

23. Crouch, *The Freedmen's Bureau and Black Texans,* 10; Calloway and Stewart, "The Black Experience," 188.

24. Jackson, "Freedom and Family," 102.

25. Crouch, *The Freedmen's Bureau and Black Texans,* 181; Smallwood, "Through the Eyes of the Freedmen."

26. Jackson, "Freedom and Family," 103.

27. Smallwood, *Time of Hope, Time of Despair,* 126–127; Cotton, *History of the Negroes of Limestone County from 1860 to 1939,* 18; Smallwood, Crouch, and Peacock, *Murder and Mayhem,* 7–73.

28. Smallwood, *Time of Hope, Time of Despair,* 127.

29. Rawick, *Texas Narratives,* 5:1823.

30. Jackson, "Freedom and Family," 65.

31. Calvert, "The Freedmen and Agricultural Prosperity," 466. For an account of the triumph of the old landowner class in the new circumstances, see Hamilton, "White Wealth and Black Repression in Harrison County, Texas," 340–359.

32. Litwack, *Trouble in Mind,* 116.

33. Glen Alyn's interviewees in Grimes and Washington counties had much to say about customary cheating at settling-up time. Their tapes and transcripts are part of the Lipscomb-Myers Collection at the Center for American History, the University of Texas at Austin. Interviewees include Bubba Bowser (1977), Lillie Lipscomb Davis (1977), Olivie "Chang" Ewing (1976), Ed Lathan (1975), Elnora Lipscomb (1973), Mance Lipscomb (1973), Willie Lipscomb (1977), and Georgia Lee Wade (1977). Descriptions of life on Brazos Valley plantation farms, as given in the above interviews, parallel in nearly every detail John Dollard's description of landowner-tenant relationships in his classic 1937 study of Sunflower County, Mississippi, *Caste and Class in a Southern Town* (see especially 109–125). Virtually every scholar of sharecropping has noted the pattern of customary cheating by landlords. See also the harsh judgments of Jack Temple Kirby (*Rural Worlds Lost,* 142–145). Anthropologist Hortense Powder-maker interviewed many African American sharecroppers and white landlords in Mississippi during the 1930s, and she estimated honest settlements in only 25 to 30 percent of the cases studied (*After Freedom,* 86).

34. Tyler and Murphy, *The Slave Narratives of Texas,* 113.

35. Rawick, *Texas Narratives,* 3:570.

36. Ibid., 3:851.

37. Sitton and Utley, *From Can See to Can't,* 45–53. See also the *New Handbook of Texas* entries on the following sharecropper communities: "Dewalt" (Fort Bend County), 2:614; "Hammond" (Harrison County) 3:436; "Harrison" (McLennan County) 3:487; and "Leigh" (Harrison County) 4:153.

38. Sitton, "Texas Freedmen's Settlements in the Context of the New South."

39. Ibid.

40. Ibid.

41. Ibid.

42. Rawick, *Texas Narratives*, 8:3198.

43. Ibid., 4:1303.

44. Ibid., 9:3703.

45. Houston County Historical Commission, "Cedar Branch Community and School."

46. Houston County Historical Commission, "Halls Bluff." Oral traditions of ex-master paternalisms have been passed down for a good many communities. See, for example, the *New Handbook of Texas* entries "Redland," 5:489, and "Shiloh" (Gregg County), 5:1028. See the marker file notes at the Texas Historical Commission for the following: Houston County Historical Commission, "Fodice"; Panola County Historical Commission, "Holland Quarters"; Tarrant County Historical Commission, "Mosier Valley."

47. Curlee, "A Study of Texas Slave Plantations," 132.

48. Rawick, *Texas Narratives*, 3:861.

49. Owens, *This Stubborn Soil*, 3.

50. Smallwood, *Time of Hope, Time of Despair*, 30.

51. Oubre, *Forty Acres and a Mule*, 159–198; Bethel, *Promiseland*, 7.

52. Rice, *The Negro in Texas*, 177.

53. Schweninger, *Black Property Owners in the South*, 174.

54. Traylor, "Harrison Barrett," 20.

55. The contention that many freedmen's settlements began as squatter communities is based on several lines of evidence, none of them strongly documented. This is not surprising. Residence on other people's property is illegal and therefore poorly recorded for the same reason that other illegalities are poorly recorded. U.S. census takers of course did not enumerate squatters (and they may have done a very inadequate job of counting actual black landowners, as James S. Fisher convincingly argued in "Negro Farm Ownership in the South," 479).

Contemporaries sometimes commented on the high frequency of land squatting in the eastern half of Texas. A critical observer of Hardin County residents noted in 1887, for example, "The people have been in the habit of using every man's land as their own for so many years they have come to believe that the land has no owners" (in Sitton, *Backwoodsmen*, 8). Oral traditions at many Texas freedmen's settlements either explicitly mention early land squatting or else recount a ten- to twenty-year gap between first settlement and first land deeds. Technically, the residents without deeds were squatters on the land, although they may have been there with full permission of the landowners. Steven A. Reich's careful study of Newton and Jasper counties found much evidence of black and white land squatters who, if challenged, often successfully established their claims on lands by the law of adverse possession. Rather commonly, squatters sold their "squatters claims" to other squatters. For example, in Newton County during 1872, freedman Richard Holmes purchased freedman Joe Hardy's claim to a tract thought to be "lost land" for 200 barrels of corn. Holmes passed this claim on to his daughter Louisa and her husband Levi Leonard. No documents changed hands in either transaction, but the Leonards later successfully established title to their land (Reich, "Searching for 'Lost Land' ").

A documentary window opens for the phenomenon of land squatting for certain East Texas counties. As Reich demonstrated, when the big lumber companies bought virgin East Texas timberlands during the period from 1885 to 1910, they found their large properties heavily infested with squatters. Many civil cases attest to this and to the strength of the law of adverse possession, "squatter's rights," in local courts. Kirby Lumber Company had over one hundred land men in the field who did nothing but negotiate with squatters, black and white.

56. Ayers, *The Promise of the New South,* 208.

57. Rawick, *Texas Narratives,* 7:2459; see also Josephine Tippit Compton's account of squatting in the Brazos River bottom after Freedom, p. 908. A similar story from the Leon River bottoms was told by Rowena Weatherly Keatts of Coryell County in an interview on May 5, 1986.

58. Sitton, *Backwoodsmen,* 66–68; Hahn, "Hunting, Fishing, and Foraging."

59. Sitton, *Backwoodsmen,* 50–51; Doughty, *Wildlife and Man in Texas,* 19; Hogan, *The Texas Republic,* 225; Dan Lay interview, August 7, 1992.

60. Margaret Session Carter and Curel Carter interview, March 19, 2000.

61. O'Connor, *Tales from the San'tone River Bottom,* 189.

62. Ibid., 104, 107.

63. Brown and Gust, *Between the Creeks,* xi; *New Handbook of Texas,* 2:909.

64. Brown and Gust, *Between the Creeks,* xiii.

65. Ibid., 81.

66. Ibid., xii.

67. Schweninger, *Black Property Owners in the South,* 174; Wilkison, "The End of Independence," 32.

68. Barr, *Black Texans,* 96; Painter, "Exodusters," 920–922; *New Handbook of Texas,* "Exodus of 1879," 2:915; Reid, "Reaping a Greater Harvest," 24.

69. Fort Bend County Historical Commission, "Kendleton"; Johnson, "Kendleton"; *New Handbook of Texas,* "Kendleton," 3:1063.

70. *New Handbook of Texas,* "Grants Colony," 3:283; Hayman, "A Short History of the Negro of Walker County," 39.

71. Rice, *The Negro in Texas,* 178.

72. Ayers, *The Promise of the New South,* 15–16.

73. Freeman, Dase, and Blake, "Agriculture and Rural Development on Fort Hood Lands," 105; *New Handbook of Texas,* "Land Grants," 4:56–58.

74. Houston County Historical Commission, "Germany"; Florarean Hall Overshown interview, August 31, 2001; *New Handbook of Texas,* "Germany," 3:146.

75. Loughmiller and Loughmiller, *Big Thicket Legacy*, 16.

76. Reich, "Searching for 'Lost Land' "; Bouvier, *Bouvier Law Dictionary*, 1:152–153.

77. Traylor, "Harrison Barrett"; Orton, "The Upshaws of County Line"; Hoskins, "Separate Streams of Discourse," 72.

78. Chumley, "Negro Labor and Property Holdings in Shelby County, Texas," 1.

79. Wilson and Ferris, *The Encyclopedia of Southern Culture*, 154.

80. Three Sadler brothers and one sister founded Negro Colony (Bosque County); the brothers Anderson and Lewis Fields, Fields Community (Dallas County); several siblings of the Hopkins family, Hopkinsville (DeWitt County); the Cartwight brothers, Possum Trot (Shelby County); Milas, Richard, and Nelson Miller, Jenks Branch (Williamson County); Abram, Alexander, George, and Philip Jones, Jones Colony (Lee County); and Guss, Jim, and Felix Upshaw, County Line (Nacogdoches County).

81. Marion Upshaw interview, August 1, 2002.

82. Caldwell County Historical Commission, "Saint John Colony."

83. Tom F. Washington interview, December 8, 1991.

84. Green, Peter, and Shepard, "Friendship," 21–74.

85. McDonald, *Out of the Darkness*, 106.

86. Washington County Historical Commission, "African-American Neighborhood Settlements"; Mears, "African-American Settlement Patterns in Austin, Texas"; *New Handbook of Texas*, "Clarksville" (Travis County), 2:142.

87. Teddlie, "Clarksville"; Mears, "African-American Settlement Patterns in Austin, Texas," 96.

88. Mears, "African-American Settlement Patterns in Austin, Texas," 99.

89. For fascinating details on the diversity of emancipation communities in and around Dallas, see McKnight, *African American Families and Settlements*.

90. *New Handbook of Texas*: "Littig," 4:226; "Harvard," 3:496; "Hufsmith," 3:769. See also James Smallwood on Wascomb Station, *Time of Hope, Time of Despair*, 76.

91. Houston County Historical Commission, "Allen Chapel"; Chester Denman interview, July 11, 2001.

92. George Francis and Vivian Francis interview, August 12, 2001; *New Handbook of Texas*, "Antioch" (Lee County), 1:207.

93. Finnegan, "Deep East Texas," 82.

94. Schweninger, *Black Property Owners in the South*, 174.

95. Camp County Historical Commission, "Center Point Community" and "Center Point School, 1889–1952."

96. Hoskins, "Separate Streams of Discourse," 42.

97. Cherokee County Historical Commission, "Cuney"; Mayfield, *Cherokee County History*, 49–50.

98. Gillard, "A Yankee Priest in Dixie Gets a Taste of Rural Mission Life," 14.

99. *New Handbook of Texas*, "Betts Chapel," 1:513; Drummond, "Descendants Sue to Regain Land."

100. Whalen, "Wynn Community Struggles, Looks for Grant Money."

101. *New Handbook of Texas*, "West Chapel," 6:891.

102. McDonald, *Out of the Darkness*, 185.

103. *New Handbook of Texas*, "Rock Springs," 5:639; Bosque County Historical Commission, "Rock Springs Cumberland Presbyterian Church"; Pierson, "Piecing Together the Past."

104. Bradford, "Families Trace Ancestry to Slaves."

105. Wesley Taylor Fobbs interview, August 10, 2001; Houston County Historical Commission, "Wheeler Springs Community."

106. Hunt and Winegarten, *"I Am Annie Mae,"* 9.

107. Houston County Historical Commission, *History of Houston County, Texas*, 4.

108. McDonald, *Out of the Darkness*, 106.

109. Grigsby, "Another Matagorda County History," 10.

110. Rawick, *Texas Narratives*, 1:291, 296. Ada Davis inserted this unusual personal note in the Texas slave narratives; apparently, she was an interviewer.

111. Donovan, "Neches River Manuscript"; Helen Darden interview, January 8, 2002.

112. Smith, "James Smith."

113. Saint Paul Reunion Association, "A Collection of Pages from the History of Neylandville and Saint Paul School," 1–11; Caston, "Built on Freedom."

114. Rawick, *Texas Narratives*, 2956.

115. Pelham Community Organization, "Memories of Pelham," 1–24; Navarro County Historical Commission, "Pelham Community."

116. Hess, "Ex-Slaves Founded Blanco Peyton Colony"; Blanco County Historical Commission, "Peyton Colony Lime Kiln"; Turner, "Boardhouse"; Coffee and Jones, "Peyton's Colony of Boardhouse"; Cathy Jones interview, August 26, 1978; Austin Jones interview, April 4, 1977; Blanco County Historical Commission, "Peyton Colony Mt. Horeb Baptist Church."

117. See the summary of initial settlement practices in Sitton, *Backwoodsmen*, 51. A similar account to Davis's about St. John is Charles Tatum's story of the founding of the Africa community of Shelby County (Tatum, *Shelby County*, 29). Hortense Powdermaker also tells a virtually identical "origins" story for an unnamed community in Sunflower County, Mississippi (Powdermaker, *After Freedom*, 95–96).

118. S. L. Davis interview, 1977; Caldwell County Historical Commission, "Saint John Colony."

CHAPTER 3

1. Rawick, *Texas Narratives*, 4:1145.

2. White and Holland, *No Quittin' Sense*, 6. C. C. White recalled this detail from around 1900, but Dora Griffith remembered that community stumps were kept

burning for this purpose at Woodville, Cherokee County, during the 1930s (Griffith, personal communication to Richard Orton, August 23, 2001).

3. Many such matters were discussed as contemporary practices in the Texas slave narratives of the 1930s. See, for example, Rawick, *Texas Narratives*, 8:3132 and 10:3965. Rowena Weatherly Keatts of Lincolnville, Coryell County, told of the dutch oven "Christmas cake" in an interview of June 9, 1986. To decorate the cake, her mother "would get little twigs of cedar, and how she got the icing on the twigs I wouldn't know. But she would decorate the cake with those twigs from the cedar tree, the most beautiful sight you've ever seen."

4. Bubba Bowser interview, August 11, 1977.

5. Cathy Jones interview, August 26, 1978.

6. James Womack interview, March 2, 1992.

7. Sitton and King, *The Loblolly Book*, 147.

8. This generalization is based on a variety of sources and lines of evidence but remains a judgment call. Poor white families, for example, also sometimes reprocessed salt from their smokehouse floors. Historian Edward L. Ayers concurred about the reason for the more intense African American frugalities. In *The Promise of the New South*, 209, he wrote, "Landowning blacks sought in every way they could to be self-sufficient and free from the snares that caught their less fortunate neighbors."

9. Grover Williams interview, November 25, 1991.

10. McDonald, *Out of the Darkness*, 304.

11. Helen Darden, personal communication to Thad Sitton, January 8, 2002.

12. Pearl Gregory, personal communication to Richard Orton, October 2, 2001.

13. Sitton and Utley, *From Can See to Can't*, 192-194. Chester Gregory's family customarily stored two full wagonloads of peas, still on the vine, in a special crib in their barn (Chester Gregory, personal communication to Richard Orton, August 22, 2001).

14. Jessie Mae Amie interview, May 27, 2001.

15. Pearl Gregory, personal communication to Richard Orton, February 6, 2002.

16. Grover Williams, Ed Lathan, and several other former residents of freedmen's settlements mentioned this conditional return to the free range in late fall, which seems to have persisted at remote communities for decades after the arrival of fence laws. For a perspective on free-range practices, see Sitton, *Backwoodsmen*, especially Chapter 6, "Rooter Hogs and Woods Cattle," 194-232.

17. Rawick, *Texas Narratives*, 4:1146.

18. Wilson, "Growing Up Black in East Texas," 49.

19. Holland, *Mr. Claude*, 3.

20. Vivian Lovelady interview, June 12, 2001.

21. Deola Mayberry Adams interview, August 4, 1987.

22. Corn cultivation was described by most memoirists and informants from freedmen's settlements. For a perspective on the importance of corn, see Hogan, *The Texas Republic*, 32; Silverthorne, *Plantation Life in Texas*, 89-106; Clark, *Frontier America*, 104; Smithwick, *The Evolution of a State*, 14, 173; and Hilliard, *Hog Meat and Hoecake*, 150-171.

23. Rowena Weatherly Keatts interview, May 5, 1986.

24. Vivian Lovelady interview, June 12, 2001.

25. Silverthorne, *Plantation Life in Texas*, 98; Sitton and Utley, *From Can See to Can't*, 60.

26. Quoted in Sitton and Utley, *From Can See to Can't*, 86.

27. Ibid., 87–88.

28. Sitton, *The Texas Sheriff*, 184.

29. Sitton, *Backwoodsmen*, 194–232.

30. Aubrey Cole interview, May 28, 1992.

31. Steven Hahn convincingly argued that southern whites saw ex-slaves' use of the free range as an important contributor to landowners' labor problems in the decades after Emancipation. White landowners thus promoted fence laws, trespass laws, game laws, and even dog taxes to force freedmen out of the woods and into sharecropping (Hahn, "Hunting, Fishing, and Foraging").

32. The comments on hunting that follow were based on numerous personal accounts, but for scholarly discussions of the special nature of African American hunting practices, see Hahn, "Hunting, Fishing, and Foraging"; and Marks, *Southern Hunting in Black and White*. A detailed general account of East Texas hunting practices may be found in Sitton, *Backwoodsmen*, 134–168.

33. Stimpson, *My Remembers*, 8.

34. Marion Upshaw, personal communication to Richard Orton, August 1, 2002.

35. Aubrey Cole interview, May 28, 1992.

36. White and Holland, *No Quittin' Sense*, 73.

37. Stimpson, *My Remembers*, 9.

38. Mance Lipscomb transcripts, 1973, Lipscomb-Myers Collection, File 2k198, Center for American History, University of Texas at Austin.

39. Aubrey Cole interview, May 5, 1992.

40. Helen Darden, personal communication to Thad Sitton, January 15, 2002.

41. W. C. Williams discussed mud and walnut poisonings in his interview of April 12, 2001. For a detailed discussion of "folk" fishing methods, see Sitton, *Backwoodsmen*, 173–193.

42. Jessie Mae Amie interview, May 27, 2001.

43. Frank Ashby interview, March 19, 1992.

44. Marion Upshaw, personal communication to Richard Orton, August 1, 2002.

45. In the two major published oral autobiographies of Texas blacks, both men describe mothers with extensive knowledge of herbal curing who attributed their knowledge to Native American sources. See Lipscomb and Alyn, *I Say Me for a Parable*, 86–89; and White and Holland, *No Quittin' Sense*, 14–15.

46. Based on his study of many recorded narratives and personal accounts, Edward L. Ayers came to the same conclusions about the special "defensiveness" of black landowners and the somewhat hostile attitudes of nearby whites (Ayers, *The Promise of the New South*, 209–210).

47. It is noteworthy that the author of the most detailed study of a freedmen's settlement also saw this defensive mode as defining the community she studied (Bethel, *Promiseland*); see also Carlson, "African American Lifeways in East Central Texas," 63–79.

48. Helen Darden, personal communication to Thad Sitton, January 15, 2002.

49. Young, *From These Roots*, 24, 37; Wesley Taylor Fobbs interview, August 10, 2001; Marion Upshaw, personal communication to Richard Orton, August 1, 2002.

50. McMath, *American Populism*, 29.

51. Larry Leonard interview, June 13, 2001.

52. Wilkison, "The End of Independence," 172–174. An excellent account of the use of the bell in community emergencies may be found in Rust, "Weeping Mary," 6. The pattern of neighbors helping neighbors in emergencies has persisted. For example, on Christmas Day, 1929, a house at Barrett in Harris County caught fire from Christmas candles and burned to the ground, but Harrison Barrett, his sons, and neighbors pitched in to build another house for the family (Will Freeman interview, August 25, 1986). Seventy-three years later, on December 21, 2002, Thad Sitton witnessed a similar community response at a rural home destroyed by fire in the Flat Prairie community of Washington County.

53. Wesley Taylor Fobbs interview, August 10, 2001. The behavior of Taylor, Patterson, Jones, and other black landlords at Texas freedmen's settlements exactly parallels that reported for other black southern landlords. See Grim, "African American Landlords in the Rural South," 408–410.

54. Andrew Lee Eleby interview, August 31, 2001.

55. Cravens, *Between Two Rivers*, 98.

56. Andrew Lee Eleby interview, August 31, 2001.

57. "Given's Hill," Historical Market File, Houston County, Texas Historical Commission, Austin, Texas.

58. Marion Upshaw, personal communication to Richard Orton, August 1, 2002; Claudie May Joyce, personal communication to Richard Orton, December 3, 1997.

59. Grover Williams interview, November 25, 1991.

60. Chester Gregory, personal communication to Richard Orton, August 22, 2001.

61. Walter Buenger discusses the social importance of the coming of parcel post in *The Path to a Modern South*, 54.

62. Ali, "Growing Up in County Line."

63. Excerpts from Cartwright's peddler's journal were published in several issues of the high school magazine *Chinquapin* during 1986–1988. A complete set of *Chinquapin* is in the Stephen F. Austin State University Library, Nacogdoches, Texas.

64. Wilkison, "The End of Independence," 143.

65. Earls, "Smith Chapel Memories," 62; Whitaker, "Appreciate Life the Way It Is," 52–57.

66. Elizabeth Silverthorne offered a useful overview of black folk medicine (and white—there seems to be little difference) in *Plantation Life in Texas*, 148–151. Re-

corded in the late 1930s, many of the several thousand personal accounts in the Texas slave narratives contribute information on the topic, often describing current practice (Rawick, *Texas Narratives*).

67. Bundick, "Settlements Develop from Early Families."

68. Sallie Norman interview, 1977.

69. Rawick, *Texas Narratives*, 7:2782. The Texas slave narratives contain numerous references to "conjur" as a living tradition of belief. See, for example, Rawick, 4:1257, 4:1430, 6:2205, 9:3867, 10:4146, and 10:4246. For a victim's account of a conjur attack, see Bubba Bowser's August 1977 interview tape.

70. Pemberton, *Juneteenth at Comanche Crossing*, 161.

71. Ibid., 160.

72. Ibid., 177–179. Frederick Young offers briefer portraits of Cologne healers in *From These Roots*, 40–43. Hortense Powdermaker's study of Sunflower County, Mississippi, reports on interviews she had with several famous "doctors" of the 1930s, and similarities to the Limestone County practitioners are striking (see Powdermaker, *After Freedom*, 288–296).

73. Grover Williams interview, May 8, 1992.

74. Rowena Weatherly Keatts interview, June 16, 1986; Dorsey, "Dr. Fred William Cariker," 57.

75. Cathy Jones interview, August 26, 1978.

76. Brophy, "The Black Texan," 174–182.

77. Helen Darden, personal communication to Thad Sitton, January 8, 2002.

78. Redwine, *History of Five Counties*, 25, 51.

79. Andrew Lee Eleby interview, August 31, 2001.

80. Rosengarten, *All God's Dangers*, 192.

81. Andrew Lee Eleby interview, August 31, 2001.

82. Redwine, *History of Five Counties*, 25.

83. W. C. Williams interview, April 12, 2001.

84. White and Holland, *No Quittin' Sense*, 73, 76.

85. Ibid., 76.

86. Ibid, 74.

87. Ibid.

88. Wilkison, "The End of Independence," 18.

89. Helen Darden, personal communication to Thad Sitton, January 15, 2002.

90. Wilkison, "The End of Independence," 4.

91. Ibid.

92. Westmacott, *African-American Gardens and Yards in the Rural South*, 90.

CHAPTER 4

1. White and Holland, *No Quittin' Sense*, 106.

2. Ibid., 107.

3. Houston County Historical Commission, "Cedar Branch Community School."

4. Titus 2:9, quoted in Silverthorne, *Plantation Life in Texas*, 43.

5. Rawick, *Texas Narratives*, 3:555.

6. Silverthorne, *Plantation Life in Texas*, 43.

7. Ibid.; Rawick, *Texas Narratives*, 2:256.

8. Ibid., 2:215.

9. Smallwood, *Time of Hope, Time of Despair*, 97.

10. Ibid.

11. Cotton, *History of Negroes of Limestone County from 1860 to 1939*, 12–13.

12. Traylor, "Harrison Barrett," 68.

13. Green, Peter, and Shepard, "Friendship," 52.

14. Vivian Lovelady interview, June 12, 2001.

15. White and Holland, *No Quittin' Sense*, 130.

16. Ibid., 141.

17. Rawick, *Texas Narratives*, 7:2627.

18. S. L. Davis interview, 1977.

19. Vivian Lovelady interview, June 12, 2001.

20. Truvillion, "Henry Truvillion of the Big Thicket," 35.

21. Brewer, *Dog Ghosts and the Word on the Brazos*, 94.

22. Andrew Lee Eleby interview, August 31, 2001.

23. Ali, "Growing Up in County Line," 34.

24. Leota Upshaw, personal communication to Richard Orton, 1995.

25. Claudie May Joyce, personal communication to Richard Orton, June 15, 2000; Marion Upshaw, personal communication to Richard Orton, August 1, 2002.

26. Ibid.

27. Cathy Jones interview, August 26, 1978.

28. Traylor, "Harrison Barrett," 71; Augusta Barrett Payne interview, 1985.

29. Vivian Lovelady interview, July 10, 2001.

30. Powdermaker, *After Freedom*, 274.

31. Ibid.; Helena Brown Patton and Zeffie White, personal communication to Richard Orton, June 28, 2001.

32. Houston County Historical Commission, "Germany."

33. For an excellent discussion of African American lodges, burial societies, and insurance societies as they operated in the 1930s, see Raper, *Preface to Peasantry*, 374–375.

34. Vivian Lovelady interview, July 10, 2001.

35. Helen Darden, personal communication to Thad Sitton, January 8, 2002.

36. Barbara Price, personal communication to James H. Conrad, June 22, 2000.

37. Rawick, *Texas Narratives*, 7:2713.

38. Wilson and Ferris, *Encyclopedia of Southern Culture*, 161–162.

39. Jordan, *Texas Graveyards*, 20–21.

40. Rust, "Weeping Mary," 8.

41. Vivian Lovelady interview, July 10, 2001.

42. Grover Williams interview, May 22, 1992.

43. Ali, "Growing Up in County Line," 108.

44. Rowena Weatherly Keatts interview, February 17, 1987.

45. Dora Session Griffith, personal communication to Richard Orton, June 25, 2001.

46. Taplin, "Picking and Pulling," 27.

47. Wisdom, Lee County Black History Files, Lee County Historical Commission, Giddings, Texas.

48. Deola Mayberry Adams interview, August 4, 1987.

49. Grover Williams interview, May 22, 1992.

50. Ali, "Growing Up in County Line," 37.

51. Anthropologist Hortense Powdermaker's fieldwork descriptions of African American revivals, church services, missionary societies, lodges, and other church matters at Sunflower County, Mississippi, in the 1930s coincide in almost every detail with those from East Texas sources (Powdermaker, *After Freedom*, 249–274).

52. Quoted in O'Connor, *Tales from the San'tone River Bottom*, 98, 99.

53. White and Holland, *No Quittin' Sense*, 3.

54. Andrew Lee Eleby interview, August 31, 2001.

55. Helena Brown Patton, personal communication to Richard Orton, June 28, 2001.

56. Jessie Mae Amie interview, August 30, 2001.

57. Chester Gregory, personal communication to Richard Orton, August 22, 2001.

58. Young, *From These Roots*, 44.

59. Larutha Odom Clay interview, February 11, 2002.

60. Chester Denman, personal communication to Thad Sitton, July 11, 2001.

61. Wesley Taylor Fobbs interview, August 10, 2001.

62. Tolbert, "On Devout Citizens of Fodice (4 Dice)," October 5, 1964.

63. Stimpson, *My Remembers*, 62; Chester Gregory, personal communication to Richard Orton, October 2, 2001; Ed Lathan interview, November 28, 1976.

64. Sitton and Utley, *From Can See to Can't*, 129–130.

65. Andrew Lee Eleby interview, August 31, 2001.

66. Some informants commented on the problem of violence in black communities, although many believed that violent incidents were less frequent in freedmen's settlements than in sharecropper communities. African American master's thesis researcher Leo B. Chumley saw much evidence of black-on-black crimes going largely unpunished in Shelby County before World War II (Chumley, "Negro Labor and Property Holdings in Shelby County, Texas," 74). Likewise, generalizing about life in County Line, Nacogdoches County, before World War II, Marion Upshaw noted that if you did something bad and got caught, you went for help to a friend, "a good strong white man that had money." Many prosecutions ended there—with the right word to the sheriff from the right man. You might end up in virtual bondage to the white friend, however (Marion Upshaw, personal communication to Richard Orton, August 1, 2002).

Writing of Sunflower County, Mississippi, psychologist and field worker John Dollard observed: "Negroes are said to have been known to kill other Negroes and get off without punishment when they have a white protector. This fact tends to make life more dangerous within the Negro group, since ordinary protection of the person by the state is not fully operative there" (Dollard, *Caste and Class in a Southern Town,* 212). Former Jasper County, Texas, sheriff Aubrey Cole said much the same as Dollard in an interview on August 14, 1992. Andrew Lee Eleby, Mance Lipscomb, and Bubba Bowers, among others, reported versions of the landowner's promise about graveyard and jail.

67. Ed Lathan interview, November 28, 1976. See also Lipscomb and Alyn, *I Say Me for a Parable,* 78–80; Sitton and Utley, *From Can See To Can't,* 243–245.

68. Ed Lathan interview, November 28, 1976.

69. Chester Gregory, personal communication to Richard Orton, August 22, 2001.

70. Nathans, "Fortress without Walls," 55–63. His description of the role played by the church at an unnamed freedmen's settlement in Georgia echoes many Texas accounts.

71. Stimpson, *My Remembers,* 108–122.

72. Several sheriffs interviewed for Thad Sitton's *Texas High Sheriffs* and *The Texas Sheriff* touched on these matters, although of course nobody admitted to taking protection money. For an account of just this phenomenon regarding a rural sheriff and a minority Hispanic community, however, see Foley, Mota, Post, and Lozano, *From Peones to Politicos,* 24–25.

73. White and Holland, *No Quittin' Sense,* 141–153.

74. Sample, *Racehoss,* 116–119.

75. Rawick, *Texas Narratives,* 8:856.

76. Jessie Mae Amie interview, August 30, 2001; Wesley Taylor Fobbs interview, August 10, 2001; Helen Darden, personal communication to Thad Sitton, January 8, 2002.

77. Matustick, "Holding On."

78. Edward Doyle, quoted in Jones, "This Juneteenth, Step Back in Time with Small Towns."

79. Williams, *Juneteenth,* 18.

80. Hill, "Clarksville," 6.

81. Neiman Johnson interview, October 20, 1978; Cathy Jones interview, August 26, 1978.

82. Williams, "Country Black," 128.

83. Pelham Community Organization, "Memories of Pelham," 10.

84. Green, Peter, and Shepard, "Friendship," 60.

85. Rawick, *Texas Narratives,* 4:1435.

86. Pemberton, *Juneteenth at Comanche Crossing,* 229.

87. Ibid., 228.

88. Ibid., 234.

89. Ibid., 238.

90. Ibid., 243.

CHAPTER 5

1. Donovan, "Neches River Manuscript."

2. Rawick, *Texas Narratives*, 8:2978.

3. Crouch, *The Freedmen's Bureau and Black Texans*, 65.

4. Ibid.; Smallwood, *Time of Hope, Time of Despair*, 83.

5. Hamilton, "White Wealth and Black Repression in Harrison County, Texas," 350; Campbell, *A Southern Community in Crisis*, 390-395.

6. Smallwood, *Time of Hope, Time of Despair*, 93.

7. Ophelia Mae Mayberry Hall interview, May 26, 1986.

8. O'Connor, *Tales from the San'tone River Bottom*, 89.

9. Carlson, "African American Lifeways in East Central Texas," 72.

10. Chumley, "Negro Labor and Property Holdings in Shelby County, Texas," 27. Hortense Powdermaker reported that in Sunflower County, Mississippi, around 1934, 85 of 122 black schools yet remained in churches (Powdermaker, *After Freedom*, 308). William J. Brophy noticed the same phenomenon in Texas and believed that black communities had good reasons for keeping their schools in churches. Only while in the church was the school fully under community control. Brophy explained, "White school boards had the authority to determine what would and would not take place in a public school building" (Brophy, "The Black Texan," 199). In her interview about the Shankleville settlement of Newton County on February 11, 2002, Larutha Odom Clay told of a major disadvantage students faced at the combined school and church—they had to participate in a great many funerals.

11. Rawick, *Texas Narratives*, 3:514.

12. Sitton and Rowold, *Ringing the Children In*, 8.

13. Bralley, *Seventeenth Biennial Report of the State Superintendent for Public Instruction*, 73.

14. *Report of the Results of the Texas Statewide School Adequacy Survey*, 240, 595, 1765.

15. Brophy, "The Black Texan," 26; Calloway and Stewart, "The Black Experience," 191.

16. For an unflinching discussion of white attitudes to blacks at the height of Jim Crow, see Glasrud, "Child or Beast?" Also see Dollard, *Caste and Class in a Southern Town*, 189-201, and Powdermaker, *After Freedom*, 304-308. Many black interviewees supported these harsh judgments.

17. Chumley, "Negro Labor and Property Holdings in Shelby County, Texas," 21-27.

18. Brophy, "The Black Texan," 34.

19. Ibid., 34-51.

20. Claudie Mae Joyce, personal communication to Richard Orton, June 15, 2000.

21. Interracial Committee, "A Report of Interracial Work in Hunt County."

22. Carlson, "African American Lifeways in East Central Texas," 87.

23. Grover Williams interview, November 25, 1991.

24. Georgia Lee Wade interview, June 14, 1977.

25. Ed Lathan interview, November 28, 1976.

26. Mrs. Corener Dean interview, June 1973.

27. White and Holland, *No Quittin' Sense*, 28.

28. Grigsby, "My Story," 91.

29. Ophelia Mae Mayberry Hall interview, May 26, 1986.

30. Rowena Weatherly Keatts interview, April 15, 1987.

31. Deola Mayberry Adams interview, August 4, 1987.

32. Dora Session Griffith, personal communication to Richard Orton, June 25, 2001. Researchers Sitton and Rowold came to very similar conclusions about the effectiveness of instruction in rural schools (*Ringing the Children In*, 16-18, 202-212), and so did the Texas School Survey of 1924.

33. Camp County Historical Commission, "Center Point Community" and "Center Point School."

34. *New Handbook of Texas*, "Center Point," 2:16.

35. Camp County Historical Commission, "Center Point School."

36. Louis R. Harlan, lead editor of *The Booker T. Washington Papers*, is the main source for the interpretation of Washington in this chapter. See especially Harlan's biography, *Booker T. Washington—The Wizard of Tuskegee*, 174-237.

37. Quoted in Ayers, *The Promise of the New South*, 323.

38. Quoted by Ishmael Reed in the preface to Washington, *Up From Slavery*, xvii.

39. *New Handbook of Texas*, "Smith, Robert Lloyd," 5:1108.

40. Ayers, *The Promise of the New South*, 326.

41. Houston County Historical Commission, "Germany."

42. Dickson, "Out of the Lion's Mouth," 53-67.

43. *New Handbook of Texas*, "Colored Farmers' Alliance," 2:231.

44. *New Handbook of Texas*, "Farmers' Home Improvement Society," 2:956; "Smith, Robert Lloyd," 5:1108. See also Carroll, "Robert Lloyd Smith and the Farmers' Improvement Society of Texas."

45. Reid, "Reaping a Greater Harvest," 30.

46. Ibid., 40-42.

47. Ibid., 154.

48. Crosby, "Limited Success against Long Odds," 278.

49. Ibid., 281.

50. Ibid., 282.

51. Reid, "Reaping a Greater Harvest," 149.

52. B. J. Pryor interview, August 3, 2002; Smallwood, *Born in Dixie*, 607.

53. *Greenville Evening Banner*, September 14, 1921.

54. Reid, "Reaping a Greater Harvest," 139.

55. Bradford, "Narrative Report, Negro County Agent Work, Cherokee County, 1928."

56. Ragsdale, "Narrative Report, Home Demonstration Work, Cherokee County, 1928."

57. Ibid.

58. Bradford, "Narrative Report, Negro County Agent Work, Cherokee County, 1928."

59. Reid, "Reaping a Greater Harvest," 154.

60. Ibid., 158.

61. Ibid., 160.

62. Ibid., 155.

63. Ibid., 162.

64. Ibid., 166.

65. Ibid., 164.

66. Ibid., 237.

67. Houston County Historical Commission, "Lula Denby Dailey"; Houston County Historical Commission, "Wheeler Springs Community."

68. *New Handbook of Texas,* "Smith, Robert Lloyd," 5:1108.

69. Dollard, *Caste and Class in a Southern Town,* 194.

70. Ibid., 192.

71. Harlan and Smock, *The Booker T. Washington Papers,* 2:330.

72. Potts, "The Negro in the Rural Areas of East Texas, 1931" 78; State Department of Education, "Negro Education in Texas," 9.

73. Riles, "The Rosenwald School Building Program in Texas," 8, 11, 97.

74. Hayman, "A Short History of the Negro of Walker County," 33.

75. Frankie Franks interview, July 16, 1979; Charlie Baylor, "Charlie Baylor Narrative."

76. State Department of Education, "Negro Education in Texas, 1934–1935," 8; Riles, "The Rosenwald School Building Program in Texas," 1–10.

77. Houston County Historical Commission, "Germany."

78. Riles, "Sweet Home Vocational and Agricultural High School."

79. Ibid.

80. Freedmen's settlements noted as having county training schools include Red Land (Van Zandt County), Neylandville (Hunt County), Kendleton (Fort Bend County), Garland's Colony (Bowie County), Galilee (Walker County), Hopewell (Houston County), and Center Point (Camp County). The following freedmen's settlements were noted as developing large rural high schools, and some of them were doubtless also county training schools: Winter's Hill (Nacogdoches County), Doak Springs (Lee County), Wellborn (Brazos County), Sand Hills (Gonzales County), Sims Colony (Freestone County), East Liberty (Shelby County), and Flint Hill (Anderson County).

81. Potts, "The Negro in the Rural Areas of East Texas," 76–78.

82. Houston County Historical Commission, "Fodice Community School."

83. State Department of Education, "Negro Education in Texas, 1931," 8.

84. Navarro County Historical Commission, "Pelham Community."

85. Pelham Community Organization, "Memories of Pelham."

86. W. C. Williams interview, April 12, 2001.

CHAPTER 6

1. Earls, "Smith Chapel Memories."

2. W. C. Williams interview, April 12, 2001.

3. Vivian Lovelady interview, June 12, 2001.

4. Ibid.

5. Susie Freeman note, Lee County Historical Commission Black History Files.

6. Leader May Sessions Turner, personal communication to Richard Orton, August 23, 2001.

7. Bethel, *Promiseland*, 98.

8. Grim, "African American Landlords in the Rural South."

9. Powdermaker, *After Freedom*, 63.

10. Hoskins, "Separate Streams of Discourse," 43-44.

11. Vivian Lovelady interview, June 12, 2001.

12. Arthur Cotton interview, March 20, 2002.

13. Freddie Eagleton interview, August 23, 1986.

14. Mary Moore note, Lee County Historical Commission Black History Files.

15. Neiman Johnson interview, October 20, 1978.

16. Jones, quoted in Azadian, *Earth Has No Sorrow*, 84.

17. Dollard, *Caste and Class in a Southern Town*, 258.

18. Porter, quoted in Pelham Community Organization, "Memories of Pelham," 21.

19. Wesley Taylor Fobbs interview, August 10, 2001.

20. Sitton, *Backwoodsmen*, 115-119; Lottie Ferguson Fields, personal communication to Richard Orton, August 22, 2001.

21. Frank Brunt interview, February 20, 1986.

22. Sitton, *The Texas Sheriff*, 160.

23. Ed Lathan interview, November 28, 1976.

24. Sitton and Utley, *From Can See to Can't*, 51.

25. Hunt and Winegarten, *"I Am Annie Mae,"* 49-52. A few years later, in separate events, Hunt's sister was kidnapped and raped and Hunt's brother-in-law abducted and murdered by the white leader of the earlier raid.

26. Oral history tapes in the Lipscomb-Meyers Collection of the Center for American History, University of Texas at Austin, contain extensive firsthand accounts of the Grimes County sharecropper farms. See the tapes of Mance Lipscomb, Elnora Lipscomb, Willie Lipscomb, Bubba Bowser, and James Wade. For a landowner's perspective, see the interview with William J. Terrell, May 9, 1995, Baylor Institute for Oral History, Baylor University, Waco, Texas.

27. Ed Lathan interview, November 28, 1976.

28. Leota Upshaw, personal communication with Richard Orton, 1995. In his oral memoir, C. C. White described a similar friendly relationship between his renter

family and that of a white landowner named Windham (White and Holland, *No Quit-tin' Sense*, 59-60). Windham treated young White almost as his own son.

29. Deola Mayberry Adams interview, August 4, 1987.

30. Freddie Eagleton interview, August 23, 1986.

31. Helen Darden, personal communication to Thad Sitton, January 8, 2002.

32. Larutha Odom Clay interview, February 11, 2002. Other freedmen's settle-ments in similar relationships to Wiergate were Cedar Grove, Indian Hill, Pleasant Hill, Saint John, Galloway, and McBride (McBride, "Out of the Depths of My Soul I Cry," 1).

33. Larry Leonard interview, June 13, 2001.

34. Many such details emerge in Mance Lipscomb's oral memoir *I Say Me for a Parable*, written with friend Glen Alyn.

35. Oscar Allen interview, March 15, 1986.

36. In an interview of September 9, 1974, Albert Ware commented on play re-lationships between children in his family at a remote freedmen's settlement and the children of a nearby white family. In early teenage years, Ware's parents forbade further social contact to protect their sons.

37. Marion Upshaw, personal communication to Richard Orton, August 1, 2002.

38. This is based on numerous oral history interviews and personal accounts, but remains a judgment call. Edward L. Ayers examined many personal sources for his study of the New South, and Ayers came to similar conclusions about back-country race relations (Ayers, *The Promise of the New South*, 134-137). In his otherwise bleak re-port on race relations in rural Mississippi, Neil R. McMillan nonetheless noted: "Indi-vidually, whites and blacks sometimes defied the rules of caste, forming deep attach-ments and lifelong friendships that served both races well. Linked by a web of feeling and mutual dependency spun by generations of intimate association, whites and blacks often managed to behave as individuals with a warmth and deeply felt concern that went beyond mere paternalism and seemed curiously out of place in a society domi-nated by race" (McMillan, *Dark Journey*, 28). Leon F. Litwack in his history of Jim Crow virtually denies the existence of genuine black-white friendships, but Litwack surely oversimplifies the situation.

39. Young, *From These Roots*, 27.

40. Chester Gregory, personal communication to Richard Orton, October 2, 2001.

41. Wesley Taylor Fobbs interview, August 10, 2001.

42. Ibid.

43. Howard Matthies interview, September 9, 1994.

44. Florarean Hall Overshown interview, August 31, 2001.

45. Green, Peter, and Shepard, "Friendship," 71-73.

46. George Francis, personal communication to Thad Sitton, August 12, 2001.

47. Sitton and Utley, *From Can See to Can't*, 238. For a discussion of the com-mon practice of cheating blacks at mercantile stores, see Ayers, *The Promise of the New South*, 148-149.

48. Cherokee County Historical Commission, "Cuney."

49. Birdie Wade, personal communication to Richard Orton, August 16, 2000.

50. King, "Mrs. Velio King," 30.

51. Andrew Lee Eleby interview, August 31, 2001.

52. Cleo Session, personal communication to Richard Orton, April 2000.

53. Texana Randolph interview, June 13, 2001.

54. Bubba Bowser interview, August 11, 1977.

55. Willie Lipscomb interview, July 16, 1977.

56. Mance Lipscomb transcripts, Lipscomb-Myers Collection, File 2k197.

57. McMillan, *Dark Journey*, 12.

58. W. A. Caplinger interview, July 7, 2001; Foote, *Farewell*, 134.

59. Glasrud, "Jim Crow's Emergence in Texas," 55.

60. Dewey Fitzpatrick interview, June 28, 1994.

61. James Wade interview, June 14, 1977.

62. Dollard, *Caste and Class in a Southern Town*, 180.

63. Sidney Green note, Lee County Historical Commission Black History Files.

64. Sitton and Conrad, *Nameless Towns*, 73.

65. Rosengarten, *All God's Dangers*, 162–169.

66. Sitton, *The Texas Sheriff*, 164.

67. McMillan, *Dark Journey*, 16.

68. Dollard, *Caste and Class in a Southern Town*, 320.

69. Ibid., 331.

70. Ibid., 359.

71. Mance Lipscomb transcripts, Lipscomb-Myers Collection, File 2k197.

72. Govenar, *Osceola*, 19.

73. White Rock note, Grayson County Historical Commission Survey Files; Rawick, *Texas Narratives*, 4:1084.

74. *New Handbook of Texas*, "Thompson, Cal," 2:4.

75. *New Handbook of Texas*, "Vann Settlement," 6:706; *Historic Matagorda County*, 1:174.

76. Dollard, *Caste and Class in a Southern Town*, 331. For racist lawmen's attitudes and policies toward rural blacks, see Sitton, *The Texas Sheriff*, 163–172.

77. Reich, "Soldiers of Democracy," 1479.

78. Ibid., 1480.

79. Buenger, *The Path to a Modern South*, 204.

80. Reich, "Soldiers of Democracy," 1502.

81. Buenger, *The Path to a Modern South*, 169.

82. Reich, "Soldiers of Democracy," 1485; Harris, "Etiquette, Lynching, and Racial Boundaries in Southern History," 398.

83. Interracial Committee, "A Report of Interracial Work in Hunt County," 4–5.

84. Sturdevant, "Black and White with Shades of Grey," 1.

85. Gilbert Osofsky, in his introduction to Raper, *Preface to Peasantry*, vi.

86. Flowers, "The Rosewood Massacre."

87. Stockley, *Blood in Their Eyes.*

88. S. L. Davis interview, 1976.

89. Buenger, *The Path to a Modern South,* 108.

90. McKenzie, "The Kellyville Incident," 39–41.

91. Akers, *Flames after Midnight,* 1–123. Lawyer Monte Akers spent years in working out the details of events at Kirvin and in Freestone County and succeeded in describing the murder, manhunt, lynching, and racial pogrom. He found strong evidence that the real murderer of Eula Ausley was the white man John Hill, who hated the girl's grandfather.

92. Ibid., 126.

93. Ibid., 128–129.

CHAPTER 7

1. Cleveland Ross, personal communication to Richard Orton, August 14, 2000. The white lawyer's name was "Cub" Denmon, and he was something of a social rebel. At that time in Nacogdoches County it was almost unheard of for a white lawyer to defend a black client against whites (Marion Upshaw, personal communication to Richard Orton, July 15, 2003).

2. Nathans, "Fortress without Walls," 62.

3. Bethel, *Promiseland,* 229–239. More fragmentary descriptions of relations between Texas freedmen's settlements and their expatriate communities exactly parallel Bethel's.

4. *New Handbook of Texas,* "Crown," 2:425.

5. *New Handbook of Texas,* "Good Hope," 3:238.

6. McKnight, *African American Families and Settlements,* 13; Mears, "African-American Settlement Patterns in Austin, Texas."

7. Hahn, "Hunting, Fishing, and Foraging."

8. Helen Darden, personal communication to Thad Sitton, January 15, 2002.

9. Smith, "The Redistribution of the Negro Population of the United States," 169; Brophy, *The Black Texan,* 18.

10. Schweninger, *Black Property Owners in the South,* 174.

11. Brown and Gust, *Between the Creeks,* xiv.

12. Lewan and Barclay, "Hundreds of Black Landowners Lost Property Through Violence, Trickery."

13. Hoskins, "Separate Streams of Discourse," 55–56.

14. Ibid.

15. McGee and Boone, *The Black Rural Landowner,* xx, 19, 64; Lewan and Barclay, "Land Traders Use Legal Ploy to Strip Black Families of Ancestral Property."

16. Interracial Committee, "A Report on Interracial Work in Hunt County," 3.

17. McMillan, *Dark Journey,* 121.

18. Steven Reich, personal communication to James H. Conrad, May 4, 2001; Flowers, "The Rosewood Massacre."

19. McDonald, *Out of the Darkness,* 145.

20. Powdermaker, *After Freedom,* 99.

21. Rawick, *Texas Narratives,* 4:1384.

22. Drummond, "Descendants Sue to Regain Land."

23. Lewan and Barclay, "Hundreds of Black Landowners Lost Property Through Violence, Trickery."

24. Ibid.

25. Barclay, Lewan, and Breed, "Black Landowners' Prosperity Made Them Targets for Violence."

26. Ibid.

27. Nathans, "Fortress without Walls," 89-101.

28. Bethel, *Promiseland,* 7.

29. W. C. Williams interview, April 12, 2001.

30. Russaw, "Winter's Hill," 43.

31. Camp County Historical Commission, "Center Point School."

32. Hunt County Historical Commission, "St. Paul School"; Adair, "A Study of the Negro Schools of Hunt County," 10-64; "St. Paul School to Close," *Greenville Herald Banner,* July 12, 1964.

33. Caston, "Built on Freedom."

34. Ibid.

35. Larry Leonard interview, June 13, 2001.

36. Houston County Historical Commission, "Lula Denby Dailey"; Houston County Historical Commission, "Wheeler Springs Community."

37. Dora Session Griffith, personal communication to Richard Orton, June 25, 2001.

38. *New Handbook of Texas,* "Germany," 3:146.

39. Bethel, *Promiseland,* 238.

40. Andrew Lee Eleby interview, August 31, 2001.

41. Jessie Mae Amie interview, August 30, 2001.

42. Quoted in O'Connor, *Tales from the San'tone River Bottom,* 102.

43. Welch, "Historic Land Lost to Tax Troubles."

44. Young, *From These Roots,* 45.

45. Grigsby, "Another Matagorda County History," 84.

46. Drummond, "Descendants Sue to Regain Land."

47. Curel Carter, personal communication to Richard Orton, March 19, 2000.

48. Helena Brown Patton, personal communication to Richard Orton, June 28, 2001.

49. Marion Upshaw, personal communication to Richard Orton, August 1, 2002.

50. Rust, "Weeping Mary," 6-14.

51. Gee, "Antioch Colony."

52. Ibid.

53. Ibid.

Bibliography

PRINT SOURCES

Abernethy, F. E., ed. *Juneteenth Texas: Essays in African American Folklore*. Denton: University of North Texas Press, 1996.

Adair, J. B. "A Study of the Negro Schools of Hunt County, 1943-44." Master's thesis, East Texas State Teachers College, 1945.

"African American Neighborhood Settlements: 1865." African American Historical Society, Brenham, Texas, n.p., n.d.

Aiken, Charles S. "A New Type of Black Ghetto in the Plantation South." *Annals of the Association of American Geographers* 80, no. 2 (1990): 223–246.

Akers, Monte. *Flames after Midnight: Murder, Vengeance, and the Desolation of a Texas Community*. Austin: University of Texas Press, 1999.

Ali, Beatrice Upshaw. "Growing Up in County Line." Unpublished manuscript, n.d.

Allyn, Glen. "Mance Lipscomb: Fight, Flight, or the Blues." In Abernethy, 69–93.

Althearn, Robert G. *In Search of Canaan: Black Migration to Kansas after Reconstruction*. Lawrence: Regents Press of Kansas, 1978.

Ayers, Edward L. *The Promise of the New South*. New York: Oxford University Press, 1992.

Azadian, Dee, ed. *Earth Has No Sorrow*. Austin: Voluntary Action Center of Caldwell County, Texas, 1977.

Baker, John Walter. *A History of Robertson County, Texas*. Waco: Texian Press, 1970.

Baker, T. Lindsay. "More Than Just Possum 'n' Taters: Texas African American Foodways in the WPA Slave Narratives." In Abernethy, 95–129.

Barclay, Dolores, Todd Lewan, and Allen G. Breed. "Black Landowners' Prosperity Made Them Targets for Violence." *Austin American-Statesman*, December 10, 2001.

Barr, Alwyn. *Black Texans: A History of Negroes in Texas, 1528–1971*. Austin: Jenkins Publishing, 1973.

Baylor, Charlie. "Charlie Baylor Narrative." Black History Files, Lee County Historical Commission, Giddings, n.d.

Bethel, Elizabeth Rauh. *Promiseland: A Century of Life in a Negro Community*. Philadelphia: Temple University Press, 1981.

Blanco County Historical Commission. "Peyton Colony Mt. Horeb Baptist Church." Blanco County Marker File, Texas Historical Commission, Austin, n.d.

———. "Peyton Colony Lime Kiln." Blanco County Marker File, Texas Historical Commission, Austin, n.d.

Bogle, Lori. "On Our Way to the Promised Land: Black Migration from Arkansas to Oklahoma, 1889–1893." *Chronicles of Oklahoma* 72, no. 2 (1994): 160–177.

Bondi, Nicole. "Detroit Producer Gives Voice to the Black West in 'Echoes,' Story of African-American Towns Created after Civil War." *Detroit News*, February 8, 1998.

Bonner, Ronald L. "Black History: Recalling a Visit to Boley, Oklahoma." *Los Angeles Sentinel*, March 4, 1998.

Bonnin, Julie. "O Little Town of Bethlehem, Texas." *Austin American-Statesman*, December 19, 1999.

Bosque County Historical Commission. "Rock Springs Cumberland Presbyterian Church." Bosque County Marker Files, Texas Historical Commission, Austin, n.d.

Bouvier, John. *Bouvier Law Dictionary*. 2 vols. St. Paul, Minn.: West Publishing Company, 1914.

Bradford, I. C. "Narrative Report, Negro County Agent Work, Cherokee County, 1928." Texas Extension Services Archives, Texas A&M University, College Station.

Bradford, Tara. "Families Trace Ancestry to Slaves." *Bowie County Citizens Tribune*, August 23, 1990.

Bralley, F. M. *Seventeenth Biennial Report of the State Superintendent for Public Instruction*. Austin: Von Boeckmann-Jones, 1910.

Brewer, J. Mason. *Dog Ghosts and the Word on the Brazos*. Austin: University of Texas Press, 1976.

Brophy, William Joseph. "The Black Texan, 1900–1950: A Quantitative History." Ph.D. diss., Vanderbilt University, 1974.

Brown, Deborah, and Katharine Gust. *Between the Creeks: Recollections of Northeast Texas*. Austin: Encino Press, 1976.

Buenger, Walter L. *The Path to a Modern South: Northeast Texas between Reconstruction and the Great Depression*. Austin, University of Texas Press, 2001.

Bundick, Marguerite. "Settlements Develop from Early Families." *Bay City Tribune*, January 21, 1977.

Burns, Richard Allen. "African American Blacksmithing in East Texas." In Abernethy, 167–193.

Caldwell County Historical Commission. "Saint John Colony." Caldwell County Marker File, Texas Historical Commission, Austin, n.d.

Calloway, Ethel, and Katie Stewart. "The Black Experience: A History of Blacks in Tyler and Smith County." In *Tyler and Smith County, Texas: An Historical Survey*, edited by Robert W. Glover, 185–200. Tyler: American Bicentennial Committee, 1976.

Calvert, Robert A. "The Freedmen and Agricultural Prosperity." *Southwestern Historical Quarterly* 76, no. 4 (1973): 461–471.

Campbell, Randolph B. *A Southern Community in Crisis: Harrison County, Texas, 1850–1880*. Austin: University of Texas Press, 1983.

———. *An Empire for Slavery: The Peculiar Institution in Texas, 1821–1865*. Baton Rouge: Louisiana State University Press, 1989.

Camp County Historical Commission. "Center Point Community." Camp County Marker Files, Texas Historical Commission, Austin, n.d.

———. "Center Point School, 1889–1952." Camp County Marker Files, Texas Historical Commission, Austin, n.d.

Caplen, John A. "Camp Big Thicket: Life in the Piney Woods, 1887." In *Tales from the Big Thicket*, edited by F. E. Abernethy, 107–113. Austin: University of Texas Press, 1966.

Carlson, Shawn Bonath. "African American Lifeways in East Central Texas: The Ned Peterson Farmstead." Reports of Investigations, no. 3. Center for Environmental Archeology, Texas A&M University, College Station, 1999.

Carroll, Robert. "Robert Lloyd Smith and the Farmers' Improvement Society of Texas." Master's thesis, Baylor University, 1974.

Caston, Kevin. "Built on Freedom: All-black Neylandville Regards Juneteenth as 'Day to Come Together.'" *Dallas Morning News*, June 19, 1994.

Chafe, William H., Raymond Gavins, and Rovert Korstad. *Remembering Jim Crow: African Americans Tell about Life in the Segregated South*. New York: New Press, 2001.

Cherokee County Historical Commission. "Cuney." Cherokee County Marker Files, Texas Historical Commission, Austin, n.d.

Chism, Fannie. "Fannie Chism." In *When I Was Just Your Age*, edited by Robert Flynn and Susan Russell, 101. Denton: University of North Texas Press, 1992.

Chumley, Leo Bertice. "Negro Labor and Property Holdings in Shelby County, Texas, 1870–1945." Master's thesis, Prairie View A&M University, 1948.

Clark, Thomas D. *Frontier America*. New York: Scribner, 1969.

Clayton, Ora L. Giddings. "The Fields Community." In McKnight, 18–19.

Coffee, Hattie, and Kathy Jones. "Peyton's Colony of Board House." In *Heritage of Blanco County, Texas*, 137–140. Blanco: Blanco County News, 1987.

Coryell County, Texas, Families, 1854–1985. Gatesville, Texas: Coryell County Genealogical Society, 1986.

Cotton, Walter. *History of the Negroes of Limestone County from 1860 to 1939*. Mexia, Texas, 1939.

Cravens, John N. *Between Two Rivers: A History of Wells, Texas*. Wichita Falls, 1974.

———. "Sweet Union." In *Cherokee County History*, 66. N.p.: Cherokee County Historical Commission, 1986.

Crosby, Earl W. "Limited Success against Long Odds: The Black County Agent." *Agricultural History* 57, no. 3 (1983): 277–288.

Crouch, Barry A. *The Freedmen's Bureau and Black Texans.* Austin, University of Texas Press, 1992.

Curlee, Abigail. "A Study of Texas Slave Plantations, 1822-1865." Ph.D. diss., University of Texas at Austin, 1932.

Daniel, Pete. *Breaking the Land: The Transformation of Cotton, Tobacco, and Rice Cutures Since 1880.* Urbana: University of Illinois Press, 1986.

Darling, Marsha Jean. "Black Land Ownership." In Wilson and Ferris, 169-170.

DeWitt County Historical Commission. "Hopkinsville: A Colony of Freedmen." DeWitt County Marker Files, Texas Historical Commission, Austin, n.d.

Dollard, John. *Caste and Class in a Southern Town.* New Haven: Yale University Press, 1937.

Donovan, Richard. "Neches River Manuscript." Unpublished manuscript, n.d.

Dorsey, Lorene. "Dr. Fred William Cariker." *Chinquapin* 8 (1979): 56-58.

Doughty, Robin. *Wildlife and Man in Texas.* College Station: Texas A&M University Press, 1983.

Drummond, Bob. "Descendants Sue to Regain Land." *Dallas Times Herald,* June 20, 1984.

Earls, Henry. "Smith Chapel Memories." *Loblolly* 6 (1982): 60-64.

Easton, Hamilton Pratt. "The History of the Texas Lumbering Industry." Ph.D. diss., University of Texas at Austin, 1947.

Ellis, John Marion. *The Way It Was: A Personal Memoir of Family Life in East Texas.* Waco: Texian Press, 1983.

Emmons, Martha. *Deep Like the Rivers: Stories of My Negro Friends.* Austin: Encino Press, 1969.

Finnegan, William. "Deep East Texas." *New Yorker* 70, no. 26 (1994): 72-97.

Fisher, James S. "Negro Farm Ownership in the South." *Annals of the Association of American Geographers* 63, no. 4 (1973): 478-489.

Flowers, Charles. "The Rosewood Massacre: From Rumor to Fact." *Seminole Tribune,* March 4, 1994.

Foley, Douglas E., Clarice Mota, Donald E. Post, and Ignacio Lozano. *From Peones to Politicos: Ethnic Relations in a South Texas Town, 1900 to 1977.* Austin: University of Texas Press, 1977.

Foote, Horton. *Farewell: A Memoir of a Texas Childhood.* New York: Scribner, 1999.

Fort Bend County Historical Commission. "Kendleton." Fort Bend County Marker Files, Texas Historical Commission, Austin, n.d.

Freeman, Martha Doty, Amy E. Dase, and Marie E. Blake. "Agriculture and Rural Development on Fort Hood Lands, 1849-1942; National Register Assessments of 710 Historic Archeological Properties." United States Army Fort Hood Archeological Resource Management Series, Research Report No. 42, January 2001.

Freeman, Susie. "Notes." Black History Files, Lee County Historical Commission, Giddings, n.d.

Friedman, Lawrence J. "Life 'In the Lion's Mouth': Another Look at Booker T. Washington." *Journal of Negro History* 59, no. 4 (1974): 337-351.

Gandara, Ricardo. "Church Homecoming Unites Relatives, History." *Austin American-Statesman,* October, 20, 1997.

Gee, Robert W. "Antioch Colony: A Living History, Coming Home Again." *Austin American-Statesman,* September 30, 2000.

Gillard, Rev. John T. "A Yankee Priest in Dixie Gets a Taste of Rural Mission Life." *Colored Harvest* 26 (1939): 7–14.

Glasrud, Bruce A. "Child or Beast?: White Texas' View of Blacks, 1900–1910." *East Texas Historical Journal* 15, no. 2 (1977): 38–44.

———. "Jim Crow's Emergence in Texas." *American Studies* 15, no. 1 (1974): 47–60.

Govenar, Allen. "Musical Traditions of Twentieth-Century African American Cowboys." In Abernethy, 195–207.

———. *Osceola: Memories of a Sharecropper's Daughter.* New York: Hyperion, 2000.

Green, Melissa M., Duane E. Peter, and Donna K. Shepard. "Friendship: An African-American Community on the Prairie Margin of Northeast Texas." Plano: Geo-Marine, Inc., 1996.

Green, Sidney. "Notes." Black History Files, Lee County Historical Commission, Giddings, n.d.

Gregg County Historical Commission. "Shiloh Baptist Church." Gregg County Marker Files, Texas Historical Commission, Austin, 1992.

———. "Shiloh School." Gregg County Marker Files, Texas Historical Commission, Austin, 1998.

Grigsby, Courtney L. "Another Matagorda County History: A Collection of Interviews, Documents, Letters, and Clippings, On the Edge of History." Unpublished manuscript, n.d. Matagorda County Historical Commission, Bay City.

Grigsby, Rebecca F. "My Story." *Chinquapin* 21 (1991): 91.

Grim, Valerie. "African American Landlords in the Rural South, 1870–1950: A Profile." *Agricultural History* 72, no. 2 (1998): 399–416.

Grindal, Bruce T. "The Religious Interpretation of Experience in a Rural Black Community." In Hall and Stack, 88–101.

Guderjan, Thomas H. "Forest Grove: A Dispersed Farming Community in East Texas." *East Texas Historical Journal* 20, no. 1 (1982): 27–31.

Hahn, Steven. "Hunting, Fishing, and Foraging: Common Rights and Class Relations in the Postbellum South." *Radical History Review* 26 (1982): 37–64.

Hall, Robert L., and Carol B. Stack, eds. *Holding On to the Land and the Lord: Kinship, Ritual, Land Tenure, and Social Policy in the Rural South.* Athens: University of Georgia Press, 1982.

Hamilton, Kenneth M. "The Origins and Early Promotion of Nicodemus: A Pre-Exodus, All-Black Town." *Kansas History* 5, no. 4 (1966): 220–242.

———. "White Wealth and Black Repression in Harrison County, Texas, 1865–1868." *Journal of Negro History* 83 (1998): 340–359.

Harlan, Louis R. *Booker T. Washington—The Wizard of Tuskegee.* New York: Oxford University Press, 1983.

Harlan, Louis R., and Raymond W. Smock, eds. *The Booker T. Washington Papers.* 14 vols. Urbana: University of Illinois Press, 1981.

Harris County Historical Commission. "The Kohrville Community." Harris County Marker File, Texas Historical Commission, Austin, 2002.

Harris, J. William. "Etiquette, Lynching, and Racial Boundaries in Southern History: A Mississippi Example." *American Historical Review* 100 (1995): 387–410.

Hayman, Bettie. "A Short History of the Negro of Walker County, 1860–1942." Master's thesis, Sam Houston State Teachers College, 1942.

Heritage of Blanco County, Texas. Dallas: Blanco County News, 1987.

Hermann, Janet. *The Pursuit of a Dream.* New York: Oxford University Press, 1981.

Hess, R. B. "Ex-Slaves Founded Blanco Peyton Colony." *Austin American-Statesman,* August 6, 1954.

Hill, Robert L. "Clarksville: The Community and Its Struggle." Unpublished manuscript, 1979. Austin History Center, Austin, Texas.

Hilliard, Sam Bowen. *Hog Meat and Hoecake: Food Supply in the Old South, 1840–1860.* Carbondale: Southern Illinois University Press, 1972.

Historic Matagorda County. 3 vols. N.p.: Matagorda County Historical Commission, 1986–1988.

History of Houston County, Texas: 1687–1979. Tulsa, Okla: Heritage Publishing Company, 1979.

History of Lee County, Texas. Giddings: Lee County Historical Survey Committee, 1974.

Hogan, William R. *The Texas Republic: A Social and Economic History.* Norman: University of Oklahoma Press, 1946.

Holland, Ada Morehead. *Mr. Claude.* College Station: Texas A&M University Press, 1984.

Hoskins, Deborah J. "Separate Streams of Discourse: Identity and the Rise of the Corporate State in East Texas, 1919–1935." Ph.D. diss., Indiana University, 1991.

Houston County Historical Commission. "Allen Chapel." Houston County Marker Files, Texas Historical Commission, Austin, 1996.

———. "Cedar Branch Community and School." Texas Historical Commission Marker File, Austin, 1996.

———. "Fodice." Houston County Marker Files, Texas Historical Commission, Austin, 1997.

———. "Fodice Community School." Houston County Marker Files, Texas Historical Commission, Austin, 1997.

———. "Germany." Houston County Marker Files, Texas Historical Commission, Austin, 1997.

———. "Givens's Hill." Houston County Marker Files, Texas Historical Commission, Austin, 1997.

———. "Hall's Bluff." Houston County Marker Files, Texas Historical Commission, Austin, 1996.

———. "Lula Denby Dailey." Houston County Marker Files, Texas Historical Commission, Austin, 1996.

———. "Richard King and Rachel Ellis King." Houston County Marker Files, Texas Historical Commission, Austin, 1997.

———. "Wheeler Springs Community." Houston County Marker Files, Texas Historical Commission, Austin, 1994.

Hunt, Annie Mae, and Ruthe Winegarten. *"I Am Annie Mae": An Extraordinary Black Texas Woman in Her Own Words.* Austin: University of Texas Press, 1983.

Hunt County Historical Commission. "St. Paul School." Hunt County Marker Files, Texas Historical Commission, Austin, n.d.

Interracial Committee. "A Report on Interracial Work in Hunt County." Hunt County File, Archives, Texas A&M University–Commerce.

Jackson, LaVonne Roberts. "Freedom and Family: The Freedmen's Bureau and African-American Women in Texas in the Reconstruction Era." Ph.D. diss., Howard University, 1996.

Johnson, Stephen. "Kendleton: City in Fort Bend County Had Its Start as a Community of Freed Slaves." *Houston Chronicle,* April 21, 1980.

Jones, Carolyn. "This Juneteenth, Step Back in Time with Small Towns." *Austin American-Statesman,* June 11, 2000.

Jordan, Terry G. *Texas Graveyards: A Cultural Legacy.* Austin: University of Texas Press, 1982.

King, Mrs. Velio. "Mrs. Velio King." *Chinquapin* 21 (1991): 30–31.

Kirby, Jack Temple. *Rural Worlds Lost: The American South, 1920–1960.* Baton Rouge: Louisiana State University Press, 1990.

Lake, Mary D. "Superstitions about Cotton." In *Southwestern Lore,* edited by J. Frank Dobie, 145–151. Dallas: Southern Methodist University Press, 1965.

Lewan, Todd, and Dolores Barclay. "Hundreds of Black Landowners Lost Property Through Violence, Trickery." *Austin American-Statesman,* December 9, 2001.

———. "Land Traders Use Legal Ploy to Strip Black Families of Ancestral Property." *Austin American-Statesman,* December 11, 2001.

Lewis, Oscar. *On the Edge of the Black Waxy: A Cultural Survey of Bell County, Texas.* Washington University Studies, New Series, Social and Philosophical Sciences, no. 7. St. Louis, 1948.

Lipscomb, Mance, and Glen Alyn. *I Say Me for a Parable.* New York: Norton, 1993.

Litwack, Leon F. *Been in the Storm So Long: The Aftermath of Slavery.* New York: Knopf, 1979.

———. *Trouble in Mind: Black Southerners in the Age of Jim Crow.* New York: Knopf, 1998.

Lotto, F. *Fayette County: Her History and People.* Schulenburg, Texas, 1902.

Loughmiller, Campbell, and Lynn Loughmiller. *Big Thicket Legacy.* Austin: University of Texas Press, 1977.

Magol, Edward. *A Right to the Land: Essays on the Freedmen's Community.* Westport, Conn.: Greenwood Press, 1977.

Marks, Stuart A. *Southern Hunting in Black and White*. Princeton: Princeton University Press, 1991.

Matustik, David. "Holding On: Peyton Colony Rich in Juneteenth Spirit." *Austin American-Statesman*, June 15, 1991.

Mayfield, Bernard. "Cuney." In *Cherokee County History*, 49–50. Jacksonville: Cherokee County Historical Commission, 1986.

McBride, Van Bette Robertson. "Out of the Depths of My Soul I Cry." Unpublished manuscript. Archives, Texas A&M University-Commerce, 1998.

McDonald, Bobby. *Out of the Darkness: The Black Face of Hopkins County, Volume III*. Self published. Archives, Texas A&M University-Commerce, n.d.

McDonald, Forrest, and Grady McWhiney. "The Antebellum Southern Herdsman: A Reinterpretation." *Journal of Southern History* 44 (1975): 147–166.

McGee, Leo, and Robert Boone, eds. *The Black Rural Landowner—Endangered Species*. Westport, Conn.: Greenwood Press, 1979.

McKenzie, Fred. "The Kellyville Incident." *East Texas Historical Journal* 37, (Spring 1999): 39–41.

McKnight, Mamie L., ed. *African American Families and Settlements: On the Inside Looking Out*. Dallas: Black Dallas Remembered, Inc., 1990.

McMath, Robert C. *American Populism: A Social History, 1877–1898*. New York: Hill and Wang, 1993.

McMillan, Eva Partee. "Upper and Lower White Rock." In McKnight, 46–52.

McMillan, Neil R. *Dark Journey: Black Mississippians in the Age of Jim Crow*. Urbana: University of Illinois, 1989.

McQueen, Clyde. *Black Churches in Texas: A Guide to Historic Congregations*. College Station: Texas A&M University Press, 2000.

Mears, Michelle M. "African-American Settlement Patterns in Austin, Texas, 1865–1928." Master's thesis, Baylor University, 2001.

———. "Freedmen Towns in the Capital City." *Medallion* 39, nos. 1–2 (2002): 6.

Medina County Historical Commission. "Mission Valley." Medina County Marker Files, Texas Historical Commission, Austin, 1986.

Meyers, Lois E. "Fellowship of Kindred Minds: Planting Cotton and Harvesting Souls of the Central Texas Plain." Paper presented to Sixth Annual Cotton and Rural History Conference of Audie Murphy/American Cotton Museum, Commerce, Texas, April 27, 2002.

Mirgan, Jessie. "East Texas Town Founded by Freed Slaves Disappearing." *Fort Worth Star-Telegram*, February 9, 2000.

Montell, William. *The Saga of Coe Ridge: A Study in Oral History*. Knoxville: University of Tennessee Press, 1970.

Moore, Mary. "Notes." Black History Files, Lee County Historical Commission, n.d.

Nathans, Sidney. "Fortress without Walls: A Black Community after Slavery." In Hall and Stack, 55–63.

Navarro County Historical Commission. "Pelham Community." Navarro County Marker Files, Texas Historical Commission, Austin, 1975.

New Handbook of Texas. 6 vols. Edited by Ron Tyler et al. Austin: Texas State Historical Association, 1996.

Newton County Historical Commission. "Shankleville." Newton County Marker Files, Texas Historical Commission, Austin, 1972.

O'Connor, Louise. *Cryin' for Daylight: A Ranching Culture in the Texas Coastal Bend*. Austin: Wexford Publishing, 1989.

———. *Tales from the San'tone River Bottom: A Cultural History*. Victoria: Wexford Publishing, 1998.

Orton, Richard. "The Upshaws of County Line: A Photographic Narrative." Text of photography exhibit, Austin, Texas, 1998.

Oubre, Caude F. *Forty Acres and a Mule: The Freedmen's Bureau and Black Landowner-ship*. Baton Rouge: Louisiana State University Press, 1978.

Owens, William A. *This Stubborn Soil: A Frontier Boyhood*. New York: Nick Lyons Books, 1966.

Owsley, Frank L. *Plain Folk of the Old South*. Baton Rouge: Louisiana State University Press, 1949.

Painter, Neil Irvin. "Exodusters." In *Encyclopedia of African-American Culture and History*, edited by Jack Salzman, David L. Smith, and Cornel West, 920–922. New York: Macmillan, 1996.

Panola County Historical Commission. "Holland Quarters." Panola County Marker Files, Texas Historical Commission, Austin, 1996.

Pelham Community Organization. "Memories of Pelham." Typescript, 1999.

Pemberton, Doris Hollis. *Juneteenth at Comanche Crossing*. Austin: Eakin, 1983.

Penningroth, Dylan. "Slavery, Freedom, and Social Claims to Property among African Americans in Liberty County, Georgia, 1850–1880." *Journal of American History* 84, no. 2 (1997): 406–435.

Pierson, Marla. "Piecing Together the Past." *Waco Tribune-Herald*, November 27, 1997.

Potts, Lawrence A. "The Negro in the Rural Areas of East Texas." Master's thesis, Cornell University, 1932.

Powdermaker, Hortense. *After Freedom: A Cultural Study in the Deep South*. New York: Russell and Russell, 1939.

Ragdale, Mrs. L. W. "Narrative Report, Home Demonstration Work, Cherokee County, 1928." Texas Extension Service Archives, Texas A&M University, College Station.

Ramos, Ralph. *Rocking Texas' Cradle*. Beaumont: Enterprise Company, 1974.

Raper, Arthur F. *Preface to Peasantry: A Tale of Two Black Belt Counties*. New York: Atheneum, 1936.

Rawick, George P., ed. *Texas Narratives*. Vols. 2–10 of *The American Slave: A Composite Autobiography*. Series 2. Westport, Conn.: Greenwood Publishing Co., 1972–1973.

Redwine, W. A. *History of Five Counties*. Tyler: 1901.

Reich, Steven A. "Searching for 'Lost Land': Squatters, Lumbermen, the Making of the Texas Lumber Industry, 1870–1920." Paper presented to the September meeting of the East Texas Historical Association, Nacogdoches, Texas, 2000.

———. "Soldiers of Democracy: Black Texans and the Fight for Citizenship, 1917–1921." *Journal of American History* 82, no. 4 (1996): 1478–1504.

Reid, Debra Ann. "Reaping a Greater Harvest: African Americans, Agrarian Reform, and the Texas Agricultural Extension Service." Ph.D. diss., Texas A&M University, 2000.

Reid, Whitelaw. *After the War: A Tour of the Southern States, 1865–1866.* New York: Harper and Row, 1966.

Report of the Results of the Texas Statewide School Adequacy Survey. Austin: State Board of Education, 1937.

Rice, Laurence D. *The Negro in Texas, 1874–1900.* Baton Rouge: Lousiana State University Press, 1981.

Riles, Karen. "The Rosenwald School Building Program in Texas, 1920–1932." Texas Historical Commission Application to National Register of Historic Places, National Park Service, 1998. Texas Historical Commission, Austin.

———. "Sweet Home Vocational and Agricultural High School." Texas Historical Commission Application to National Register of Historic Places, National Park Service, 1998. Texas Historical Commission, Austin.

Rose, Harold M. "The All-Negro Town: Its Evolution and Function." *Geographical Review* 55, no. 3 (July 1965): 362–381.

Rosen, Joel N. "Mound Bayou, Mississippi." *Encyclopedia of African-American Culture and History,* edited by Jack Salzman, David L. Smith, and Cornel West, 1872–1873. New York: Macmillan, 1996.

Rosengarten, Theodore. *All God's Dangers: The Life of Nate Shaw.* New York: Knopf, 1974.

Ross, Judge Donald R. "Black Sacred Harp Singing Remembered in East Texas." In Abernethy, 15–19.

Russaw, Annie B. "Winter's Hill." *Chinquapin* 1 (1976): 42–43.

Rust, Carol. "Weeping Mary." *Houston Chronicle Magazine,* April 19, 1998, pp. 6–14.

Saint Paul Reunion Association. "A Collection of Pages from the History of Neylandville and Saint Paul School." Neylandville, Texas, 1988. Archives, Texas A&M University–Commerce.

Sample, Albert Race. *Racehoss: Big Emma's Boy.* Austin: Eakin Press, 1984.

Schaadt, Robert, ed. *Hardin County History.* Dallas: Hardin County Historical Commission, 1991.

Schlosser, Jim. "Black Town Outgrows Role at Pinehurst." *Greensboro News & Record,* June 20, 1999.

Schweninger, Loren. *Black Property Owners in the South, 1790–1915.* Urbana: University of Illinois Press, 1990.

Scott, Herman. "County Negress, 95, Recalls Reb Soldiers." *Greenville Banner,* June 18, 1956.

Shanklin, Annie Mae Thomas. *Precious Memories.* Charles R. Drew Alumni Association, 1997.

Sharpless, Rebecca. *Fertile Ground, Narrow Choices: Women on Texas Cotton Farms, 1900–1940.* Chapel Hill: University of North Carolina Press, 1999.

Shepard, Donna K. "Historical/Archival Research and Oral History Study of an Area East of the Wallisville Townsite and the Associated African American Community, Wallisville Lake Project, Chambers County, Texas." Wallisville Lake Project, Technical Series Reports of Investigations, no. 1, 1995.

Shine, Dan. "Enjoying the Simple Life of Frog." *Dallas Morning News,* April 29, 1991.

Silverthorne, Elizabeth. *Plantation Life in Texas.* College Station: Texas A&M University Press, 1986.

Sitton, Thad. *Backwoodsmen: Stockmen and Hunters along a Big Thicket River Valley.* Norman: University of Oklahoma Press, 1995.

———. "Texas Freedmen's Settlements in the Context of the New South." Paper presented to East Texas Historical Association, Nacogdoches, Texas, Fall 2000.

———. *Texas High Sheriffs.* Austin: Texas Monthly Press, 1988.

———. *The Texas Sheriff: Lord of the County Line.* Norman: University of Oklahoma Press, 2000.

Sitton, Thad, and James Conrad. *Nameless Towns: Texas Sawmill Communities, 1880–1942.* Austin: University of Texas Press, 1998.

Sitton, Thad, and Milam C. Rowold. *Ringing the Children In: Texas Country Schools.* College Station: Texas A&M University Press, 1987.

Sitton, Thad, and Dan K. Utley. *From Can See to Can't: Texas Cotton Farmers on the Southern Prairies.* Austin: University of Texas Press, 1997.

Sitton, Thad, and Lincoln King, eds. *The Loblolly Book: Omnibus Edition.* Austin: Texas Monthly Press, 1986.

Smallwood, James M. *Born in Dixie: Smith County from 1875 to Its Centennial Year.* Austin: Eakin, n.d.

———. "Through the Eyes of the Freedmen: Reconstruction in Texas." Paper presented to East Texas Historical Association, Texarkana, Texas, March 2001.

———. *Time of Hope, Time of Despair: Black Texans during Reconstruction.* Port Washington: Kennikat Press, 1981.

Smallwood, James M., Barry A. Crouch, and Larry Peacock. *Murder and Mayhem: The War of Reconstruction in Texas.* College Station: Texas A&M University Press, 2003.

Smith, Jarvis. "James Smith." African-American History Files, Lee County Historical Commission, Giddings, Texas, n.d.

Smith, T. Lynn. "The Redistribution of the Negro Population of the United States, 1920–1960." *Journal of Negro History* 51, no. 3 (1966): 151–169.

Smithwick, Noah. *The Evolution of a State: Old Texas Days.* Reprint, Austin: University of Texas Press, 1983.

State Department of Education. "Negro Education in Texas." *Bulletin 295,* September 1931, 9–19.

State Department of Education. "Negro Education in Texas: 1934–1935." *Bulletin 343,* March 1935, 7–16.

Stimpson, Eddie ("Sarge"), Jr. *My Remembers: A Black Sharecropper's Recollections of the Depression.* Denton: University of North Texas Press, 1996.

Stockley, Grif. *Blood in Their Eyes: The Elaine Race Massacres of 1919.* Fayettville: University of Arkansas Press, 2001.

Stovall, Frances, Dorothy Wimberley Kerbow, Maxine Storm, Louise Simon, Dorothy Woods Schwartz, and Gene Johnson. *Clear Springs and Limestone Ledges: A History of San Marcos and Hays County.* Austin: Nortex Press, 1986.

Strahan, Opal. "The Church of God in Shankleville Community." In *Crosscuts: An Anthology of Memoirs by Newton County Folks,* edited by Newton County Historical Commission, 211–213. Austin: Eakin, 1984.

Sturdevant, Paul E. "Black and White with Shades of Grey: The Greenville Sign." Typescript, April 30, 2002. Archives, Texas A&M University–Commerce.

Taplin, Dave. "Picking and Pulling." In *Hidden Memories,* edited by Pamela McGlaum, 27–31. Burton: Burton High School, 1979.

Tarrant County Historical Commission. "Mosier Valley." Tarrant County Marker Files, Texas Historical Commission, Austin, 1982.

Tatum, Charles Edward. *Shelby County: In the East Texas Hills.* Austin: Eakin, 1984.

Taylor, Quntard. "Black Towns." In *Encyclopedia of African-American Culture and History,* edited by Jack Salzman, David L. Smith, and Cornel West, 369–374. New York, Macmillan, 1996.

Teddlie, Anne. "Clarksville: An Austin Community." Typescript, 1973. Austin History Center, Austin.

Tolbert, Frank X. "Boardhouse Folk Are 'Just Content.'" *Dallas Morning News,* December 8, 1963.

———. "The Changes around Weeping Mary Town." *Dallas Morning News,* August 11, 1970.

———. "On Devout Citizens of Fodice (4 Dice)." *Dallas Morning News,* October 5, 1964.

———. "Ninety-two-year-old Twins Called Big and Dee." *Dallas Morning News,* January 21, 1973.

———. "Visit to the City of Weeping Mary." *Dallas Morning News,* February 24, 1964.

———. "Weeping Mary Should Be Called 'Crying Candace.'" *Dallas Morning News,* October 16, 1972.

Traylor, Ronald D. "Harrison Barrett: A Freedman in Post-Civil War Texas." Master's thesis, University of Houston, 1999.

Truvillion, Jesse. "Henry Truvillion of the Big Thicket: A Song Worth Singing." In Abernethy, 21–39.

Turner, Allan. "Boardhouse: Remains of Century-Old Dreams." *Austin American-Statesman,* November 5, 1972.

Turner, Morris. *America's Black Towns and Settlements: A Historical and Reference Guide.* Rohnert, Calif., 1998.

Tyler, Ronnie C., and Lawrence R. Murphy, eds. *The Slave Narratives of Texas.* Austin: Encino Press, 1974.

Van Ryzin, Jeanne Claire. "A Personal Journey across the Racial Divide." *Austin American-Statesman,* February 5, 1999.

Washington, April M. "All-Black Town Grew from Idealism." *Denver Rocky Mountain News,* October 19, 1999.

Washington, Booker T. *Up From Slavery.* Reprint, New York: Signet, 2000.

Washington County Historical Commission. "African-American Neighborhood Settlements, 1865." Brenham, Texas, n.d.

Welch, Wenda Latham. "Historic Land Lost to Tax Troubles." *Austin American-Statesman,* July 1, 1989.

Westmacott, Richard. *African-American Gardens and Yards in the Rural South.* Knoxville: University of Tennessee Press, 1992.

Whalen, Ken. "Wynn Community Struggles, Looks for Grant Money." *Tyler Courier-Times-Telegraph,* March 9, 1996.

Whitaker, Buford. "Appreciate Life the Way It Is." *Chinquapin* 3, no. 2 (1981): 52–57.

White, C. C., and Ada M. Holland. *No Quittin' Sense.* Austin: University of Texas Press, 1969.

Wilkerson, Floyd. "Booker T. Washington Edition." In McKnight, 16–17.

Wilkerson, Valerie Culp. "The Old Iron Pot." *Lufkin Daily News,* November 21, 1990.

Wilkison, Kyle. "The End of Independence: Social and Political Consequences of Growth in Texas, 1870–1914." Ph.D. diss., Vanderbilt University, 1995.

Williams, David A. *Juneteenth: Unique Heritage.* Austin: Texas African-American Heritage Organization, 1992.

Williams, Lorece P. "Country Black." In *The Folklore of Texas Culture,* edited by Francis E. Abernethy, 118–129. Austin: Encino Press, 1974.

Williams, Michael. *Americans and Their Forests: A Historical Geography.* Cambridge: Cambridge University Press, 1989.

Wilson, Charles Reagan, and William Ferris, eds. *Encyclopedia of Southern Culture.* Chapel Hill: University of North Carolina Press, 1989.

Wilson, William H. "Growing Up Black in East Texas: Some Twentieth-Century Experiences." *East Texas Historical Journal* 32, no. 1 (1994): 49–54.

Winegarten, Ruthe, Janet G. Humphrey, and Frieda Werden, eds. *Black Texas Women: 150 Years of Trial and Triumph.* Austin: University of Texas Press, 1995.

Wisdom, Emma Jackson. Untitled manuscript, n.d. Black History Files, Lee County Historical Commission, Giddings.

Wonzer, Shauna. "Pastor Says Integration Not Always Positive for Blacks." *Tyler Morning Telegraph,* July 2, 2002.

Woodson, Carter G. *The Rural Negro.* New York: Russell and Russell, 1930.

Wright, Cheryl. "I Heard It Through the Grapevine: Oral Tradition in a Rural African American Community in Brazoria, Texas." Master's thesis, University of Houston, 1994.

Yeats, E. L., and E. H. Shelton. *History of Fisher County, Texas.* Roby, Texas, 1971.

Young, Frederick. *From These Roots.* Houston: Southern University Press, 1973.

ORAL SOURCES

Adams, Deola Mayberry. Taped interview with Rebecca Sharpless, 1987. Baylor Institute for Oral History (hereafter BU).

Amie, Jessie Mae. Taped interview with Thad Sitton, 2001. Houston County Historical Commission, Crockett, Texas (hereafter HCHC).

Ashby, Frank. Taped interviews (3) with Thad Sitton, 1992. East Texas Collection, Stephen F. Austin State University, Nacogdoches, Texas (hereafter SFA).

Ball, Mrs. Tom D. Taped interview with James Conrad, 1991. Archives, Texas A&M University–Commerce (hereafter A&M)

Ball, Tom D. Taped interview with James Conrad, 1991. A&M.

Berry, Eldon. Personal communication to Thad Sitton, July 11, 2001.

Berry, Leslie M. Personal communication to Thad Sitton, July 11, 2001.

Berry, Rhoda Bowers. Taped interview with Corrinne E. Crow, 1973. A&M.

Bowser, Bubba. Taped interview with Glen Alyn, 1977. Lipscomb-Myers Collection, Center for American History, University of Texas at Austin (hereafter LMC).

Brown, Israel L. Taped interview with Marguerite Bundick, 1977. Matagorda County Historical Commission Archive, Bay City, Texas (hereafter MCHC).

Brown, Lorraine. Taped interview with Marguerite Bundick, 1977. MCHC.

Brunt, Frank. Taped interviews (2) with Thad Sitton, 1986. Center for American History, University of Texas at Austin (hereafter CAH).

Byars, Lula. Taped interview with Thad Sitton, 1979. CAH.

Calvert, Ruth. Personal communication to Richard Orton, 2000.

Canton, Soporhia Dennis. Taped interview with Dan Scurlock, 2002. A&M.

Caplinger, W. A. Taped interview with James H. Conrad, 2001. A&M.

Carpenter, George. Taped interviews (2) with Thad Sitton, 1985–1986. SFA.

Carpenter, Oscar. Taped interview with Margaurite Bundick, 1975. MCHC.

Carter, Curel. Personal communication to Richard Orton, 2000.

Carter, Margarite Session. Personal communication to Richard Orton, 2000.

Clay, Larutha Odom. Taped interview with James H. Conrad, 2002. A&M.

Click, Cutic. Taped interview with Dan Scurlock, 2002. A&M.

Click, Joseph C. Taped interview with Dan Scurlock, 2002. A&M.

Cole, Aubrey. Taped interviews (2) with Thad Sitton, 1992. SFA.

Cotton, Arthur. Taped interview with Dan Scurlock, 2002. A&M.

Darden, Helen. Personal communication to Thad Sitton, 2002.

Davis, Jennie Tillie. Personal communication to Richard Orton, 2002.

Davis, Lillie Lipscomb. Taped interview with Glen Alyn, 1977. LMC.

Davis, Mige Priestly. Personal communication to Richard Orton, 2002.

Davis, S. L. Taped interview with Dee Azadian, 1976. CAH.

Dean, Mrs. Corener. Taped interview with Corrinne E. Crow, 1973. A&M.

Denman, Chester. Personal communication to Thad Sitton, 2001.

Dennis Charles. Taped interview with Dan Scurlock, 2002. A&M.

Dixon, Addie Mae Barrett. Taped interview with Ronald D. Traylor, 1996. R. D. Traylor Collection, Houston, Texas (hereafter RDTC).

Eagleton, Freddie. Taped interview with Addie Mae Barrett Dixon, 1986. RDC.

Earls, Horace. Taped interview with Marguerite Bundick, 1977. MCHC.

Earls, Lizzie Brown. Taped interviews (2) with Marguerite Bundick, 1977. MCHC.

Eleby, Andrew Lee. Taped interview with Thad Sitton, 2001. HCHC.

Ewing, Olivie ("Chang"). Taped interview with Glen Alyn, 1976. LMC.

Fields, Lottie Ferguson. Personal communication to Richard Orton, 2001.

Fitzpatrick, Dewey. Taped interviews with Corrinne E. Crow, 1978; with Fred Allison, 1994. A&M.

Fletcher, Cleveland. Taped interviews (2) with Marguerite Bundick, 1975–1977. MCHC.

Fletcher, Corina Bell. Taped interview with Marguerite Bundick, 1975. MCHC.

Fobbs, Wesley Taylor. Taped interviews (2) with Thad Sitton, 2001. HCHC.

Francis, George. Personal communication to Thad Sitton, 2001.

Francis, Vivian L. Personal communication to Thad Sitton, 2001.

Franks, Frankie. Taped interview with Thad Sitton, 1979. CAH.

Freeman, Will. Taped interview with Addie Mae Barrett Dixon, 1986. RDC.

Gracey, Minnie Lang. Taped interview with Addie Mae Barrett Dixon, 1986. RDC.

Gregory, Chester. Personal communication to Richard Orton, 2001.

Gregory, Pearl Lee. Personal communication to Richard Orton, 2001, 2002.

Griffith, Dora Sessions. Personal communication to Richard Orton, 2001.

Hall, Ophelia Mae Mayberry. Taped interviews (2) with Rebecca Sharpless, 1986. BU.

Hancock, Earnest. Taped interview with Thad Sitton, 1994. BU.

Hardeman, Hiram. Taped interview with Dee Azadian, 1977. CAH.

Hardeman, Rosie Lee. Taped interview with Dee Azadian, 1977. CAH.

Harris, Richard. Taped interview with Louise O'Connor, 1992. Texas Coastal Bend Collection.

Henderson, Ada. Taped interview with Marguerite Bundick, 1975. MCHC.

Henderson, Roscoe. Taped interviews (3) with Marguerite Bundick, 1975. MCHC.

Henson, Roosevelt. Taped interviw with Dan Scurlock, 2002. A&M.

Johnson, C. L. Taped interview with Dan Scurlock, 2002. A&M.

Johnson, Eunice Brown. Taped interviews (2) with Rebecca Sharpless, 1986–1987. BU.

Johnson, Jack. Taped interview with Allen Turner and Catherine Jones, 1975. CAH.

Johnson, J. E. Personal communication to Richard Orton, 2000.

Johnson, Nieman. Taped interview with Allen Turner and Catherine Jones, 1978. CAH.

Jones, Austin. Taped interview with Allan Turner, 1977. CAH.

Jones, Cathy. Taped interview with Allan Turner, 1978. CAH.

Jones, Nelson. Taped interview with Dee Azadian, 1977. CAH.

Joyce, Claudie May. Personal communications to Richard Orton, 1997, 2000.

Keatts, Rowena Weatherly. Taped interviews (5) with Rebecca Sharpless, 1986–1987. BU.

Lathan, Ed. Taped interviews (2) with Glen Alyn, 1975–1976. LMC.

Lathan, Ed. Taped interview with Thad Sitton, 1995.

Law, Roosevelt. Taped interview with Marguerite Bundick, 1977. MCHC.

Lay, Daniel W. Taped interviews (2) with Thad Sitton, 1989–1992. SFA.

Leonard, Larry. Taped interview with Thad Sitton, 2001. HCHC.

Lincecum, Charlie. Taped interview with Dan K. Utley, 1992. BU.

Lipscomb, Elnora. Taped interviews (3) with Glen Alyn, 1973–1975. LMC.

Lipscomb, Mance. Taped interviews (11) with Glen Alyn, 1973–1975. LMC.

Lipscomb, Willie. Taped interview with Glen Alyn, 1977. LMC.

Loud, Jonnie. Taped interview with Thad Sitton, 1994. BU.

Lovelady, Vivian. Taped interviews (2) with Thad Sitton, 2001. HCHC.

Manning, Ruth Weatherly. Taped interview with Rebecca Sharpless, 1987. BU.

Mathis, Alma Martin. Taped interview with Thad Sitton, 2001. HCHC.

Mayberry, Louis Edward. Taped interview with Rebecca Sharpless, 1987. BU.

Meiden, Janie Canton. Taped interview with Dan Scurlock, 2002. A&M.

Mitchell, Earlean Anderson. Personal communication to Richard Orton, 2001.

Mount Horeb Baptist Church, "100th Aniversary Service." Taped by Allan Turner, 1974. CAH.

Noble, Harry P. Taped interview with Dan Scurlock, 2002. A&M.

Norman, Sallie. Taped interviews (2) with Marguerite Bundick, 1977. MCHC.

Overshown, Byron. Taped interview with Thad Sitton, 2001. HCHC.

Overshown, Florarean Hall. Taped interview with Thad Sitton, 2001. HCHC.

Overshown, Vivian. Taped interview with Thad Sitton, 2001. HCHC.

Patton, Helena Brown. Personal communication to Richard Orton, 2001.

Payne, Augusta Barrett. Taped interviews (2) with Addie Mae Barrett Dixon, 1985–1986. RDC.

Powell, Walter. Personal communication to Richard Orton, 2001.

Pryor, B. J. Taped interview with James H. Conrad, 2002. A&M.

Randolph, Texana. Taped interview with Thad Sitton, 2001. HCHC.

Robbins, Jeff. Taped interviews (2) with Marguerite Bundick, 1975. MCHC.

Robinson, Connie. Taped interview with James H. Conrad, 2002. A&M.

Ross, Cleveland. Personal communication to Richard Orton, August 14, 2000.

Session, Cleo. Personal communication to Richard Orton, 2000.

Shaw, E. P. Taped interview with James H. Conrad, 2001. A&M.

Sidney, Alex Coleman. Taped interview with Marguerite Bundick, 1976. MCHC.

Singleton, Shad. Taped interview with Dan Scurlock, 2002. A&M.

Smalley, Laura. Taped interview with John Henry Faulk, 1941. CAH.

Smith, Carl. Taped interview with Dan Scurlock, 2002. A&M.

Smith, Harriet. Taped interview with John Henry Faulk, 1941. CAH.

Sorrels, Willis. Taped interview with John Henry Faulk, 1941. CAH.

Spencer, Harriet. Taped interviews (2) with Marguerite Bundick, 1975. MCHC.

Steagall, Curtis. Personal communication to Richard Orton, 2000.

Stolz, Skeeter. Taped interview with Glen Alyn, 1980. LMC.

Strickland, Elnitia Berry. Personal communication to Thad Sitton, July 11, 2001.

Terrell, William J. Taped interview with Thad Sitton, 1995. BU.

Turner, Leader May Sessions. Personal communication to Richard Orton, 2001.

Upshaw, Leota Freeman. Personal communication to Richard Orton, 1995.

Upshaw, Marion. Personal communications to Richard Orton, 2002, 2003.

Wade, Birdie. Personal communication to Richard Orton, August 16, 2000.

Wade, Georgia Lee. Taped interview with Glen Alyn, 1977. LMC.

Wade, James ("Beck"). Taped interview with Glen Alyn, 1977. LMC.

Ward, Martha. Taped interviews (2) with Marguerite Bundick, 1975-1977. MCHC.

Ware, Albert. Taped interview with Corrinne E. Crow, 1974. A&M.

Washington, Davis. Taped interview with Glen Alyn, 1977. LMC.

Washington, Tom F. Taped interview with Kyle Wilkison, 1991. A&M.

Weatherd, James. Taped interview with Dan Scurlock, 2002. A&M.

White, Zeffie. Personal communication to Richard Orton, 2001.

Whitener, Oliver. Taped interviews (3) with Thomas L. Charlton and Dan K. Utley, 1992. BU.

Williams, Grover, Sr. Taped interviews (5) with Dan K. Utley, 1991-1992. BU.

Williams, Joel, Jr. Taped interview with Marguerite Bundick, 1975. MCHC.

Williams, Joel, Sr. Taped interview with Marguerite Bundick, 1975. MCHC.

Williams, Rufus. Personal communication to Richard Orton, 2000.

Williams, W. C. Taped interview with Thad Sitton, 2001. HCHC.

Womack, James. Taped interview with Thad Sitton, 1992. SFA.

Woodward, Hattie Lee. Taped interview with Marguerite Bundick, 1975. MCHC.

Woodward, Jimmie. Taped interview with Marguerite Bundick, 1975. MCHC.

Index